REBUILDING COMMUNITIES IN AN
AGE OF INDIVIDUALISM

For Emma and Anna

Rebuilding Communities in an Age of Individualism

PAUL HOPPER

University of Brighton

ASHGATE

© Paul Hopper 2003

Published by
Ashgate Publishing Limited
Gower House
Croft Road
Aldershot
Hampshire GU11 3HR
England

Ashgate Publishing Company
Suite 420
101 Cherry Street
Burlington, VT 05401-4405
USA

Ashgate website: http://www.ashgate.com

British Library Cataloguing in Publication Data
Hopper, Paul
    Rebuilding communities in an age of individualism
    1. Community 2. Social capital (Sociology) 3. Individualism
    I. Title
    307

Library of Congress Cataloging-in-Publication Data
Hopper, Paul, 1963-
    Rebuilding communities in an age of individualism / Paul Hopper.
        p. cm.
    Includes bibliographical references and index.
    ISBN 0-7546-1438-7
    1. Community life. 2. Individualism. 3. Community development. I. Title.

HM761 .H66 2002
307--dc21

2002038262

ISBN 0 7546 1438 7

Printed in Great Britain by Antony Rowe Ltd, Chippenham, Wiltshire

Contents

Introduction

The focus of this book is upon the condition of community and social life in Western societies. It is an area that is receiving increasing attention, with many commentators maintaining that we are witnessing the erosion of 'social capital'. The concept of social capital has been variously interpreted and employed, but is understood here in its broadest sense as essentially the glue that binds or holds societies together, and enables them to function effectively. There needs to be, for example, habits and attitudes of sociability, co-operation and reciprocity in order to generate trust, social solidarity and civic engagement – that is, social capital – within a society. And local communities or neighbourhoods are important arenas where such attitudes and behaviour can develop. Yet it will be argued they face considerable challenges in the contemporary period. It is for this reason that this work is concerned with how we can maintain and revive local communities and community life in these increasingly individualistic times.

The book is divided into two parts. In Part I, the processes shaping our late modern age, such as post-Fordism or post-industrialism (Chapter 1), detraditionalization (Chapter 2) and globalization (Chapter 3), are examined in terms of their impact upon advanced industrial societies. These processes, it will be claimed, are eroding the structures, institutions and practices – such as the welfare state, the full-time job, work-based communities and stable family life – which for much of the twentieth century provided people with a sense of purpose, identity and security. It has resulted in a shift towards more individualistic and private-orientated modes of behaviour as citizens adjust to the new conditions. More significantly, this greater individualism has been to the detriment of local communities, social capital and civic engagement (Chapter 4).

A lack of stability and security, and concomitant feelings of anxiety and uncertainty, is not of course a universal experience. Some people are doing very well under current conditions: they might enjoy financial security, be confident about employment prospects, belong to caring and supportive families, and so on. There are also arguments – which will be addressed later – that recent developments are liberating and empowering, and provide us with greater control over our own lives. But it will be stressed there is widespread concern about such matters as job security, welfare provision, rising crime, drugs, the loss of community, the break-up of families, the decline of morality and the excessive pursuit of self-interest (see Blair, 1996; Etzioni, 1995a, 1997b; Gray, 1993).

Identifying insecurity and individualism in our own time is not meant to imply that Western societies were once harmonious, integrated and co-operative places in which to live. Whether such societies existed in the past, and if so when, has generated much research and remains a source of debate (see Black, 1984; Durkheim, 1964; Gierke, 1900; Parsons, 1951; Tönnies, 1957). Indeed, some commentators are deeply sceptical of the notion that Western societies were more integrated in the past (see Archer, 1988; Abercrombie, 1980; Laslett, 1965). For example, Abercrombie and his colleagues (1980) contend that factors such as poor or non-existent communications and transport systems undermined social integration in the pre-modern period.

While the primary processes of late modernity encourage greater individualism, this manifests itself to varying degrees within different Western democracies. In part, this is because these are not uniform processes affecting all societies in the same manner; their impact and the responses they provoke will therefore be uneven. It is also the case that the national cultures of these societies will shape the nature of this interaction. These points, and above all this complexity, should be taken into account with the analysis presented in Part I, which is based upon identifying and describing broad trends.

The justification for this approach is that these are powerful forces likely to produce similar outcomes, often overriding national cultures. Moreover, all advanced industrial societies are in some way experiencing these processes, and cannot remain immune to them. Consequently, even those societies often considered rich in social capital, such as Germany, may well have to confront its diminution in the future. Likewise, Asian societies like Japan and South Korea may find aspects of their social and cultural life, such as the family and respect for authority, under increasing pressure from these developments.

Having outlined the challenges facing local communities, in Part II it is argued such forms of community are a necessary and important component of human life, and therefore measures must be taken to preserve and rebuild them within advanced industrial societies. In this respect, a case is made for modern governance being more geared towards fostering a public-spirited culture. In defending this position, it is shown how strategies encouraging public-spirited activity – examples of which are outlined (Chapters 5 and 8) – could help to revive local communities and replenish stocks of social capital. Such measures might actually build more vibrant, inclusive and mutually supportive local communities, which is an environment able to facilitate human flourishing (Chapter 7). This also begins to address another major development of our time: the retreat by some people into forms of identity politics, often based upon exclusivity and intolerance, which is in part a response to the insecurity that exists in our late modern age (Chapter 6).

An Age of Individualism

From the outset it is necessary to define key terms and concepts, and in this respect the definitions provided by *The Concise Oxford Dictionary* (1990, 8th edition) will be employed. Individualism is defined as:-

> **1** the habit or principle of being independent and self-reliant. **2** a social theory favouring the free action of individuals. **3** self-centred feeling or conduct; egoism. (8th edition, 1990: 602)

As this book concentrates upon society, rather than social theory, individualism will be understood to mean the habit of being independent and self-reliant; behaviour that can lead to self-centred feeling or conduct.

The reason for defining individualism is because it is receiving increasing critical attention, often in relation to individualization (see Bauman, 2001; Beck and Beck-Gernsheim, 2002). Some of this discussion has centred upon interpreting the meaning of these concepts. In this regard, Ulrich Beck and Elisabeth Beck-Gernsheim (2002) view 'individualization' as a structural concept; that is, in the sense of it being institutionalized individualism. To paraphrase them, certain institutions of modern society such as paid employment are now geared to the individual and not to the group. They contend that ongoing individualization is destroying 'the given foundations of social coexistence', but view it as 'becoming *the social structure of second modern society itself*' (2002, xxii; emphasis in original). As will be seen, there is some common ground with the claims made here. In this book, it is argued that the primary processes or developments of late modernity are producing profound changes by undermining existing social structures, institutions and practices, which in turn is encouraging greater individualism.

Finally, it needs to be made clear what is meant in this work by an 'age of individualism'. It is not the intention to deny or ignore the fact that there might be a history of individualism within many Western societies. For example, Alan Macfarlane in his classic work *The Origins of English Individualism* (1978) traces England's long individualist tradition, arguing its roots can be found in the medieval age. But the claim here is, to repeat, simply that the defining processes of our late modern age are encouraging greater individualism within advanced industrial societies to the extent that some of the forms of common life, such as local communities and social capital, are threatened.   Hence this book is entitled: 'Rebuilding Communities in an Age of Individualism'.

The Importance of Community

There are many different types of community, and people can and do belong to multiple communities. Trade unions, professional organizations, workplace environments, clubs, associations and pressure groups can all be considered as operating as forms of non-kinship based communities. However, the focus of this work is upon local or neighbourhood communities because these are the locations where people live, and often work, and consequently are an important part of all our lives.   A neighbourhood or local community could be a village or an area within a town or city; it might also be a housing estate. Indeed, for each of us what constitutes our local community or neighbourhood is a subjective perception. There can be no universal definition. As Rachel Spence has noted in her discussion of this issue:-

> ... for some neighbourhoods are perceived as being defined by natural borders such as roads or rivers, while for others, they are marked by alterations in housing design – from council estate to private dwellings for example – or by where we shop, or catch the bus. (Spence, 2002: 5)

Any discussion of local communities has to recognise that citizens of advanced industrial societies are more geographically mobile than ever before. For example, a British citizen in the 1950s would travel on average approximately five miles per day; today the figure is over 30 miles, and is set to increase in the future to an estimated 60 miles a day in 2025 (Ledgard, 2002). Our contemporary 'hypo-mobility' is leading, it is claimed, to the anonymous society where individuals have little attachment to particular local communities or neighbourhoods. While this is a discernible trend, nevertheless it remains the case that most people live in particular neighbourhoods or local communities whether they are villages or areas within towns and cities such as suburbs and housing estates. We have to return to these areas after our working day is complete, and some people will both live and work in these areas. Nearly all of us therefore are likely to feel a degree of attachment to what we consider 'our' neighbourhood for as long we are living there. It is in these areas that our public-spirited behaviour can be focused and, as will be shown, is likely to be most productive.

It is also important not to exaggerate the extent of our geographical mobility. This is evident from a recent study in the UK produced by the performance and innovation unit, a Cabinet Office think-tank. It revealed that four out of 10 people still live within the local authority in which they were born (Walker, 2002).

The emphasis here upon local communities is not intended to detract from the importance of other forms of community and association, such as religious groups, professional bodies, arts groups, sports clubs, protest movements, political parties and trade unions. These bodies are a prerequisite of a vibrant civil society. Moreover, they are also an important determinant of the condition of local communities. As Charles Leadbeater (1997) has noted, associations and clubs are a good way of fostering mutuality: we freely join them from personal interest and enjoyment, and through them develop trusting, supportive and reciprocal relationships. They also give us a sense of belonging and attachment to others, and thereby a greater stake in our local communities and wider society; and there is even some evidence that people are likely to live longer if they belong to clubs and associations. For these reasons it is essential that amateur clubs and associations are encouraged by government, whether through the provision of facilities, grants and loans, forms of tax relief, or other such measures.

However, many people already belong to clubs and associations. It will therefore require more than this type of activity to rebuild local communities. Furthermore, the work of Robert Putnam (2000) and others suggests there is a diminishing amount of this type of civic and community involvement going on within countries such as the United States. Consequently, it will be argued that reviving local communities also necessitates encouraging citizens to act in a more public-spirited manner in the form of undertaking community and neighbourly activity. This proposal will provoke some unease in that it constitutes an attempt to change or modify people's behaviour, and because government would play an important role in this process. Nevertheless this approach will be defended throughout Part II.

The Economic Dimension of Community

There will be many economic considerations or factors involved in regenerating local communities. For instance, such communities rely upon employment opportunities and a degree of economic development if they are to survive. And it is regarded as axiomatic here that poverty hinders community activity. It is an obvious point, but it is hard to be public-spirited if you live in inadequate housing conditions and suffer from poor health. You will have more pressing considerations.

Inequality can also act as an obstacle to community. For example, in the UK, for much of the twentieth century policies such as distributive taxation, the universal welfare state and comprehensive system of education were widely regarded – and not just by social democrats – as the means of producing greater equality, which in turn could help create a common citizenship. If income differences are smaller, and we all go to similar schools and hospitals, it is likely that we will feel we have much in common with our fellow citizens. These common experiences lead to the development of shared interests and concerns, entailing that we find it easier to associate and work with each other. And these are the very ingredients or elements that go to make-up social capital and community.

Furthermore, in conditions of extreme inequality, those who are very poor might feel a strong sense of injustice, as well as hostility towards the wealthy, and would understandably not want to participate in their local communities or societies. Similarly, those who prosper from a society of unequal rewards might consider there is little point in trying to change it. Thus any government concerned with the diminution of social capital and the decline of local communities and community life would concentrate upon poverty, inequality and employment, and devote sufficient resources to them.[1] However, it would need to strike the right balance between equality and liberty in its decision-making. For example, if some groups in society are taxed so heavily that they feel a sense of injustice, they will be unlikely to participate in their local community and wider society; many will consider they have already made their contribution.

To repeat, it is taken as self-evident that there will be strong economic considerations behind any attempt to revive local communities and social capital. For this reason – while not ignoring or underestimating the importance of the economic dimension of community – the main focus of this work is upon the attitudes and behaviour of citizens, and in particular the prospects of developing a public-spirited culture within advanced industrial societies.

Encouraging Public-spiritedness

The Concise Oxford Dictionary definition of public-spirited is 'having a public spirit' and 'a willingness to engage in community action' (1990: 966). And this is how the term will be employed in this work. Being public-spirited is therefore essentially an outlook or attitude towards other people, not just family and friends, but also neighbours, fellow citizens and strangers; it is about thinking beyond our own particular interests and being prepared to become more involved in our local communities for the benefit of others. Thus public-spiritedness entails both thought and action because as Aristotle observed in *The Politics*, 'there is no such thing as a man's or a state's good action without virtue and practical wisdom' (1981: 393).

The case made here for fostering a public-spirited culture avoids making claims upon people's time in terms of their duties and responsibilities as citizens. This approach therefore differs from that of the New Labour government in the UK, which seeks to link rights and responsibilities. Indeed, a defining speech of the New Labour project, given by Tony Blair in London on 22 March 1995, is entitled 'The Rights We Enjoy, the Duties We Owe' (Blair, 1996). There are two reasons such a connection will not be made here. Firstly, the language or vocabulary of duty is beginning to appear rather dated in an increasingly individualistic age. Secondly, as was mentioned earlier, to reinvigorate local communities also requires people simply joining and participating in clubs and other societies and generally engaging in the social and civic life of their communities. This has little to do with notions of duty and responsibility to the state and to one's fellow citizens. It may seem strange to suggest that people should be encouraged to join and participate in clubs, societies and other community-based groups as many people already undertake such activity. But as will be shown in Part I, developments influencing the nature of work and leisure within advanced industrial societies are encouraging more private-orientated modes of behaviour.

While criticisms may be raised over the particular strategies outlined here for encouraging public-spirited behaviour, the overall purpose of this work is to establish the importance of Western democracies devoting more attention and resources to regenerating local communities and community life. This it will be argued is an appropriate and necessary response to living in 'an age of individualism'.

The Approach of this Work

This work pursues an interdisciplinary approach, combining politics and political philosophy with a social and economic analysis of the nature of contemporary societies. Indeed, the political arguments and political philosophy are dependent upon, and justified by, the preceding analysis. The intention is therefore to steer away from abstract theorizing; however, given the scope and nature of this work this is unavoidable.

Many of the references and examples in this work are drawn from the UK and the United States. Undoubtedly, this is in part because of my own background – I am a British citizen. It also reflects the fact that much of the recent writing on issues to do with community and social capital is American-based or orientated. Following on from this last point, it might be considered the greater individualism identified in this book is simply an

American, or at most Anglo-American, phenomenon.   Indeed, the insecurity and individualism described here are almost certainly more pronounced in these countries.   But as has been stated, the primary processes of late modernity are, to a varying extent, affecting all advanced industrial societies.   For example, the pressures of globalization will not simply bypass, say, Germany or Japan.   It will have some impact upon their respective economies and societies.   The claim here is simply that this is likely to lead towards more individualism.

This book is based on my DPhil thesis, and I am very grateful to my supervisor, Luke Martell, for his support and critical comments.   It has also benefited from the thoughts and recommendations of my examiners, Paul Hirst and Darrow Schecter.   My DPhil thesis was submitted in September 1997.   It has been substantially updated, nevertheless the overall approach and central claims remains the same.   Lastly, I would also like to thank my brother, Shaun Hopper, for his help in sorting out my endless computing problems.   This book is dedicated to my family, and in particular my nieces, Emma and Anna Hopper.

PART I
AN AGE OF INDIVIDUALISM

Introduction

Part I seeks to demonstrate a growing shift towards more individualistic and private-orientated modes of behaviour within Western democracies. It is argued that this is to the detriment of civic and community life within these societies. This position is based upon an examination of the primary processes of the contemporary period.

In Chapter 1, recent changes in technology, the workplace and the organization of modern economies, which have come to be termed 'post-Fordism' or 'post-industrialism', are considered. A significant feature of the post-Fordist transformation has been the undermining of co-operative and collectivist patterns of behaviour and organization in the workplace. This it will be claimed is fostering economic insecurity, which in turn is encouraging individualistic and entrepreneurial responses.

In Chapter 2, 'detraditionalization' is examined in terms of its role in fostering individualism. The steady diminution of traditional or established forms of authority and practices, ranging from organized religion to marriage, has removed many constraints acting upon people leaving them freer to pursue their own individual life-styles. However, there are negative aspects to detraditionalization, especially with regards to the functioning and cohesiveness of communities and societies. Moreover, many of these 'traditional' practices and institutions have historically provided sources of support and security for citizens.

Globalization, it is argued in Chapter 3, is also likely to lead to greater individualism. Even sceptical accounts of globalization are confronted with an increasing number of Western governments that regard it is as an economic reality, and are formulating policies accordingly. For ordinary citizens, this entails having to become more self-reliant in order to adjust to the new economic circumstances.

There are a number of aspects to Chapter 4 but all centre upon a consideration of the decline of local communities in the contemporary period. A recurring theme is an examination of the impact of the key forces of late modernity – post-Fordism, detraditionalization and globalization – delineated in the previous chapters. It is concluded that the greater individualism and insecurity these processes foster diminishes forms of social capital, such as trust, sociability and co-operation, thereby undermining an important prerequisite of community life.

Endeavouring to demonstrate the growth of individualism in advanced industrial societies is clearly a difficult, not to say massive, task. Moreover, such a wide-ranging analysis is inevitably susceptible to counter-evidence – of examples of people leading gregarious, altruistic lives, and so on. However, the concern here is simply to identify major trends, and above all to establish there are developments currently discouraging and running counter to civic and community activity.

In summary, the argument of Part I is that the social and economic processes identified in this work – globalization, post-Fordism and de-traditionalization – are deep-rooted and have come to shape our late modern age. They are creating widespread anxiety and uncertainty. Above all these processes encourage greater individualism and a preoccupation with the private realm to the detriment of civic and community life.

Chapter 1

Post-Fordism and Individualism

Post-Fordism is the term or concept used to describe recent changes in the structure, organization and processes of modern economies. It is primarily an economic and technological development, but its impact has been wide-ranging, including upon the realms of culture, politics and gender. Although broadening concepts associated with production to embrace wider social and economic developments such as trade unionism, community life and patterns of individual behaviour is rejected by some academic commentators (see Clarke, 1988, 1992). However, this is the approach undertaken here because it is difficult to imagine how it is possible to separate changes in the nature of production and the labour process from wider society.[1] And as Stuart Hall (1989) has noted, post-Fordism insists 'that shifts of this order in economic life must be taken seriously in any analysis of our present circumstances' (ibid., 119).

In accordance with the overall purpose of this work, the aim of this chapter is to demonstrate the ways in which aspects of post-Fordism foster individualistic and private-orientated modes of behaviour. This is an area, which has received relatively little academic attention to date. It will also entail a consideration of whether the shift towards a post-Fordist economy ushers in new forms of co-operation and solidarity.

Fordism and Post-Fordism

Both Fordism and post-Fordism have been subjected to criticism, and even to doubts about their legitimacy and existence. Some commentators question whether the nature of production and work organization is undergoing fundamental change. For example, John Tomaney (1994) contends recent developments 'represent an intensification of existing tendencies' and 'are conditioned by deeply embedded traditions of industrial practice' (ibid., 157-8). They should not be considered as constituting a radical break with past practices. In a similar vein, the Marxist position would be that the condition or nature of modern societies has not changed to the extent that the exponents of post-Fordism claim. The private ownership of the means of production and the system of wage-labour continue to be the primary organizing mechanisms of contemporary capitalism. Yet as will be shown during the course of this chapter, for an increasing number of people their experience of work, employment prospects and relationship with other workers or citizens, has changed quite considerably in the recent period.

What then is post-Fordism? And how does it differ from Fordism? Before answering these questions it is important to note that in the transition from one paradigm or epoch to another there is an inevitably an overlap and elements of continuity (Jessop, 1994). Many firms will employ a combination of Fordist and post-Fordist methods and practices to suit their particular needs. This means that what is presented here therefore is inevitably somewhat of an ideal-type description of Fordism and post-Fordism.

Many commentators consider the Fordist regime of capital accumulation began 'to run out of steam in the 1960s' (Murray, 1989b: 56).[2] The Fordist era was one of mass production and consumption, characterized by the division of labour and standardized production ('assembly line') techniques and products. Such production methods necessitated stable patterns of work which, in turn, paved the way for collectivist forms of behaviour in the form of trade unions and communities growing-up around the workplace.

In contrast, within the post-Fordist epoch there is a shift towards specialized patterns of consumption and the development of flexible production methods, machines and systems, in order to meet changing consumer demand. It is also characterized by technological and organizational innovation; a reliance upon new microelectronic technologies; the movement towards a service and information economy; and, a rise in the number of white-collar workers (professional, technical and managerial staff) with a concomitant decline in the proportion of the manual working class. In particular, 'flexibility' and 'flexible specialization' are the buzz-words, especially when applied to labour markets and the labour process. This encourages a movement away from 'Taylorist' forms of work organization – with its emphasis upon the division of labour and close management supervision – towards cell or group manufacturing whereby small teams of multi-task workers produce entire products. Companies now increasingly require, and expect, a labour force and technology capable, at short notice, of adapting to rapidly shifting markets. For the individual worker, this has entailed learning new skills and competencies, and being prepared to retrain for other jobs. It has also meant a reduction in the number of permanent jobs available. For example, in the United States, according to a report in the *New York Times* (17 March 1988), during the first half of the 1980s almost one third of the ten million new jobs created could be classified as 'temporary' (Harvey, 1989: 152).

In accounting for the emergence of post-Fordism a number of factors and processes have been identified by commentators. Firstly, it was made possible by technological advances in the field of communications and information technology, with computers and computerized knowledge becoming the principal new force of production. Secondly, the growing competition faced by Western producers from regions like East Asia led to the search for new models of efficiency (Mathews, 1989). Thirdly, the post-Fordist model is considered by many employers to be more responsive to consumer demands than mass production techniques, and therefore more profitable. Fourthly, there have been other advocates of these developments, ranging from academics to trade unionists, who consider they can usher in better working practices for workers – the 'new optimists' as Tomaney has called them. For these reasons there is likely to be an extension of such methods in the future.

Post-Fordism and Individualism

Having outlined some of the debates surrounding post-Fordism, it is now possible to indicate how the shift towards this industrial paradigm has encouraged individualism and private-orientated modes of behaviour. There are a number of aspects to this process, and five will be discussed here.

To begin with a notable feature of the post-Fordist epoch has been – as a result of the greater competition from other regions in the world as a result of the spread of the global market – a degree of de-industrialization in many Western countries. This is especially evident in the decline or 'restructuring' of traditional industries such as coal, iron, shipbuilding and steel, as well as some sections of manufacturing, such as the automobile industry. For example, in the United States, the number of workers employed in manufacturing has dropped by 9 per cent in twenty years: in the early 1990s it was 17 per cent, compared to 26 per cent in 1970 (U.S. Bureau of the Census 1993: 409). In particular, forms of de-industrialization in countries like Britain, the United States and Sweden has had a devastating impact upon the regions where such industries are located.[3] As well as eroding standards of living in these areas, it has contributed to the break-up of working-class communities, undermining community life and associated co-operative forms of organization. For. instance, Stanley Aronowitz (1992) has described how some areas of America's industrial heartland, 'from western Pennsylvania to Chicago,

Detroit to Cincinnati' (ibid., 3), have become 'ghost towns'. Economic activity is an essential prerequisite of community, and the shift by firms to post-Fordist practices as a result of operating within a global economy, introduces instability into this relationship. As W.Paul Cockshott and Allin Cottrell (1993) have noted:-

> There is a great deal of official cant going around about the 'community'. We hear talk about Community Care, Community Programmes and so on at the very time that economic development is destroying any organic basis for community. A community can only exist on the basis of shared cooperative activity. (Cockshott and Cottrell, 1993: 165)

The disruption of communities and community life is therefore one way in which the post-Fordist transformation paves the way for greater individualism.

Secondly, the shift from mass production to flexible specialization under post-Fordism has facilitated changes in modern consumption patterns. There has been a movement away from mass consumption to the fragmentation of markets, evident in more differentiated purchasing and the individualization of choice. This theme, and how it contributes to individualism and a greater emphasis upon our private lives, will be discussed in more detail in Chapter 4. For now all that needs to be stated is that the new technologies enable producers to be more receptive to the demands of the individual consumer, paving the way for niche marketing and greater product differentiation. This has also resulted in the increasing displacement of mass culture by a postmodernist culture, which emphasizes image and life-style (Jameson, 1984).

Thirdly, the developments in information and communications technologies that provided much of the momentum behind the shift towards a post-Fordist economy are also encouraging a return to the private realm. In particular, personal computers, modems and fax machines has enabled an increasing number of people to work from home.[4] This form of working provides some obvious benefits for employees, notably in terms of spending more time with their family, working in a more comfortable environment, and not having to commute to work.

However, there are disadvantages and costs involved in so-called 'telecommuting'. It entails less regular contact with fellow workers and with it their everyday support and co-operation, and can lead to feelings of estrangement and loneliness. The workplace is an important arena for social interaction: a forum that enables us to develop our social and communication skills, socialize and form friendships (Connelly, 1995). Home-workers can also feel detached from the running of the firm, especially in terms of having less direct input into the day-to-day decision-making processes.

Overall this development runs counter to collective activity in our working lives. With the workforce more scattered because of home-working, the shared experience and solidarity which comes from working in a single workplace is increasingly missing, making it much more difficult for trade unions to organize and function. The wide range of occupations engaging in telecommuting also entails there is probably insufficient commonality to set-up a Teleworkers Union (Holderness, 1995). This in turn means there is a greater risk of exploitation; a point supported by the history of home-working before the arrival of telecommuting. In general home-workers, the majority of whom are women, suffer from low-status and are low-paid being employed on the basis of piece-rates (Hill, 1995).

Yet it is likely that more of us will be 'telecommuters' in the future. Home-centred working has obvious environmental benefits because it is likely to mean fewer people travelling to work each day. This will appeal to national governments with internationally agreed environmental targets to meet, and some may well actively promote these new patterns of work. While for employers, telecommuting is usually more cost-effective: they need less office and factory floor-space, and can more easily employ home-workers on a freelance or subcontracting basis. This in turn can contribute to the development of a 'flexible' workforce less able to insist upon pension schemes and redundancy payments, nor sickness and holiday pay. There will therefore be a strong temptation for firms to seek the 'casualization' of existing workforces, and encourage more of their employees to become 'telecommuters'. Already there is an increasing tendency for Western firms to outsource work to developing societies where wage levels are lower. Again it is the new technology which has made this both possible, and relatively easy to set-up.

In a number of works Alvin Toffler (1981) has argued that we are about to witness a rapid rise in the number of what he terms 'electronic cottages' leading to the home becoming the centre of society, something last in evidence in pre-industrial times. And there is some statistical evidence to suggest this process has already begun. For example, in Canada more than a million people now work from home (Nadwodny, 1996). In America, 6 per cent of the workforce are telecommuters (Barnes, 1994); other writers point to market research indicating that in 38 per cent of U.S. households there is at least one person working at home (Dunkin and Baig, 1995).

Yet there are variations in the statistical data on this area making it ~~ult to determine exactly what is going on. This can be seen in the case : United States. For example, one survey conducted in the early 1990s classifies almost 25 per cent of the workforce as home workers (Popcorn, 1992: 52). While the U.S. Census of Population Survey of 1991 reveals that only 14.5 per cent of people worked more than 35 hours a week at home (Edwards and Field-Handley, 1996). But what can be concluded from this research is that despite the variations significant numbers of people are now working from home. And as we have seen there are financial and environmental incentives for this to continue apace in the future, further enhancing the importance of the private realm within contemporary life.

Fourthly, the advent of post-Fordism has introduced new divisions into the workplace and wider society, and challenged working class collective identity.[5] The movement away from mass production techniques to flexible specialization demands a different type of workforce. New technology and more sophisticated consumer demands means fewer workers need to be employed in the production process, but they must be highly trained, computer-literate and multi-skilled. Under the influence of Japanese management practices, these core workers will often have the security of a job-for-life, as well as corporate welfare systems in the form of company pension schemes and health provision. In return they will be expected to be extremely adaptable, able to work in small teams, and capable of undertaking a variety of tasks within the firm, ranging from manufacturing and maintenance to the improvement of the products and processes. They therefore have a direct input – through such ideas as quality circles – into the production process (Murray, 1989a: 45-8). And as a result of the continuous training they receive, and high level of investment in them, the core worker becomes difficult to replace – hence the job-for-life guarantees – and consequently their status is enhanced. Indeed, Rank Xerox has tried 'to change its accounting system so that machinery becomes a cost, and labour its fixed asset' (ibid., 49). All of which has impacted upon the nature of modern management leading to an erosion of traditional managerial hierarchies as these new 'flexible' workers are granted greater autonomy and the chance to use their own initiative.

For firms, these practices enable them to 'downsize' and to shed those who are viewed as non-core workers, with any additional work being sub-contracted out. This also provides companies with greater control over wage levels for workers that fall into this category (Harrison, 1994). The post-Fordist transformation therefore establishes two types of division in modern society. Firstly, there is a division between the core and 'peripheral' workforce.[6] Work for the non-core majority becomes increasingly of the part-time, short-term contract, job-sharing variety. Denied regular access to the levels of training that their full-time counterparts receive, there is the danger that those on the periphery will find themselves being left behind. And invariably excluded from the medical and pension schemes of companies as a result of their status, they have to rely upon provision from an 'overloaded' state (Huntingdon, 1975). This in turn helps to foster differences in terms of the welfare provision received by citizens.[7]

A second form of division under post-Fordism exists beyond the core-periphery division, between those inside and those effectively outside of modern society. This is the so-called 'underclass', which is being increasingly identified within many advanced industrial societies. The permanently unemployed who have effectively disappeared from the labour market; many of whom are simply falling by the wayside and becoming non-citizens under the new economic conditions. As David Harvey has observed, 'flexible accumulation', as he terms it, 'appears to imply relatively high levels of structural (as opposed to frictional) unemployment' (Harvey, 1989: 147-50). Whereas thirty years ago there was sufficient work available for the low-skilled, now such work is drying-up and they are confronted with bouts of temporary work and unemployment, which risks their marginalization from mainstream society. Thus in a very direct way advances in technology have reduced the employability of less skilled workers. This general development has been noted by a number of commentators. For example, André Gorz identifies the emergence of a new 'non-class of non-workers' within modern societies (1982: 7). William Julius Wilson (1987) contends what he calls 'the truly disadvantaged' now exist in most OECD countries. While in the case of Britain, Will Hutton (1996) argues that a 'thirty, thirty, forty society' has emerged in the recent period.

There is tangible evidence of growing income inequality – what Ralf Dahrendorf (1996) has called 'inequalization' – in modern societies. In the United States, income inequality has increased dramatically in recent years to the point where it has the largest wage gap of any major industrial nation (Wright, 1995). For example, the U.S. Bureau of the Census (1990) reveals that between 1980 and 1987 the aggregate income of the poorest two-fifths of families decreased from 16.7 per cent to 15.4 per cent; during the same period the share of for the wealthiest one fifth their share increased from 41.6 per cent to 43.7 per cent (ibid., 451). Growing income inequality is also evident in the UK. British Government figures for the period 1979-1996 indicate the income of the poorest sections of the population fell by 17 per cent, and that the wealthiest people became 62 per cent better off (Blair, 1996: 301).

There will be many reasons for these disturbing figures, including the domestic policies of the British and American governments during this period. Nevertheless, given the implications it has for employment opportunities and wage-levels, the post-Fordist transformation must be viewed as a contributory factor to growing income inequality. Indeed, increasing wage differentials between high and low skilled workers is becoming a characteristic feature of knowledge-based economies (*The Economist*, 28/9/96). This is reinforced by a number of recent investigations, which have concluded technological change helps to explain increasing income inequality, and in particular identify a correlation between computer usage and individual wage levels (Krueger, 1993; Wright, 1995).

Finally, post-Fordism and associated developments challenge the role and influence of trade unions and other labour organizations. Such bodies are reliant upon large numbers of workers located within a single workplace. But with the increase in telecommuting and the general shift by firms towards subcontracting, outsourcing and the use of agency-temporaries, it becomes more difficult to establish a mass membership and to organize collective action. Moreover, the emphasis upon multi-skilling and flexibility within post-Fordism also creates problems for some trade unions in terms of trying to incorporate this type of worker into its membership. For instance, which category of 'trade' should this type of worker fall under? This is not an insurmountable problem, but it has required a degree of adjustment on the part of trade unions.

As well as its membership being eroded in its traditional industrial heartlands, organized labour has found it difficult to establish itself in those regions that are the new employment growth areas. These are the post-industrial districts, such as the silicon valleys and glens that have emerged in many advanced industrial societies. They are typified by craft production techniques, heavy utilization of information and communications technologies, and service-sector employment (Piore and Sabel, 1984). For some people this type of work offers the prospect of lucrative careers, which may in part explain why trade unions have often been unable to attract significant levels of support and membership in these areas.

Trade unions are also hampered by being primarily national players, but having to operate in an increasingly global economic environment. This makes it possible for MNCs and TNCs to play off trade unions in different countries against each other, especially because they can threaten to relocate.[8] In the past, trade unions have shown little capacity for transnational co-operation and solidarity; the international labour federations have generally not inspired deep commitment. As Nigel Harris has noted, '[a]lthough capital can go international, this is much more difficult for labour' (1986: 199).

Thus the shift towards a post-Fordist regime would appear to challenge the role and influence of trade unions, primarily because they are finding it more difficult to operate under the new conditions. An important form of group solidarity and co-operative behaviour is therefore threatened by the post-Fordist transformation. While trade unions and other labour organizations do not exactly replicate the ethos and philosophy of the guilds they have replaced – and many people join them through motives of economic self-interest – they are nevertheless founded upon principles of mutual support and collective action for the furtherance of common aims. And their affiliated clubs and facilities meant that during the Fordist era they used to function as important centres in the social life of many communities. Antony Black (1984) contends such work groups bind people together and serve as a source from which to derive our values (ibid., 238). Indeed, for Black it is the dearth of collective groups in modern society that 'has led to an impoverishment of our social being and our social consciousness' (ibid., 239).

Unable to depend as heavily upon trade unions and fellow workers for job advancement, and having to deal with greater job insecurity under post-Fordism, the individual has to rely more upon their own abilities and endeavour in order to earn a living. For example, he or she may have to do a number of part-time jobs, including freelance and contract work. Often the flexibility needed to find work entails an individual being geographically mobile and moving to another region, and possibly even another country. Regularly moving for work can disconnect us from our surroundings, making it difficult to establish meaningful attachments and deep-rooted ties. Above all greater geographical mobility further disrupts communities and can weaken social bonds and ties, placing strains upon families and friendships. In a number of respects therefore social and community life faces considerable obstacles under contemporary working conditions. The post-Fordist transformation encourages individual, not collective or group, responses.

Some people undoubtedly regard the new working patterns as liberating, enabling more choice and variety in forms of employment as well as providing greater scope for individual initiative and enterprise. There is some merit to this argument. Fordist structures and culture, while often affording greater security and stability, contained much that was unattractive, notably greater emphasis upon centralized planning, hierarchical organizations, rigid job descriptions and Taylorist scientific management. Moreover, the work itself could be extremely monotonous: the skill element of craft production was effectively removed as the worker became part of the standardized, mass production conveyor belt requiring little or no mental labour or initiative.

However, monotonous undemanding jobs can still be found in the post-Fordist epoch. As has been shown, challenging work requiring a range of skills and allowing for individual initiative is mainly the preserve of a select number of workers. Furthermore, it has also been demonstrated that there are a number of negative aspects bound-up with the shift to post-Fordism which need to be weighed against any potential gains in terms of individual freedom. These include the disruption of communities; the creation of new divisions in society; the erosion of co-operative forms of behaviour; greater inequality and the emergence of an underclass; job insecurity; new forms of exploitation; and for many a greater sense of isolation and estrangement from others.

Post-Fordism and Co-operation?

In examining the social and economic implications of post-Fordism, it is also necessary to consider whether it ushers in new forms of solidarity and co-operation. And one potential area where such behaviour is possibly being fostered is the move towards working in teams within the workplace. As was mentioned earlier in this chapter, the flexible worker is increasingly expected to be able to work in small teams or 'flexible manufacturing cells' to ensure the completion of particular projects. Employees in their teams are encouraged to co-operate with each other, to discuss issues and problems, share decision-making, and so on. It is an approach that has been very much influenced by Japanese working practices and management concepts (see Elger and Smith, 1994; Jürgens, 1989; Murray, 1989).

While the sheer diversity of the different types of team-working practices make formulating conclusions difficult, some commentators nevertheless regard this type of work organization as enabling greater participation by workers in the running of firms. In this respect, considerable attention has been directed at the potential of Quality Circles, which in theory provide employees with some input into the production process. For the employer, it has the advantage of utilizing the ideas and talents of their workforce, as well as ensuring the continuous monitoring and improvement of products and services.

It is an approach that has been adopted by companies in many parts of the world, notably in Japan and the United States, and has been particularly embraced by major automobile manufacturers, such as Ford and General Motors (Jürgens, 1989: 204).

Yet in many countries Quality Circles are seen as simply a form of quality control, rather than the basis for worker participation in the management of companies. Christian Berggren (1989) in a study of the incorporation of what he terms 'new production concepts' in Sweden, concurs with this view arguing that Quality Circles do not constitute an attempt to change existing patterns of authority and hierarchy within the firm. More broadly, John Tomaney (1994) contests the notion that flexible specialization marks a fundamental challenge to the nature of management, noting that even skilled work 'may be subordinated to managerial control' (ibid., 163).

Linked to the emphasis upon teamwork, a further way in which the transition to post-Fordism may lead to new forms of co-operation and community is in relation to craft production. Michael Piore and Charles Sabel, *The Second Industrial Divide* (1984), contend that flexible specialization – with its emphasis upon skilled adaptable workers able to operate multi-use equipment and capable of making various models – 'amounts to a revival of craft forms of production that were emarginated at the first industrial divide' (ibid.,17). Moreover, they maintain that had mass production not replaced mechanized forms of craft production 'we might today think of manufacturing firms as linked to particular communities' rather than as independent organizations (ibid., 6). For Piore and Sabel therefore the return of craft processes creates the prospects of a link once again between production and community, and for the building of what they term 'collective individualism'. Craft production 'depends on solidarity and communitarianism' (ibid., 278): it requires regional co-ordination, industrial districts and the integration of production into the local community. Because of such benefits, as well as the enhanced intellectual role of the worker in the production process, craft production should be viewed as a positive development 'regardless of the place accorded to unions' within this type of activity (ibid.). Indeed, Piore and Sabel suggest that trade unions will have to come to terms with these new developments and rethink their role within the workplace.

Piore and Sabel identify these forms of craft production in the networks of small 'artisan' manufacturing firms in central and northwestern Italy, but also see such practices spreading to large-scale industries. However, they suggest that even though we are living through the second industrial divide it is not certain which path or strategy – whether flexible specialization or mass production (and their many variations) – will be pursued in any one country (ibid., 4). They simply view the former with its revival of craft production as offering the more promising future, particularly for workers who are confronted with the prospect of more meaningful and challenging work.

However, there have been criticisms raised against the claims made for craft production. Some commentators cite the lack of evidence for Piore and Sabel's quite bold assertions about the potential of the computer (see Coriat, 1991). They consider it to be a machine which 'meets Marx's definition of an artisan's tool'; as 'an instrument that responds to and extends the productive capacity of the user'; and above all that the 'advent of the computer restores human control over the production process' (Piore and Sabel, 1984: 261). It is pointed out that with a few exceptions, computerization has thus far been more geared towards enhancing mass production and central control of the production process, than facilitating flexible specialization in the form of a rapid change-over of products in response to shifting market demand (Coriat, 1991; Tomaney, 1994).

More generally, for a number of reasons, it is questionable whether the introduction of craft production and team-working into the workplace heralds the emergence of new forms of co-operation and solidarity. To begin with it is clear that the incorporation of methods or programmes of team-working and craft production varies considerably between different countries and companies. For instance, in the case of Quality Circles, while many companies in Japan and the United States employ such processes, in Britain, Germany and Sweden there has been less of an attempt to introduce such methods. Indeed, such practices have encountered a degree of resistance, for different reasons, from both unions and employers in these countries. Ulrich Jürgens (1989) contends their implementation has been hampered by the difficulty of incorporating them into existing industrial relations, as well as lack of acceptance by lower- and middle-level management. While some trade unions in the UK have viewed participation in such schemes as constituting unpaid additional work.

It is also the case that not all employees are being encouraged to work in such manner in the modern workplace. While allowing for the variations that exist within particular countries and companies, there nevertheless remains a tendency for such forms of work organization to be concentrated upon the more skilled core workers. In contrast, the flexibility expected of non-core workers is often on the basis of low-level transferable skills with little opportunity for them to use their initiative, either individually or collectively. And here we return to the point discussed earlier about the shift to post-Fordism ushering in new divisions amongst workers. In the specific case of team-working there is the prospect of it encouraging the formation of a skilled elite within a company that by the nature of their work experience feel separated or aloof from other workers, and more likely to identify with the company (Mathews, 1989: 89).

This in turn raises the question of who are the real beneficiaries of team-working and craft production? It is possible to make a case that it is employers who will derive most benefit from their implementation. As was mentioned earlier, many employers consider the incorporation of these new practices and technologies make their company more responsive to consumer demands, and therefore more efficient and profitable.

Furthermore, implementing these new approaches entails significant re-organization of the workplace, and with it the prospect of challenging the role and position of trade unions, particularly on the shop-floor. Moreover, if an employee identifies with their particular team within the workplace, they are of course ultimately committing themselves to the company. Team-working can therefore obscure the true nature of the relationship between the employee and his or her company, a relationship which can be exploitative. A team can also instil its own disciplines and encourage hard work, and in this sense operates very much in the interests of the company.

For employers, the erosion of the role of trade unions and the less distinct managerial hierarchies brought about by forms of team-working, offers the prospect of a reduction in divisive industrial relations. In a similar vein, the co-operative behaviour encouraged by team-working and craft production is less likely to pose a threat to industry and business than past forms of collective action by workers, which were based upon occupational and class solidarity. Indeed, greater emphasis upon team-working and transferable skills can serve to undermine occupational solidarity. And while these new 'flexible' workers may socialize with each other outside of work, there is little evidence that it is leading to them undertaking joint activity to achieve shared goals within the workplace, through such measures as industrial action.

Some critics consider the erosion of older forms of solidarity has been a deliberate policy on the part of many employers, in alliance with right-wing governments, to ensure a more pliable and productive workforce (Mathews, 1989). As Catherine Casey (1995) has noted with regards to the United States, 'the effort to divest unions of their social and political power has made precarious the social solidarity function they once provided' (ibid., 134).

The social solidarity function once provided by the trade union now increasingly falls to the company. Again the influence of Japanese conceptions of the role of the company can be seen here. However, companies are generally unsuited to perform this social solidarity role given that many consider improved productivity and profitability is best attained by fostering competition and individualization within the workplace. For example, most companies – even those implementing team-working and craft production – seek to encourage individual motivation, and thereby hard work, by offering a range of personal incentives, including financial bonuses and productivity or performance related pay schemes.

Yet many of these incentives, as well as encouraging competition and individual motivation, can also foster divisions amongst the workforce. For example, performance related pay schemes, particularly when they have been introduced into the public sector, have created tensions and disagreements amongst workers. In the UK, this has been evident within the staff-rooms of some schools as a result of the government's attempt to link the salary of teachers to performance. Interestingly, this was reflected in divisions amongst the major teaching unions over whether to accept the government proposals. Thus we are a long way from the forms of social solidarity and collective endeavour that existed during the Fordist epoch, and which were promoted by trade unions.

Some commentators consider the developments discussed in this chapter – team-working, craft production as result of developments in technology, and the incorporation of Japanese labour processes and models of production – as leading to a more co-operative relationship between management and workers. This is seen as part of a broader trend. It is reflected in the establishment of workplace 'works councils' of managers and employees as part of the Social Protocol or Chapter, which is annexed to the Treaty on European Union. The Works Council directive specifically requires employers to consult employees before making major changes in the workplace. This trend it is claimed even applies to countries like the UK which in the past have been plagued by poor industrial relations. For example, Jonathan Freedland (2000), as part of his attempt to identify forms of collectivism in the new millennium, sees evidence of this within British industry, especially in the emphasis upon 'partnership' between management and workers (ibid.,12).

However, it is far too soon to be making such pronouncements. And in the particular case of the UK, collectivism is far too strong a word to describe the contemporary situation within industry. If anything in the recent period British industry has become more share-holder driven, rather than stakeholder orientated as writers like Will Hutton (1999) have argued for. This means that British managers are first and foremost accountable to shareholders rather than workers. Above all this rather tenuous notion of 'partnership' between management and workers can not really be regarded as a form of collectivism.

It has also been shown in this chapter that there are problems with viewing team-working and craft production as new forms of co-operation and solidarity. Likewise, the adoption of Japanese models of work organization would seem to hold little prospect of fostering such forms of behaviour. This is particularly evident with Japanese unions which, compared to other industrialized countries, are more tied to individual companies rather then organized nationally upon the basis of a particular trade or occupation. Critics argue this has led to company unions lacking critical detachment, highlighting the often close relationship that can exist between the union leadership and management (Deutschmann, 1987).

Based upon their study of the social organization of the labour process in the Japanese automobile industry, Dohse and colleagues (1985) consider company unionism, and the lack of a strong independent union movement, to be a reflection of the relative power positions of workers and management. They coin the term 'Toyotism' to describe this state of affairs, but essentially see it as an extension of Fordist mass production techniques 'under the conditions which management prerogatives are largely unlimited' (ibid., 141). Thus for Dohse (1985) and Sayer (1986) company or corporate unionism in Japan has merely facilitated the imposition by management of the patterns of work organization which it desires, reflected in the speed and intensity that employees are expected to work and symbolized by the just-in-time system. From this perspective company unionism merely entails that workers are participating in their own exploitation.

Conclusion

In summary, the argument of this chapter is that the shift to a post-Fordist economy within advanced industrial societies encourages individualistic and private-orientated modes of behaviour. While there are examples of co-operative and group behaviour within the workplace under post-Fordism, this has been at the expense of established forms of solidarity and collectivism which were essentially class and occupation-based formations. Moreover, the new forms of work-based co-operation differ in form and nature from that which they are replacing. They are less secure and often rather tenuous, maintained under the auspices of the firm or company rather than developing organically. Occupational solidarity, community-support and trade union branch meetings are increasingly being supplanted by an emphasis upon the transferable skills and professional development of the individual worker.

Chapter 2

Detraditionalization and the Rise of Individualism

'Detraditionalization', the decline of tradition, is one of the defining developments of our time. It is an area currently receiving considerable attention from sociologists, historians and other commentators (see Beck, 1994; Giddens, 1994; Heelas, 1996). This chapter will begin by outlining the nature of detraditionalization as well as identifying the most plausible explanations for its emergence. The second part of this chapter will consider some of the consequences and implications of detraditionalization. It will be argued, in the line with the rest of this work, that detraditionalization has greatly contributed to the rise of individualism in the contemporary period.

The depiction of tradition and detraditionalization employed here will be, for the sake of clarity of argument, something of a Weberian 'ideal-type'. This has meant largely ignoring certain debates about the extent and nature of detraditionalization.[1] For example, Nikolas Rose (1996) has questioned the validity of the linear conception of history which lies behind the detraditionalization thesis. Nevertheless, it will be argued there are strong grounds for viewing the contemporary period as marking an irreversible retreat from tradition; a process best described as detraditionalization. This is not to deny there remain forms of traditional authority, such as organized religion, that retain some influence over the behaviour of many people; it is just that their status and authority has been fundamentally challenged and consequently their influence is waning. Similarly, Giddens (1991) and Beck (1994) contend that within early modernization elements of tradition remained, but in recent times as modernization has continued we have entered a period of 'late modernity' in which the hold and influence of tradition upon our behaviour is diminished.

What is Detraditionalization?

Detraditionalization, as the word implies, marks a rethinking of attitudes and a diminution of established institutions, structures and practices in the sense that they no longer shape our behaviour and influence us as once they did. In particular, within advanced industrial societies, organized religion, political authority, class, the family and other forms of common life are regarded as having been exposed to 'detraditionalizing' influences or forces (which will be discussed in a moment). As a result, in a variety of ways, the relevance of these traditional institutions appears to be waning, and with it their authority and status.

For instance, in terms of organized religion there has been a steady decline in levels of church attendance in Western societies for many decades. In the UK, less than 1 in 10 people now go to church on Sunday (Bates, 2000). The family structure and the nature of family life have also undergone significant change. For a variety of reasons (including higher divorce rates, the decline in extended families, bereavement in a greying society and through personal choice) less people now live within familial households. This is reflected in a rapid growth in single home ownership: single people now make up a quarter of all British households (Heelas, 1996: 1); and trends indicate that by 2020 one in three people will be living alone (Office for National Statistics, 1997).

Traditional forms of political authority in Western societies have also been confronted with a number of challenges. Opinion polls in recent years increasingly reveal disillusionment with national politics amongst electorates (Nye, 1997). This is reflected in low voter turnout at elections, and a lack of trust in political parties and politicians, verging upon cynicism. For example, in Sweden in 1994, 72 per cent of people agreed with the statement 'parties are only interested in people's votes, not their opinions'; significantly this figure had been only 49 per cent in 1968 (*The Economist*, July 17, 1999).

So, how can we explain detraditionalization? The answer lies in the cumulative effect of a number of developments and processes – the most significant of which will now be outlined – that each in someway challenge traditions and traditional forms of authority. The latter are of course not immutable; they have evolved over time and have been invented and reinvented (Hobsbawm and Ranger, 1983).

Modernity and Modernization

One of the earliest challenges to traditions and traditional authority came from the project of modernity and the forces of modernization.[2] Such forces date back to the Enlightenment, and possibly before this time, and include the growth of secularism, rationalism and individualism. For example, the origins of individualism can be traced to the Reformation and the emergence of Protestantism, which with its emphasis upon the importance of liberty of conscience, came to challenge ritual and established authority. More broadly, the social and political project of modernity undermined traditional beliefs and practices such as religion, the principle of the Divine Right of Kings, feudal hierarchies, and so on. In turn, such ideas or patterns of thinking paved the way for the rise of modern ideologies like liberalism, socialism and fascism that further served to displace religion in the modern world (see Eccleshall, 1984; Vincent, 1992).

The forces of modernization also include certain social and economic developments, such as the emergence of capitalism, industrialization and urbanization that all have disrupted the traditional social order and patterns of living. Indeed, modern society contains within it a momentum that is destructive of tradition, where 'all that is solid melts into air' (Marx, 1977: 224). While for Max Weber rationalization was the defining feature of the modern world because of its efficiency and productivity even though it was destroying the traditional values and practices that gave meaning and purpose to life. Yet because it was essential to the operation of large-scale industrial societies and facilitated the creation of material abundance, Weber regarded rationalization and the destruction of tradition as inevitable. For Weber this is the 'fate of our times'.

However, modernity and modernization do not form an extensive part of the literature on detraditionalization. The latter is widely viewed as a defining feature of late modernity, and consequently more recent developments and processes tend to be given greater consideration. These will now be discussed.

Reflexive Modernization

Tradition is further eroded by 'reflexive modernization'. This is a concept developed by writers such as Ulrich Beck (1992, 1994), Anthony Giddens (1990, 1991) and Scott Lash (1993). As the term suggests, 'reflexive modernization' has many features in common with the modernization thesis. Indeed, it has been viewed as being merely an extension of modernization (Thompson, 1996). Of more relevance to this work, reflexive modernization is premised upon the notion that in a world increasingly devoid of the constraints imposed by tradition, the individual has more freedom, but must carve-out their own life-styles and make their own decisions (Beck, 1994: 177). As a consequence, an element of self-reflexivity is introduced: the individual becomes aware of his or her ability to forge their own life-paths and hence more aware of themselves. For example, deciding whether to get married or to remain within a marriage becomes increasingly a matter of personal choice. Our conduct is not as influenced or guided by custom and traditional authority as it was for previous generations. Heelas (1996) describes detraditionalization as entailing 'a shift of authority: from "without" to "within"' (ibid., 2).

Self-identity and self-constitution are therefore at the heart of reflexive modernization. It is as if, as Scott Lash puts it, the sensibility and outlook of high modernity has filtered down to the rest of society (Beck, 1994: 212). While this point is less applicable to the poorest groups in contemporary societies who for financial reasons will continue to find it difficult to forge their own life-paths, nevertheless they are also confronted with the declining influence of traditional authority and their behaviour will adjust accordingly.

Globalization

Globalization constitutes a challenge to tradition in a number of ways. To begin with, the developments in communications and information technologies facilitating globalization can also be viewed as contributing to detraditionalization (Heelas, 1996). In this respect, Giddens (1991) and Thompson (1996) – stressing the importance of mediated experience in the process of self-identity – point out that this is given a new dimension with the emergence of mass electronic communications. We have entered a period when, as Giddens puts it, 'the influence of distant happenings on proximate events, and on intimacies of the self, becomes more and more commonplace' (1991: 4). Thus the developments in communications and information technologies contribute to the process of self-identity and reflexivity which as we have seen challenge tradition.

One popular account of globalization views it primarily in terms of the emergence of a homogenized global culture. This is often considered to be essentially a form of Western – more specifically American – cultural imperialism that threatens national and local cultures and traditions (see Strinati, 1995, ch.1).[3] A homogenized global culture is reflected in the fact that towns and cities across the industrialized world are looking increasingly alike. They have the same banks, fast-food restaurants, major shopping stores, and so on; they are decorated by the same advertisements for products that can be purchased anywhere in the world. Above all, it is claimed, consumerist values and patterns of behaviour are being promoted by this global culture. George Ritzer (1993) goes further and contends the world is undergoing a process of 'McDonaldization' in which the organizing principles of the fast-food restaurant – such as efficiency, predictability and calculability – are being universalized. This provides people with a different set of behavioural guidelines, other than tradition and custom, to follow.

In contrast to the idea of a homogenized global culture, some commentators consider the most significant aspect of globalization is it has brought us all into closer contact with the beliefs and values of other cultures through increased levels of international trade, travel and migration. Yet this also can potentially undermine local and national traditions. Presented with the opportunity to sample a variety of cultural experiences, people have a chance to 'mix-and-match': to incorporate aspects of other cultures, and to question or dispense with some of the guidelines and constraints imposed by the traditions of their own particular societies. It is this diversity of options that undermines tradition (Giddens, 1991: 5). For instance, some people in the West are more attracted by the teachings and approach to life of Buddhism than the cultural values and practices of the societies in which they live. The New Age Movement is another example of this form of cultural hybridization. Thus writers like Arjun Appadurai (1990) and Mike Featherstone (1990, 1995), in opposition to the idea of a homogenized global culture, talk of cultural complexity when describing contemporary developments. This very complexity leads Featherstone to conclude that, rather than a global culture it is more appropriate to talk of a plurality of global cultures being produced by globalizing processes (1990: 10).

Linked to this challenge to the notion of a homogenized global culture, some writers discuss the possibility of globalization paving the way for the construction of so-called 'third cultures' (Featherstone, 1995; Gessner and Schade, 1990). Such cultures exist beyond the confines of national boundaries and national cultures, and emerge as a result of the increased flows of information, goods, services and above all peoples and the general disembeddedness produced by such developments. This helps to produce a different outlook and a merging of cultural influences in the formation of a new more cosmopolitan perspective. Greater intercultural communication is also necessitated by the expansion of international organizations, such as the UN and the European Union. Those engaged in such intercultural interaction and communication are at present still mainly professionals, the diplomats, international lawyers and other legal specialists, business people and academics. There is of course no guarantee that the cosmopolitan outlook produced by third cultures will spread to all sections of society (Featherstone, 1990: 9); yet it still must be regarded as presenting an ongoing challenge to national cultures and traditions.

In a variety of ways therefore the authority wielded by traditions and traditional institutions at the local and national level is eroded by globalization. As we have seen the common theme of a number of the interpretations of this phenomenon – of a homogenized global culture; cultural complexity or diversity; and the formation of third cultures – is the decline of tradition.

The Spread of the Market

The spread of markets and the establishment of the market mechanism as the basis for organizing society further challenges tradition. This is because markets encourage practices and forms of behaviour, which can be destructive of tradition and traditional institutions. For example, in the UK, on the basis of market principles such as freedom of choice, the British Government and local councils have been allowing shops and shopping centres to open on Sundays. And with the majority of British people choosing to go shopping rather than to church on that day, the free operation of the market can be seen as further eroding a traditional institution and form of authority.

There are other ways in which market principles shape the contemporary period. In late modernity, traditional forms of authority become simply products within the market undergoing commodification and commercialization. This further undermines their authority and their aura. For example, in the case of religion, the production of souvenir mugs, posters and tee-shirts of the Pope in the recent period has done little to enhance his authority. Similarly, in the UK, the royal family, political parties and governments have undergone similar marketing processes, and this may in part account for the decline in their esteem. Subjected to the same commodification processes as other cultural forms the influence of traditional sources of authority wanes. Their voice has to compete with pop stars, celebrities and sports people to be heard. And some citizens will choose to listen to the pop star's views on, for instance, drug taking, rather than the politician or the bishop.

For many, the driving force behind the implementation of market principles or mechanisms is capitalism and profit making. For example, the major retailers have been the most active in campaigning for Sunday-opening in the UK. This is undoubtedly because of the prospect of higher profits. Likewise, forms of commodification and commercialization – such as mugs and posters – will in many cases be driven by a similar motive. While for some commentators, especially those on the Left, capitalism is also the real motor behind the detraditionalizing processes identified here, such as modernization or rationalization, and globalization.

Market capitalism is not only an integral part of Western democracies, but is rapidly establishing itself in new regions such as Eastern Europe and parts of South-East Asia. The threat to tradition therefore looks set to continue apace. This even applies to countries with a long history of market capitalism, like the UK, where market principles are being extended into previously non-market areas, such as education and welfare provision.

In summary, the first part of this chapter has endeavoured to demonstrate how certain processes have contributed to the diminution of tradition and traditional forms of authority in the contemporary period. The implications and consequences of this development will now be considered.

Detraditionalization: Consequences and Implications

Positive Aspects of Detraditionalization

There are many positive and liberating aspects to detraditionalization. As Giddens has noted 'tradition is repetition, and presumes a kind of truth antithetical to ordinary "rational enquiry"...' (1994: 66). In particular, detraditionalization paves the way for greater autonomy and – as has been shown – self-reflexivity. No longer confined and conditioned by traditional authority and practice, the individual has greater freedom to make decisions and to forge their own life-styles. This means, as Ulrich Beck and Elizabeth Beck-Gernsheim have observed, 'that something that was earlier expected of a few – to lead a life of their own – is now being demanded of more and more people' (Heelas, 1996: 11). And not only is this a liberating experience, but it enables the development of personal responsibility and maturity.

Above all, detraditionalization means no longer having to accept 'one's place'. For instance, the position of women in modern society has improved due to the diminution of certain traditional practices. In particular, the erosion of the authority and influence of institutions and practices such as organized religion, marriage, and the nuclear family, has provided women with more autonomy. Likewise, homosexuals have suffered considerable discrimination and exclusion as a result of the practices and moral codes promoted by certain traditional institutions.

Detraditionalization and Individualism

However, detraditionalization can also lead to greater individualism.[4] This is because tradition is part of the collective conscience, or as Durkheim would have put it, 'the collective sentiments'; it is shared values and practices.   Indeed, Durkheim believed that without this collective conscience there could be no society and social life would be impossible (Durkheim, 1961).   With the erosion of tradition, the individual is less influenced or guided by the collective conscience. It means our decisions and behaviour are no longer shaped to the same extent by reference to past collective experiences, nor to shared beliefs and cultural practices emanating from particular communities or societies.[5] This can encourage each of us to develop a subjective morality, whereby our behaviour and codes of conduct suit our own interests, and have little reference to the collective sentiments or conscience that go to make up a common moral culture.   In this regard, Paul Heelas notes that detraditionalization is premised upon the notion that people no longer 'think of themselves as belonging to the whole' (1996: 4). '

Zygmunt Bauman (1993, 1996a) contends that rather than viewing the breakdown of tradition as the end of morality as we know it; he considers it to be the end of morality 'as we have all learned to see it' (1996a: 57). For Bauman, this is an important distinction. Rather than, as in the past, morality being simply given to us or imposed upon us from some external source, whether secular or sacred, the way is open for us to fall back upon ourselves; to undertake a 'voyage of self-discovery' in an 'age of contingency' (ibid., 58).   We are now in a post-modern period – '[p]ostmodernity is the condition of *contingency*' (ibid., 51) – where the very notion of morality coming to us from an external source and based upon universal principles is in retreat. Postmodernism has thrown into doubt the very idea of universal principles. We have, according to Bauman, seen through all of this; we have identified the power-relations upon which they were constructed.

The decline of tradition and particular traditional institutions and practices, such as organized religion, does not mean that modern societies are becoming less moral.[6] It is just that those sources of morality are changing. And perhaps it is simply a matter of getting used to the idea of a diminishing foundational morality emanating from reassuring traditional sources. It is about having confidence in human endeavours and capacities. After all, as Nietzsche argued, these traditional sources were originally the invention of human beings. From now on we will have to return to 'the moral impulses, skills and competences of men and women living with, and above all *for* each other' (ibid., 58). Yet Bauman concedes there 'is no guarantee that this grounding will prove to be sound enough to sustain a moral community' (ibid.).

Zygmunt Bauman responds to the difficulty of forming a moral community by placing faith in 'sociation' rather than socialization (1996a: 58). And this does resonate with contemporary developments where there has been heightened awareness of the value of friendship, with greater emphasis upon forming networks of friendships. ¡ Some people, for example, join identity-based groups and organizations for this very purpose. However, while valuable and essential, friendships are not geared towards the inculcation of values in the way that families, churches and schools are. Indeed, some friendship networks – such as alternative subcultures and gangs or groups of young people – can actually encourage or generate anti-social behaviour and crime.

Thus we still need agencies of socialization, such as the family and the educational system, and cannot leave this, as Bauman infers, to chance or, as he puts it, to the 'wondrous aptitudes of sociation' (ibid.). Detraditionalization, however, has made the role of these agencies in the socialization of children and young people more difficult. To demonstrate this point the family will briefly be considered, especially in relation to the family meal and the 'traditional Sunday'.[7]

In the case of the family meal, Matthew Fort (1996) notes this ritual often provides the only opportunity for all the family to be together, and therefore serves as an important forum for communication and the strengthening of family ties. It also provides parents with the chance to teach their children social skills and good habits, and for children to put these into practice. Yet despite this the family meal is taking place less and less in many Western societies. Fort refers to a survey of one thousand British school children, undertaken in 1996, which revealed one in three of them had not sat down to a meal with his or her family in the preceding week (ibid.). Even in France where the decline of the family meal is nowhere near as marked as it is in Britain and the United States, the French government has become concerned that the average French family now only spends eighty minutes over a meal as opposed to two-and-a-half hours in 1965.

Fort cites a range of reasons for this trend, such as the popularity of convenience food (the so-called 'TV dinners') and television. However, he also identifies a number of factors, which are related to the processes of detraditionalization. These include longer working hours (market capitalism) and the dramatic increase in divorce (reflexive modernization).

The demise of the family meal is part of a more general trend vexing many people, ranging from politicians to teachers: the deteriorating effectiveness of the family as a source of moral and social guidance and values. Increasingly there is, as Fort puts it, 'no transfer of the experience and values of one generation to the next. Each generation now seems to be making them up as it goes along' (ibid.). In the UK, it is widely believed this is a contributory factor in the anti-social behaviour of some young people, and the much-reported difficulties that teachers are facing in keeping control within the classroom. In response, New Labour has introduced a combination of measures, such as parenting classes and fines for parents of disruptive children.

Numerous explanations have been postulated to account for this development, and again many of which can be seen as a product of detraditionalization. For example, in both the UK and the United States, so-called 'absentee fathers' have been criticized for their selfishness and lack of responsibility (see Cohen, 1998; Popenoe, 1996). There will be a variety of reasons why some men choose to behave in this way, but reflexive modernization – whereby many of the constraints imposed by tradition upon the individual are absent enabling people to carve-out their own life-styles – will be a contributory factor. It means absentee fathers face diminishing pressure from custom and social convention to 'do the right thing' and play a full and equal role in raising their children, enabling them to focus upon their own lives.

The 'traditional Sunday' is also disappearing in many Western societies. While it is always unwise to generalize – and perhaps what is presented here is an idealised version – there were three defining features of the 'traditional Sunday': church attendance; visiting and being with family; and the Sunday dinner. All three activities have declined, for reasons and processes already delineated, and with them therefore a further opportunity for the dissemination of societal and cultural values is lost. Indeed, research evidence consistently suggests that more and more people are shopping or working on Sundays; that is, using Sunday as simply a day to 'catch-up'.

The waning of such traditions, and others like it, entails a diminution of opportunities to establish guidelines and principles to structure behaviour. This potentially has implications for social order because there would seem to be fewer constraints acting upon the individual. Thus the downside of the greater autonomy resulting from detraditionalization is that it can only be hoped the individual will use it positively and act in a fair and just, and not in an anti-social, manner. But Bauman's claim about 'sociation' and a 'voyage of self-discovery' cannot ensure this point. It contributes nothing practicable to ensuring children will not be disruptive at school; that people will not turn to crime; politicians will resign when it is discovered they have accepted bribes; that business leaders will not award themselves or accept huge salary increases, and so on. Traditional institutions and practices before detraditionalization were of course never able to prevent such behaviour. Yet they did serve to provide a more distinct moral framework for acceptable and unacceptable conduct. In a detraditionalizing era, actions are to a greater degree guided by individual preference. It is for this reason that the final chapter of this book is on citizenship, and a case is made for the necessity of devising strategies designed to disseminate and instil civic values.

All this is not to argue, to return to a point made earlier, that people are now constructing their own ethical codes of conduct completely independent of any social, historical and moral constraints. Tradition in the form of, for example, religion continues to influence the behaviour and outlook of many people. But the key point is that once traditional institutions and forms of authority have been challenged, once traditional ideas and patterns of behaviour show signs of breaking down, it is very hard, perhaps impossible, to resurrect them. The initial foundations or beliefs upon which they were based are fatally undermined.

Another example of how detraditionalization is impacting upon societal cohesion is that the lack of trust within Western democracies – which is discussed in more detail in Chapter 4 – is being widely debated (see Anderson, 1993; Ashford and Timms, 1993; Beck, 1992; Giddens, 1990, 1991, 1992). For instance, the issue of trust dominated, and perhaps defined, the British General Election of 1997. Barbara Misztal (1996), contends trust is becoming of much greater significance under contemporary conditions, which are characterized by contingency and the erosion of existing or previous certainties, and the search for new forms of integration (ibid., 3). As Misztal points out, commentators across a range of academic disciplines see trust as fulfilling this role and providing the necessary social cement. Yet crucially trust requires many of the conditions which tradition provides and reinforces. In particular, the development of trust between members of a society is aided by conditions of stability, familiarity and predictability. In this sense therefore detraditionalization can run counter to social integration.

A further problem with detraditionalization is that the erosion of common moral codes and shared practices can lead to egoistic and even narcissistic behaviour. Thus a rather unappealing form of individualism can emerge, one based upon a preoccupation with the self. This will be demonstrated by briefly examining Michel Foucault's work on this area.

Foucault and the Ethics of Pleasure

Foucault never actually wrote about 'detraditionalization', yet he effectively recognized and welcomed this development, especially in his later works (Foucault, 1987, 1988a, 1988b). He declared in an interview: 'the idea of morality as obedience to a code of rules is now disappearing, has already disappeared' (Foucault, 1988a: 49). It is for this reason that Foucault undertook a study of aspects of Greek and Roman antiquity arguing they replicated in various ways the contemporary situation: 'certain questions pose themselves to us in the same terms as they were posed in antiquity' (ibid., 253). He portrays the ancient world that he is interested in as one largely devoid of moral codes and constraints upon individual behaviour. His work might therefore offer some insight into the potential consequences of detraditionalization should it continue apace. While there are obvious differences between the two periods especially in terms of the degree of economic and political development, it is in the areas of morality, individual behaviour and social cohesion that comparisons will be made.

For Foucault, during the Hellenistic and Imperial periods, unlike under Christianity, there is an absence of a universal system of moral codes and obedience to a system of rules. This leads to the search for a personal ethics. There is an emphasis upon the care and cultivation of the self, and the employment of 'techniques of the self' such as self-mastery and stylization. The latter, in particular, was central to the self-constitution of the individual as an ethical subject. Stylizing emphasized the individual's freedom, and usurped the role of codes of conduct, universal norms and the role of moralists and others in positions of authority in the Greco-Roman era. It was an approach to morality which, Foucault maintained, culminated in the elaboration of one's life as a personal work of art (ibid., 49). More significantly, he believed that in our own period there is 'a return to some form of Greek experience' (ibid., 248), and urged us also to cultivate ourselves as a work of art and pursue an 'aesthetics of existence'.

However, there are some unappealing aspects to Greco-Roman antiquity, which by extension might also be found in societies undergoing detraditionalization. The common theme linking the various practices or techniques by which the individual constitutes herself as an ethical subject is a concern with the self. As Foucault admitted: 'I don't think that one can say that the Greek who cares for himself should first of all care for others... One must not have the care for others precede the care for self' (Martin et al., 1988: 7). The individual therefore goes about their daily tasks (stylizations) – whether it is engaging in relations with others, participating in politics or organizing the household – in terms of their own self-interest. Foucault's ethical subject is egoistic; his notion of ethics is a form of ethical individualism or egoism.[8]

The problem with ethical individualism is that it can encourage atomization within society (Dews, 1989: 40). Society becomes, as Terry Eagleton has observed, 'just an assemblage of autonomous self-disciplining agents, with no sense that their self-realization might flourish with bonds of mutuality' (1990: 393). The psychologist Erik Erikson (1965) contends trust in other people is founded upon reciprocity or mutuality of involvement, and this in turn is the basis of a stable self-identity. There are also practical difficulties for the organization of society if everyone is pursuing their own self-interest, especially in terms of engendering societal norms and values to live by. Foucault therefore presents us with an ethics of personal pleasure, which would be unable to form the basis of a functioning society in terms of providing a legal system, a political framework, social co-operation and economic organization.

The natural concomitant of this preoccupation with the self, and the quest for self-identity and self-development, is a reduced concern for the wider community. We enter a period when, as Giddens puts it, 'the old communal orders have broken down, producing a narcissistic, hedonistic concern with the ego' (1991: 122). Indeed, there is little mention of community life, friendship or politics in the second and third volumes of Foucault's *The History of Sexuality*. In describing the practices which constituted the 'cultivation of the self', Foucault declares the attention of citizens in the Hellenistic world could not 'be dissipated in an idle curiosity, either that of everyday agitations and of absorption in the lives of others' (Foucault, 1988b: 65). The emphasis in imperial times was to 'please oneself' and to experience pleasure in oneself (ibid., 66). To avoid disturbances to our body and mind, including disengaging from politics as a way of ridding oneself of the stresses that it entails: 'One must leave politics to take better care of the self' (Martin et al., 1988: 31). There is therefore the prospect in a detraditionalized era of more individuals being not only self-preoccupied, but also politically apathetic. And there may already be evidence of such behaviour. In many Western societies levels of voter turnout at elections and membership of political parties have been in steady decline for a number of years.

Another potential consequence of a preoccupation with the self is that it can foster narcissism. This scenario is encouraged by many passages in Foucault's later writings. For example, in volume 3 of *The History of Sexuality*, he discusses the dilemmas of the citizens of the Roman World in deciding how much of their day should be devoted to the cultivation of the self. As Foucault puts it: 'There is the care of the body to consider, health regimens, physical exercises without overexertion, the carefully measured satisfaction of needs' (1988b: 51).

Again it would seem this aspect of antiquity is already with us in our detraditionalizing era: the rise of narcissism has received considerable academic attention (see Fornas, 1995; Giddens, 1991; Lasch, 1979; Sennett, 1986). For example, Richard Sennett (1986) traces the recent development of narcissistic tendencies to the decline of community and public life and the concomitant rise of the private realm. While Christopher Lasch (1977, 1979) identifies what he terms a 'culture of narcissism' afflicting modern societies.[9] It is a world where the focus or gaze of the narcissistic subject, as in antiquity, is turned inwards to concentrate upon the self: 'life becomes a never-ending search for health and well-being through exercise, dieting, drugs, spiritual regimens of various kinds, psychic self-help, and psychiatry' (Lasch, 1977: 140).

The 'culture of narcissism' can be observed in a variety of forms in the contemporary period. It is reflected in the growth of the cosmetics, fashion and leisure industries; the vast range of diet and health products; the veneration of the beautiful and the fashionable; the plethora of magazines and television programmes providing life-style advice; and the rapid turnover of popular fashions or crazes. The common theme of these developments is a preoccupation with appearance and style. Of course such attitudes can be traced as far back as the salons of France in the eighteenth century, the courts and palaces of Europe during the *ancien regime* and beyond. In the past, however, this was primarily the domain of the idle rich. What is distinct about the last few decades is the way in which such concerns have assumed popular appeal. While the 'stylization' of antiquity would seem to be paralleled by postmodernism's endless creation of images; celebration of surfaces, collage, ephemeral fashions; and, non-judgemental receptivity of the spectacle and the new (Harvey, 1989).

Further evidence of the current preoccupation with the self can be seen in the emergence of what might be called 'the therapeutic self'. In an age of uncertainty, characterized by the absence of structures and security, the counselling and therapy industries have boomed. People are increasingly turning to such sources for help because traditional forms of support are fragmenting, weakened by the very processes of late modernity identified in this work. For example, the extended family is no longer as able to function as effectively as a support mechanism for its members. Higher levels of divorce, as well as the pressure upon individuals to be 'flexible' and relocate to different regions in search of work, makes it more difficult for the extended family to perform this role.

The absence of structures and routines shaping everyday life may also partly explain the increase in Western societies of obsessive behavioural patterns such as workaholics, shopaholics, fitness fanatics, and so on. As a result, accompanying the burgeoning counselling and therapy industries, there has been a trend in telephone help-lines offering support and advice on problems ranging from alcoholism to eating disorders.

Any attempt to undertake a comparison between Greco-Roman antiquity and the contemporary period would be considered by many people to be a rather dubious exercise. However, this brief discussion has identified possible similarities and parallels between the two epochs. While some historians might question the historical accuracy of aspects of Foucault's portrayal of antiquity, he nevertheless saw his role as undertaking 'histories of the present': examining the past to better understand the present. His work suggests that when a common moral framework is diminished or largely absent in a society – which it has been argued here is one of the consequences of detraditionalization – egoism, narcissism and atomization may well follow.

Detraditionalization and 'Rightsism'

Further evidence of detraditionalization can be seen in the increasing emphasis upon 'rights' within Western societies. This is a logical consequence of the diminution of a common moral culture and greater individualism. Many commentators consider it is appropriate to employ the term '*rightsism*' to describe this recent development. This is because the conviction and passion with which many individuals and organizations assert or demand 'their rights' often resembles an uncritical commitment to an ideology.

The problem with making an appeal to rights is that it makes negotiation, compromise and even the recognition of the arguments of one's opponents extremely difficult. A rights-based politics can therefore undermine the basis for democratic governance. And there are a number of recent cases where such an approach has exacerbated a dispute, and even encouraged extremism. For example, the issue of abortion is articulated and contested in the language of rights. Anti-abortionists stress the right to life of the unborn foetus; in contrast, the arguments of their opponents are often based upon the right of women to have control over their own bodies. As a result the dispute has been running for many years and shows little sign of being resolved. And in the United States this issue has resulted in a number of people being physically attacked and even killed. Similarly, in the UK, a few animal rights supporters have resorted to forms of violence to further their cause. Moreover, the twentieth century was littered with terrorist acts carried out by groups and individuals on the basis of their right to national self-determination. *Rightsism* therefore has the potential to become a form of fundamentalism.

A number of writers (see Etzioni, 1995; Fukuyama, 1995; Glendon, 1991; MacIntyre, 1981; Sandel, 1982; Taylor, 1992) are now arguing that *rightsism* has gone too far; that it is having negative and divisive consequences for societies. In particular, rights are used to justify a whole range of undesirable and anti-social behaviour: from violent pornography to the taking of drugs to the distribution of racist literature. Personal desires or interests are simply couched in the vocabulary of rights. Rights become a 'cover for selfish individuals to pursue their private aims without any regard for the surrounding community' (Fukuyama, 1995: 316).

The problems created by a rights-based individualism are most evident in the United States. One notable example is the issue of gun control. As is well known there are thousands of shootings every year in America. Yet the U.S. government is unable to introduce significant gun control measures because opponents, notably the powerful gun lobby, cite the Second Amendment of the American Constitution which established the right of Americans to bear arms. Hence you have the bizarre situation of American citizens being killed as an indirect consequence of their rights being upheld.

Fukuyama (1995) contends that the 'culture of rights' in America is uncompromising and not balanced by a sense of duty, responsibility and obligation to other people. He claims it has reached the point where '[a] Good Samaritan in the United States is much more likely to be sued for administering the wrong kind of help than rewarded for his or her troubles' (1995: 315). Similarly, Etzioni (1995) has called for a moratorium on the establishment of new rights in the United States, arguing that the continued issuance of rights through the country's legal process has devalued their moral claims to the point of absurdity (1995: 5). In one case legal scholars, in order to protect beaches from development, sought to claim that sand has rights (ibid., 9).

Conclusion

It has been argued in this chapter that detraditionalization is fostering individualism. As has been shown, this is taking a number of forms, but in particular it means tradition and community are increasingly no longer the source or foundation of a common moral culture.

But what are the prospects of creating new moral cultures? This was briefly addressed in relation to Bauman's emphasis upon sociation and self-discovery – and as we saw there are problems with such an approach. However, the modern progressive view would be that such a culture or framework can emerge through our capacity to reason and via democracy. Reason and democracy present us with the opportunity of constructing our own codes of behaviour free from the constraints of tradition. And this is increasingly what has happened in most Western nations since the end of Second World War.

Yet this does not completely address the issue of individualism. As we have seen, this period has also been marked by a greater preoccupation with the self and a more assertive pursuit of individual rights and interests, behaviour that pays diminishing regard to a common moral culture, either traditional or modern. This is because the institutions and practices, including the agencies of socialization, needed to transmit the values and moral codes agreed upon through our rational democratic processes, such as our legislative assemblies, have been weakened. Detraditionalization has, in various ways, undermined their status and authority, and this includes the political institutions and forms of governance of many Western societies. As stated earlier in this chapter, there is evidence of increasing cynicism towards aspects of the political system, which is reflected in declining voting figures. Thus in the shift to a post-traditional society we must ensure effective mechanisms and processes exist to enable the individual to gain a sense of ethical and moral conduct. In this respect, in Part II it is argued that developing a public-spirited culture can contribute to this end.

While the claim of this chapter has been that detraditionalization is leading to greater individualism, this is not to deny the many problems traditional practices and institutions have generated. A return to the past is simply not possible, nor desirable. For example, do we really want our morality based upon a supernatural being? Many consider this morality oppressed and discriminated against many groups in society, notably women and homosexuals. There should therefore be no attempt to go back to some alleged 'golden age' – often considered by those on the political right to be the 1950s – because quite simply for many groups in Western societies it was far from being 'golden'. Indeed, many of the positive aspects of detraditionalization have been highlighted here, notably the greater autonomy it affords individuals. Yet it has also been shown, that the individualism encouraged by detraditionalization presents many difficulties and challenges for contemporary societies, some of which are addressed in Part II.

Chapter 3

Globalization and the Individual

The purpose of this chapter is to consider the ways in which globalization might be fostering individualism within advanced industrial societies. However, such a discussion is made more difficult by the lack of consensus over the nature of globalization, with some writers even doubting its existence. Indeed, it is possible to identify three broad approaches to globalization. These approaches consist of writers who, while making their own particular contribution to the globalization debate, might be defined as *strong globalizers*, *sceptics* and *transformationalists* (see Held et al., 1999). It will be argued that despite these different interpretations, the resort to individualism is likely to be a common response to globalization within Western democracies.

Strong Globalization

Writers who might be classified as strong globalizers include Greider (1997), Guéhenno (1995), Julius (1990), Ohmae (1990) and Wriston (1992). A common theme in their writings is a belief that contemporary developments and processes constitute a new condition or phase within human history. They describe the emergence of an integrated global economy with the breaking-down of national borders and more open markets, reflected in the growing volume of international trade. Production is now a global process. This can be seen in the greater mobility of finance and capital, increased levels of foreign direct investment (FDI), and in the ways in which multinational corporations (MNCs) and transnational corporations (TNCs) are increasingly restructuring production across national boundaries, and in so doing establishing geographical specialization and greater economic interdependence.

The diminution of the role and influence of national governments is a constant theme amongst strong globalizers, with some regarding globalization as marking the end of the nation-state (Ohmae, 1990). Such views are supported by claims that the policies of national governments are largely determined by their involvement in an integrated and interdependent global economy. Global movements of financial capital, rather than payments for trade, dominate foreign exchange markets and hinder the ability of national governments to follow independent economic management.

This point is perhaps evident in the area of taxation. Vito Tanzi (2001) contends globalization will make it progressively more difficult for governments to provide current levels of social protection, in the form of adequately funded welfare states, through their tax systems.[1] Quite simply, aspects of globalization make national taxation systems more difficult to implement and enforce. For instance, more and more individuals and companies are doing business outside their home countries; there is an increasing amount of intra multinational trade; and there is also a growing use of electronic commerce and electronic transactions which operate across borders. All of these areas and others, Tanzi maintains, are difficult to tax and this may be reflected in the fact that in most industrial countries in recent years 'the tax level has stopped growing and, in a few, there has actually been some decline' (Tanzi, 2001: 193). One alternative way of securing sufficient revenue is to increase existing levels of taxation upon domestic populations. But this is also likely to be problematic as companies and high-skilled individuals are now more mobile and faced with high tax rates will look to relocate to another country (ibid., 192).

For the strong globalizers, the diminished power and influence of national governments in relation to global financial markets was revealed on so-called 'Black Wednesday' in September 1992. The British government was forced to withdraw from the Exchange Rate Mechanism (ERM) after failing to maintain the price of sterling in the face of hostile speculation on the money markets. But it is not just the British government that has had to adjust its national economic policy in order to maintain the confidence of international financial markets. The French government in 1991 and the Swedish government in 1994 also undertook policy changes in response to external economic pressures (see Gamble and Wright, 1998: 2).

Government leaders are increasingly concerned to maintain the confidence of the financial markets and to attract new investment. The former head of Citibank, Walter Wriston, concedes that currency traders now 'conduct a kind of global plebiscite on the monetary and fiscal policies of governments' (Burbach, 1997: 70). It is a plebiscite that national governments are extremely sensitive to often feeling compelled to subordinate the domestic economy and society to the imperatives of the international economy (Harris, 1991). Such imperatives include labour market flexibility, deregulation and international competitiveness.

These constraints make it more difficult for governments to finance welfare systems and consequently to protect their citizens from the harshness of the new economic environment.[2] While the levels of expenditure on welfare states have not yet noticeably decreased, many Western governments are increasingly adopting less interventionist financial policies. As Will Hutton (1996) has argued, tax and welfare systems are regarded 'as burdens in the fight for competitiveness' (Hutton, 1996: 16). For example, in the 1990s social democratic states like Canada and Sweden have been seeking to curb welfare expenditure (Burbach, 1997). Based on their research, Lash and Urry (1987) point to a general movement by many European countries towards an American system of welfare provision: a two-tiered structure comprising the state and the private sector (1987: 231). And as part of this trend many states have effectively given up on fulfilling certain traditional commitments to their citizens, notably the commitment to full employment.

Another theme of the strong globalizers is the challenge the nation-state faces from the rise of MNCs and TNCs. They regard MNCs and TNCs as having little sense of allegiance to a particular country, making decisions primarily for the good of the corporation. But their investment decisions can have a significant impact upon a national economy, especially upon the level of unemployment, which in turn enables them to exert political influence upon national governments and national politics. For example, during the UK General Election of June 2001, the global head of Nissan, Carlos Ghosn, warned that continued British abstention from the Euro would result in his company shifting investment to continental Europe.

With the strong globalization approach it is relatively straightforward to see how globalization might contribute to greater individualism. From this perspective, a primary feature of globalization is not only that it is based upon interdependence or interconnectedness, it is also an impersonal process driven by complex and unpredictable global markets. An economic downturn in Japan, for example, can potentially harm the employment prospects of many European workers because it might lead to Japanese firms reducing their levels of foreign investment. In this regard, John Tomlinson believes a particular culprit is the role played by the 'complex and anarchic' world financial markets. As he puts it: 'Rumours about the United States economy can produce activity on the Tokyo market which may have the effect of increasing interest rates, and thus mortgages, in the United Kingdom' (Tomlinson, 1991: 176). It is this very randomness which engenders feelings of insecurity amongst ordinary citizens. This is reinforced by the perception that their respective national governments are increasingly powerless to protect them from the forces of globalization. In response, the global citizen will increasingly have to resort to individual initiatives and strategies to cope with the changing economic conditions.

This is particularly the case in the area of welfare provision. It has been well documented that a growing number of Western societies are finding it increasingly difficult to finance existing levels of demand (Offe, 1984; Rose and Peters, 1977), with much of the recent literature blaming globalization (Amin, 1996; Cox, 1997; Gill, 1995; Gray, 1996 1998). For example, because of the pressures of globalization – as well as developments such as an ageing population – a number of governments in the European Union are struggling to finance existing state pension schemes and are examining new forms of funding (Ryle, 1996). Indeed, soon after being elected in May 1997 the New Labour government in Britain declared it was planning to overhaul the state pensions system. It has culminated in British citizens being increasingly urged to start their own personal or 'stake-holding' pension schemes, and not to rely solely upon state provision.

Taken together these developments begin to suggest the nation-state will find it more difficult to perform its role as protector of its citizens in the future. In the modern period the nation-state is often viewed as performing a night-watchman role, looking-out for and protecting its citizens from hostile external forces in the form of aggressive neighbouring states. Today's hostile external forces – in the shape of global financial markets – are different in nature. Yet in some ways are more powerful as their impact is less predictable.

In a similar vein, the role of the state as provider for its citizens is increasingly being pared back in a number of Western democracies. Many of the functions formerly carried out by the state and public authorities such as the provision of postal services, railways, public utilities (such as water, gas and electricity) and prisons are being privatized. While Eric Hobsbawm (1996) considers many states in the contemporary period are having difficulties in protecting their citizens from internal forces or developments, especially rising crime and the breakdown of law and order (ibid., 59).

Globalization may also be contributing to the sense of a diminishing state in political terms by reducing the significance of voting within modern societies. This is because, from the strong globalization perspective, substantive decision-making lies increasingly beyond the influence of the nation-state and with financial and capital markets and non-state bodies, such as MNCs and TNCs. If this is the case, then it undermines the purpose of voting for ordinary citizens. As John Tomlinson (1991) has noted: 'We cannot vote in or out multinational corporations or the international market system, and yet these seem to have more influence on our lives than the national governments we do elect' (ibid., 176). This may partly explain the growing apathy towards national politics in many Western democracies, evident in lower voter turnout at elections and declining membership of national political parties – a theme returned to later in this work.

The Sceptical Position

As might be expected the sceptical position towards globalization is critical of the accounts and interpretations of the strong globalizers. Again there are a range of writers who might be said to adhere to this position. For example, many Marxists regard globalization as simply a further expansion of international capitalism and deny it constitutes a new epoch (MacEwan, 1994).

From a different perspective, Paul Hirst and Grahame Thompson (1996) take issue with what they term the 'myths' of globalization. Based upon their research they maintain that the world economy is far from being genuinely 'global'. Rather trade, investment and financial flows are concentrated in a triad of Europe, Japan and North America and this dominance they contend seems set to continue. Other sceptics note that while there is an increasing role being played by East and South-East Asia, 'other regions on the globe have been excluded from this supposedly "global" restructuring process' (Ruigrok and van Tulder, 1995: 151).

Furthermore, Hirst and Thompson – as well as writers like Gordon (1988) – believe there are historical precedents for current levels of trade and capital flows. They argue that between 1870-1914 the world economy was if anything even more integrated or internationalized than it is now. Such integration was possible because of factors like a system of international submarine telegraph cables being laid during this period (Hirst and Thompson, 1996: 197).

Hirst and Thompson also challenge claims associated with TNCs. Based on their research they contend that genuinely transnational companies are relatively rare with most companies nationally based and operating in a small number of countries (1996: 198). This should not be viewed as surprising because it is expensive for firms to relocate, requiring new factories to be built, new workforces to be trained, and so on (Harman, 1996). But perhaps most significantly, Hirst and Thompson maintain that the majority of MNCs accept the respective governmental policies of the countries in which they are located.

As a result of their investigation Hirst and Thompson consider it is more accurate to describe developments within the international economy as a process of internationalization rather than full globalization. It leads them to challenge the notion that national governments are no longer able to pursue independent economic management. Such a view has been politically expedient for governments, enabling them to play down their responsibility for the management of their respective economies. They maintain that the major economic nations of the world retain the capacity, especially if they co-ordinate policy, to exert governance over financial markets and non-state economic actors. Global markets are therefore not beyond regulation and control. Indeed, an obvious example of how national governments shape the global agenda is that neo-liberalism, which has done so much to facilitate globalization, was actively promoted by the Reagan and Thatcher administrations in the 1980s.

The sceptical position towards globalization would seem to pose a considerable challenge to the argument of this chapter. Quite simply, if globalization does not exist then it cannot be fostering individualism. However, many writers who are critical of the strong globalization case recognise significant changes have been taking place within the international economy. And Hirst and Thompson concede this has placed 'constraints on certain types of national economic strategy' (1996: 4) and that in general 'the economies of nation states are less subject to the actions of "government"' (ibid., 199).

But the major reason the sceptical globalization thesis does not challenge what is being argued for here is that globalization has become a new orthodoxy, especially within business, academic and political circles. Irrespective of debates about whether it exists or not, it is widely perceived as the economic reality to which we all must adjust, and national governments in particular have been pursuing strategies and implementing policies accordingly.[3] This is evident in the way in which exponents of the 'third way' – who dominate much recent centre-left thinking – have internalized this view of globalization. For example, the New Labour government in the UK considers globalization to be self-evidently the condition of our time from which we cannot escape. As Tony Blair declared in a speech given in Chicago in April 1999: 'We cannot refuse to participate in global markets if we want to prosper' (Giddens, 2000: 23-4). Indeed, an oft-repeated theme in New Labour rhetoric is the difficulties countries will face if they are left behind and do not participate in, or adapt to, the 'new global economy'.

But rather than seeing globalization as a threat, the rhetoric of New Labour invariably portrays it as an 'opportunity' or a 'challenge'. This is the case throughout the industrial world, especially amongst political leaders, with globalization regarded as something to be embraced ushering in many benefits such as the promise of an interdependent world where old rivalries become redundant (Ruigrok and van Tulder, 1995: 168).

More importantly, a consensus is emerging amongst Western governments on how they should respond to globalization. Unable to control global capital and financial flows, and therefore manage demand, the view is taking hold that there are limits to what governments can do to shape their economies. According to this logic, the primary aim and role of a national government must be to promote economic stability and incentives for capital investment. Again this view has been fully incorporated by the New Labour government in the UK. Blair declares in his book *New Britain: My Vision of a Young Country*: '... if companies are to invest they must have relatively stable macro-economic framework in which to plan' (Blair, 1996: 79). In practical terms this means, as Gordon Brown (the British Chancellor of the Exchequer) frequently declares, ruling out any looseness with inflation, tax rises and public spending. This in part helps to explain why the level of expenditure on public services in the UK continues to be lower than that of comparable Western democracies.

New Labour considers a further way of attracting capital investment is by restraining government interventions in the economy. It therefore not only accepts globalization, but effectively seeks to extend it through its support of neo-liberal initiatives that, for example, expand free trade: '... to compete in the new global market... [a] country has to dismantle barriers to competition and accept the disciplines of the international economy' (Blair, 1996: 118). This has meant MNCs enjoy considerable freedom to operate in the UK. It is an example of how globalization, once established as a new orthodoxy, becomes a self-fulfilling prophecy. New Labour considers capital to be highly mobile in the contemporary period and hence does little or nothing to control it thereby contributing to its very mobility.

This governmental attitude to globalization has considerable implications for ordinary citizens. It is another encouragement for us to become self-reliant, adaptable and entrepreneurial. Many exponents of the third way maintain that for individuals to cope in the new global age they must be 'flexible'. And in accordance with the logic of their approach to globalization, influencing the supply and quality of labour is one of the few areas the New Labour government feels able to intervene in the economy. It prioritizes supply-side economics in the form of the provision of education and training, encapsulated in the oft-quoted phrase: 'Education, Education, Education'.

This effectively entails a departure from traditional social democratic policies, and an acceptance of a changed and in many ways reduced role for government. It is something that Tony Blair has publicly acknowledged. In a speech to European Socialists in Malmö (6 June 1997) he outlined how the role of government was now 'to give people the education, skills and technical know-how they need to let their own enterprise and talent flourish in the new market-place' (Blair, 1997).

The promotion of the flexible worker also has implications for the level of inequality in the UK. Under New Labour the emphasis upon universalizing access to opportunities has been accompanied by a reluctance to pursue more direct forms of income redistribution (Oppenheim, 2001). This means there is greater onus upon the individual, rather than government, to improve their own economic position through their education and skills. It has echoes of attitudes of the late nineteenth century. In this respect Colin Crouch (1999) considers New Labour's polices mark something of a revival of the new liberalism or social liberalism of the late nineteenth century and entails it has given up on the notion of protecting its citizens from market forces. In this respect, many critics of New Labour consider its welfare-to-work programme is designed primarily to discourage welfare dependency.

For business and industry, the flexible worker has distinct advantages. Such a model worker is able to rely upon his or her own talents and abilities, and therefore has less need to belong to a trade union to ensure job advancement and better pay and working conditions. This has been reflected in the individualization of pay bargaining, notably the spread of performance related pay schemes. Above all it makes resistance by organized labour more difficult because it tries to create the impression that it is unnecessary in a more competitive global age.

So far the focus of this discussion has been upon the third way and in particular New Labour's view of the role of government in the new global economy. However, it is not just a substantial part of the centre-left in the UK that has come to accept this approach to globalization. Successive administrations in the United States have of course been pursuing and actively promoting such policies for many years. But a similar adjustment to what are perceived as the new economic circumstances has been taking place within other Western democracies. In particular, the recent shift to the centre-right in Europe – notably in Spain, Italy, Denmark, Austria, France, Portugal and the Netherlands – has seen the election of governments broadly in tune with Blairite ideas. This was reflected in the Barcelona summit of March 2002, which saw the member states of the European Union take further steps towards economic liberalization, especially in terms of establishing more 'flexible' energy and labour markets. Indeed, a consensus appears to be emerging amongst mainstream political parties in Western societies on how best to respond to the new global economic conditions. The form that it is beginning to take will now be outlined.

To begin with the market economy has come to be universally accepted. Many Western leaders advocate the benefits of trade liberalization entailing that their respective governments will generally refrain from regulating economic markets. Moreover, many social democratic parties have become, if not pro-business, then certainly more aware of the important wealth-producing and employment-generating function of business. As Blair and Schroeder declared in a joint paper on the third way project: 'The development of prosperous small and medium-sized businesses has to be a top priority for modern social democrats' (Blair and Schroeder, 1999: 34). There is also less reliance within many states upon traditional Keynesian forms of economic management. Indeed, the whole idea of national management, in both an economic and political sense, is less evident within recent social democratic thinking. Instead there is greater emphasis upon both devolved and multi-level governance (Gamble and Wright, 1999: 5).

Welfare reform is also high on the political agenda of many Western governments, with many of them looking for ways to reduce budgets and avoid deficit spending. For example, Germany's Chancellor Gerhard Schroeder has taken up 'the Clinton-Blair welfare-to-work approach and the commitment to restrain public spending' (Michel and Bouvet, 1998: 143). One aspect of the rethinking of welfare provision has been a shift in emphasis away from spending on social benefits to social investment (e.g., skills, education and training). This is considered – and not only by New Labour – as the best way to prepare citizens for coping with globalization and constitutes an acceptance of the need for labour market flexibility. In this regard, early in 1999 Tony Blair and the Spanish Premier Aznar launched a Joint Declaration calling for a revision of the employment policies of the European Union with greater emphasis upon de-regulation (Coates, 1999: 3). Similarly, the outcome of a meeting between Blair and Silvio Berlusconi in February 2002 was an Anglo-Italian agreement to promote economic liberalization within the European Union, with the focus upon overhauling its 'rigid' labour laws (Carroll, 2002).

There has also been widespread rejection of big government. Collectivist approaches in the form of nationalization programmes have been abandoned across Europe. More generally, there is increasing acceptance of the role the private sector in the running of public services, especially because it is seen as a way of curbing public spending. For example, the former French socialist Prime Minister, Lionel Jospin, privatized more state companies than his centre-right predecessor. In particular, it is claimed that Jospin effectively supported the partial privatization of France Telecom and Air France (Michel and Bouvet, 1998). Although again New Labour has gone further in this regard than its European counterparts, advocating private sector solutions to many of the problems facing the UK, and actively promoting public-private partnerships and the contracting-out of public services.

As a result of this new thinking there has been a blurring of the lines between 'market and state, between public and private' (Gamble and Wright, 1999: 5). It also entails changes in the nature of modern governance, especially in terms of the relationship between government and citizens with greater emphasis upon individual self-reliance. In this respect, Tony Blair stated in an interview given on 27 October 1997 that 'the role of government is to organise and secure provision rather than fund it all' (Michel and Bouvet, 1998: 140). He elaborated upon this by referring to the example of pension reform, declaring that 'people will have to provide more of their own financial independence' with government playing 'a role in organising that system' (ibid.).

This growing consensus over the nature of modern governance has been noted by a number of writers. For example, Donald Sassoon considers globalization has brought about a convergence, especially in European politics, between Left and Right – 'and largely unavoidably on the terms set by the Right' (Sassoon, 1998: 95). This is because globalization has 'contributed significantly to a realignment of the European Left away from its traditional terrain: a "national" social democracy based on a welfare state and full employment' (ibid., 95). Debates about equality, for instance, are increasingly about attaining equality of opportunity rather than, as in the past, equality of outcome through forms of economic redistribution such as taxation: 'equality, though still appealing as a goal, may be tempered by the need to preserve incentives and competition' (ibid., 96). As Sassoon puts it: 'The new pan-European Left has accepted the constraints of the new global capitalism' (ibid., 95). And in a comparison of New Labour with other examples of social democracy in Europe, Sassoon contends that on many issues 'Blair's modernisers are part of the mainstream' (Sassoon, 1999: 30).[4] Frédéric Michel and Laurent Bouvet (1998) also detect similar examples of convergence, but note that many continental governments are coalitions which means that social democratic parties have to make compromises rather than simply assert their own agenda.[5]

This broad consensus over policies and the lack of ideological debate between major political parties perhaps further helps to explain why growing numbers of citizens in Western democracies are becoming disengaged from mainstream politics.[6] Political disputes are increasingly about technical competence and leadership abilities rather than ideological principles, often focussing upon image and personality politics. This is not to deny that there are counter-examples and counter-movements, such as the anti-globalization movement, to the political consensus outlined here.

However, as with previous chapters, the aim is to identify and delineate broad historical processes and trends. And the fragmented nature of the anti-globalization movement reflects the lack of a coherent alternative with wide popular appeal, to what is being pursued by mainstream parties in Western societies.

To recap, while strong globalizers and sceptics provide radically different accounts of globalization, for the citizen it seems likely that they will have to formulate their own individual responses to this development. This is due to the impact of globalization upon the nation-state, whether this impact is real or perceived. More specifically, globalization is in a variety of ways entailing that the nation-state appears less able to protect its citizens, and is thereby forcing them to rely upon their own initiatives and strategies to cope with the new economic conditions. As we have seen, strong globalizers consider the nation-state is increasingly powerless to resist the forces ranged against it. While the sceptical thesis suggests there is greater scope for national governments to act autonomously and pursue traditional social democratic policies, for reasons that have been outlined many are not acting in this manner.

The Transformationalist Approach

David Held and his co-writers present a detailed account of the transformationalist approach to globalization in their book *Global Transformations* (1999). And they consider Anthony Giddens (1990) and James Rosenau (1997) to be leading exponents of this approach. In contrast to the strong and sceptical approaches – which focus upon whether or not globalization is an established condition – the transformationalist position is that it is a long-term, but far from uniform, historical process. Transformationalists also regard contemporary global interconnectedness – in terms of economic, political, migratory and cultural flows – as historically unprecedented (Held et al., 1999: 7-10). Above all globalization is seen as a powerful dynamic force responsible for massive change within societies and world order, and national governments are having to formulate new strategies in order to adapt to the new conditions (Rosenau, 1997).

Transformationalists consider the driving force behind globalization to be the combined forces of modernity. Thus globalization is not just motored by capitalism, but also by processes already identified in this work such as developments in technology, post-Fordism and detraditionalization. And in a number of ways this is likely to encourage individualism. This is because, as we have seen in the previous chapters, such processes constitute the condition of late modernity: an era of greater choice and individual freedom.   For example, the choice and opportunity afforded by globalization include the prospects for greater travel and geographical mobility. But equally importantly from the transformationalist perspective, it is also a time of risk and insecurity. As David Held notes, 'states and societies across the globe are experiencing a process of profound changes as they try to adapt to a more interconnected but highly uncertain world' (Held et al., 1999: 2). This is linked to the fact that globalization, for transformationalists, is not only a long-term process but the direction it is taking is unpredictable; it has no clear or obvious historical destination.

For citizens, as well as the greater uncertainty of employment prospects mentioned earlier, there are other forms of risk and insecurity associated with globalization. In particular, the fluid and therefore inherently unstable nature of international financial markets can wipe out or dramatically reduce people's savings and investments.   Downturns in the global economy can decimate the price of people's houses and the value of their mortgages. There is also the worry that a rapidly changing global economy will render obsolete a person's skills and training.   Other aspects of globalization which create anxiety for many citizens are the spread of communicable diseases from other parts of the globe as a result of increased travel and concerns that the incorporation of new regions into the global economy will produce more environmental disasters. Pollution of course, as Ulrich Beck (1992) has noted, does not recognise national borders.

With each of these risks there are limits to what a national government can do to protect its citizens. Tony Blair is one political leader who has conceded this is a period in which there are considerable feelings of insecurity: '... with globalisation comes its offspring – insecurity. People feel, and are, less economically secure than ever before' (Blair, 1996: 120). This vulnerability is likely to encourage people to look out for themselves, and to formulate their own coping strategies, much more than has been the case in modern societies in the recent past. The only exception to this trend is likely to be the United States where historically the federal government has played, in comparison with the governments of Western Europe, a more limited role in terms of welfare provision for its citizens.   In general therefore Americans have already become more accustomed to adapting to this economic reality.

The   transformationalist   perspective   comes   closest   to   the interdisciplinary approach of this work with its emphasis upon the multi-dimensional nature of globalization.   It does not solely focus upon economics, but incorporates politics, social change and culture as part of a continuous   process.   Little   insight   can   be   gained   from   viewing developments within the international economy – that have come to be termed 'globalization' – in isolation. It is essential to recognise that they are embedded within contemporary societies and should be considered in relation to, or intertwined with, other major developments of our time such as shifts in technology, post-Fordism and detraditionalization. And the cumulative impact of these processes entails we enter, certainly in Western societies, a new phase in human history that can most appropriately be described as 'late modernity'. This phase, as the term implies, has continuities with the modern age. Moreover, as will be discussed later, there are reactions against it in the form of the rise of religious fundamentalism and ethnic and national revival. This is only to be expected. Under modernity there were similar contradictory and competing developments. Key aspects of the Enlightenment, such as rationalism and ideas of individual liberty and universal citizenship provoked reactions or counter-movements in the shape of Romanticism and conservative forms of nationalism.

Conclusion

In this chapter, three major approaches to globalization have been outlined. While each approach provides a distinctive insight into this issue, from the perspective of ordinary citizens, globalization would seem to entail that they are going to have to be increasingly entrepreneurial and self-reliant in the future. Whether this is because, as transformationalists maintain, they will have to deal with the risk and uncertainty of changing global economic conditions or, as strong globalizers claim, their governments will be less able to manage their national economies and provide adequately-funded welfare states. And while those writers who are sceptical about globalization raise important arguments, their case is confronted with the problem that globalization has become a new orthodoxy, and governments and citizens are acting accordingly. In the next chapter, some of the consequences of this greater individualism are considered in relation to social and community life within Western democracies.

Chapter 4

Community and Social Capital

This chapter draws together the analysis of the three preceding chapters and thinks through some of the claims that were made. More specifically, the consequences of the shift towards more individualistic and private-orientated modes of behaviour, engendered by the primary processes of late modernity, are considered. It will be argued this development is almost certainly having a detrimental impact upon local communities and social capital within many advanced industrial societies. In this regard, the linkage between heightened forms of insecurity in our late modern age and the lack of civic and community engagement will be stressed. As with the rest of this work, the aim is merely to delineate key contemporary trends, rather than establish irrefutable facts, and this is reflected in the nature of analysis presented here.

The chapter will also look at other developments potentially undermining local communities such as the rise of a consumer society, changing leisure patterns and aspects of urban life. Some of these developments are of course intertwined with, or influenced by, the forces of late modernity identified here. For instance, the development of a consumer society has been aided by the emphasis upon flexible specialization within post-Fordism by paving the way for greater consumer choice. However, rather than seeking to make these connections – though some will be made – the overriding aim will be to outline how these developments challenge local community life and erode social capital in the contemporary period.

The Consequences of Insecurity

Insecure Times

For many people in advanced industrial societies, the combined effect of globalization, post-Fordism and detraditionalization is to introduce greater uncertainty, and therefore anxiety, into their daily lives. This insecurity assumes many different forms, but is mainly generated by the diminution of the structures, institutions and practices, such as a stable family life and secure employment, which help to shape everyday life. As we have seen the traditional sources of support and solace for the individual – such as the welfare state, the family, the church and trade union – are all facing significant challenges from the processes of late modernity. In many cases these support mechanisms or institutions are fighting rearguard actions to preserve their traditional roles at a time when the need for them has never been so great. Above all it leaves the citizen in a more vulnerable position. This is evident in the changing role of the modern state.

In many Western democracies reliance upon the state has increased partly because the co-operative tradition and forms of mutuality which once existed, particularly in a number of industrial countries in Europe during the nineteenth century, has waned. For example, in the UK mutuality was evident in the emergence of different forms of mutual aid and welfare organizations, such as Friendly Societies and the Co-operative Movement (see Black, 1984; Godsden, 1961, 1973; Thompson, 1968). E.P. Thompson in his classic study *The Making of the English Working Class* (1968), argues working-class life in the early industrial period consisted of many 'rituals of mutuality' (1968: 456).[1] However, today this tradition has declined in Britain to the extent that the Co-operative Wholesale Society (CWS) was subjected to a hostile take-over bid from financial speculators in April 1997.[2] This decline is largely because the task of welfare provision was taken over by the British state after 1945 and citizens have come to rely upon this source. A pattern repeated in other countries of Western Europe and beyond. Recently, however, as a result of the developments and ideologies associated with globalization – discussed in Chapter 3 – the modern state is facing a range of pressures in the performance of this role. For the citizen, it is not knowing whether they can rely upon the state, especially in the long-term, for such as essentials as health care provision and pensions, which is fostering insecurity (Vail, 1999).

Another source of insecurity is the amount of risk associated with living in late modernity. This phenomenon has been identified by a number of writers, notably Ulrich Beck (1992, 1994) and Anthony Giddens (1990, 1991). They talk of the emergence of a 'risk society' that is bound-up with reflexive modernization and assumes many different forms – only one aspect of which will be dealt with here.

Risk stems from the nature and level of human development, ranging from the global expansion of trading relationships to the spread of industrial and technological processes, that constitutes our late or high modern age. Our very attempt to control the natural and social worlds has brought new uncertainties and new forms of unpredictability. It means events are no longer confined to local situations, but have implications for everyone living on the planet.   An industrial accident, like the one at Chernobyl, can impact upon the planet's ecosystem; a human error can lead to a global nuclear war; financial speculation concerning one national economy can reverberate across the international money markets (Giddens, 1990: 125).   While the accumulation of knowledge and critical scrutiny which lie at the heart of the project of modernity merely reveals to us the limits of our knowledge and raises doubts about what we formerly viewed as certainties (Smart, 1993: 105).   As Zygmunt Bauman has noted 'the growth of knowledge expands the field of ignorance' (Bauman, 1991: 244).

However, a distinction needs to be made between short- and long-term risks.   The risks identified above are all possibilities in the future; they do not constitute an everyday lived experience.   Indeed, both Giddens and Beck regard these dangers as potentially catastrophic or 'high consequence', yet currently low-probability, risks.   In contrast, job insecurity, redundancy and periods of unemployment is a constant concern for most people in our global society making it difficult to take decisions about the future, such as having children and taking-out mortgages.   Linked to this, as Nikolas Rose (1996) has argued, are the greater risks associated with living in a detraditionalized era.   As we saw in Chapter 2, with the diminution of traditional forms of authority to control and advise us, each of us must increasingly determine our own life-plan and make decisions over such matters as diet and health, sexual conduct, financial management, home ownership, careers and pensions (ibid., 320).   Undoubtedly, this is a liberating experience, but it also means should we make the wrong choices and decisions we are more likely to have to face the consequences on our own.

Insecurity and Individualism

The increased insecurity felt by many people in the contemporary period is encouraging greater individualism.   Unable to rely upon traditional forms of support, the citizen increasingly has to depend upon their own enterprise and actions.   They have to be more 'flexible' in the job market; to undertake their own private health care provision; to take-out mortgage insurance schemes in case of loss of earnings, and so on.   Indeed, many Western governments are actively promoting individual self-reliance.   In the UK, as was mentioned in Chapter 3, it has become government policy to dissuade British citizens from relying solely upon the state pension, and to make their own private provision.   It is an approach to dealing with an ageing population, which is receiving considerable attention from other member states within the European Union.

Greater individualism has in turn implications for both local communities and the modern state. If people get into the habit of being independent and self-reliant there is less need to engage in civic and local community activity. Moreover, why should people engage in public life if they do not feel secure within, or protected by, that society or state? For instance, if they no longer feel they can rely upon the state for adequate welfare provision their commitment to it is likely to diminish. These are factors or considerations that make us feel we have a stake in the society and communities in which we live.

Anthony Giddens (1990) provides a more positive interpretation of how people are responding to contemporary conditions. Rather than just resorting to individualism, he identifies a range of adaptive reactions to, as he puts it, 'the risk profile of modernity' (ibid., 134). These range from *pragmatic acceptance* to *cynical pessimism*, but most importantly include *radical engagement*. This entails mobilization and taking 'contestory action' to confront common problems and dangers. It is an approach in which social movements perform a key role. Thus for Giddens social activism and not just private retreatism forms part of the response to changing circumstances. His work is a useful reminder that there can never be a single universal reaction to the developments of late modernity.

However, this more optimistic analysis of our late modern age is not entirely convincing, especially with regards to the nature and purpose of social movements. Roger Burbach (1997) contends that social movements are rooted in what he terms the 'new individuality'; 'they reflect a quest to satisfy individual needs and individual desires that is unprecedented in the history of civilization' (ibid., 51):-

> What are the gay and human rights movements, if not an attempt by each and every person to pursue his or her individual sexual identity?... The environmental movement is also rooted in an individual, personal quest for a better life, a life free from visual, commercial and environmental pollution. And the environmental movement is also an attempt to define one's relationship and identity in relation to other species. (ibid.)

Burbach perhaps slightly overstates his case. For instance, many members and supporters of the environmental movement will be driven by altruistic motives and a concern with the fate of the whole of humanity. Although of course social movements are primarily concerned to promote their particular causes, and in this sense differ from political parties which have to represent a wide range of interests if they want to be elected. Indeed, Alberto Melucci (1989), one of the foremost writers on contemporary social movements, goes further and regards them as facilitating greater individual self-expression. Such movements are a reflection of the very differentiation and individualization of complex societies. He views them as potentially paving the way for a new type of politics, one which avoids the preoccupation with capturing state power and maintaining disciplined political organizations. Social movements, unlike conventional party systems which are unable to cater for individual needs and experiences, are geared towards 'the need for self-realization in everyday life' (1989: 23).

Thus the very agency which Anthony Giddens identifies as the primary vehicle for social activism would also seem to be imbued with the new individualism. Yet in fairness to Giddens, he also notes the political engagement of the new social movements is orientated towards the promotion of 'life politics', and of lifestyle choices and human self-actualization (Giddens, 1991: 9). As he puts it: 'Social movements have played a basic role in bringing life-political issues to the fore, and forcing them on public attention' (ibid., 228).

Trust and Social Capital

Another way in which insecurity and individualism can be viewed as being detrimental to community life centres upon the issue of trust. For local communities to function it necessitates its members being sociable and co-operating, which in turn is dependent upon the amount of trust that exists between them. Thus trust has come to be regarded as part of the 'social capital' – the customary behaviour or shared norms and values – communities and societies need if they are to operate (see Ehrenhalt, 2000a; Fukuyama, 1999; Lichterman, 2001). But recently 'trust' has been receiving considerable attention, largely because of the growing perception that there is a diminishing amount of it in many Western societies (see Fukuyama, 1995; Gambetta, 1988; Luhmann, 1979, 1988; Misztal, 1996; Putnam, 1995, 1996). This will now be considered.

There are different forms of trust and it serves many functions (see Misztal, 1996). The focus here will be upon the everyday trust existing between or amongst citizens because of its significance for local communities. It is difficult to determine whether there has been a decline in this form of trust because, as Fukuyama (1995) has noted, there are considerable variations within modern societies in terms of the amount of trust that exists. In fact Fukuyama distinguishes between 'high-trust' and 'low-trust' societies. However, considerable insight can be gained from assessing this issue in relation to the major forces and developments shaping our age.

In this regard, it is likely the processes of late modernity work against trust being produced and disseminated. This is because, as we have seen, these processes facilitate greater individual freedom and choice making it more difficult to maintain lasting or permanent relationships. In a post-traditional era, we are more able to walk away from relationships when we do not feel satisfied by them. This in turn encourages scepticism about whether other people can be trusted, thereby eroding some of the social capital which is a prerequisite of community life. Zygmunt Bauman (1996a) has also made this connection:-

> Everything seems to conspire these days against distant goals, life-long projects, lasting commitments, eternal alliances, immutable identities… One cannot build the future around partnership or the family either: in the age of 'confluent love', togetherness lasts no longer than the satisfaction of one of the partners, commitment is from the start 'until further notice', and today's intense attachment may only intensify tomorrow's frustrations. (Bauman, 1996a: 51-2)

And in response to the more insecure nature of human relationships many of us will develop certain defence mechanisms for dealing with other people. As Christopher Lasch (1991) has noted these include:-

> … a certain protective shallowness, a fear of binding commitments, a willingness to pull up roots whenever the need arose, a desire to keep one's options open, a dislike of depending on anyone, an incapacity for loyalty or gratitude. (ibid., 239)

Self-reliance, 'protective shallowness' and 'fear of binding commitments' all suggest an erosion in the amount of trust in contemporary life.

There is a further way in which detraditionalization might be eroding trust and making us more wary of others. As we saw in Chapter 2, detraditionalization entails the shared practices and moral codes of a society are not only challenged in the contemporary era, they are increasingly not passed on, leaving greater scope for individuals to construct their own codes of conduct. Inevitably, the diminution of a common moral culture makes human behaviour less predictable. This means we can no longer be as sure about the actions and conduct of the people we meet. Such attitudes might well be reflected in the decline of hitchhiking. One commentator on this development, Frank Barrett, observed in an article entitled 'A hitch-hikers' guide to growing up' (1992):-

> In the Sixties everybody hitch-hiked; in the Nineties practically nobody seems to. What has happened?… For one thing, the world has changed: it became less safe to hitch-hike. (Barrett, 1992: 43)

This greater wariness of others can also be seen in the so-called 'stranger danger' phenomenon. Parents concerned about the safety of their children are increasingly accompanying them to school until a much older age; many are choosing to drive their children to school. In the UK, for example, the number of children walking to school has significantly reduced: only 44 per cent of 11 to 15-year olds now walk to school, compared to 53 per cent ten years ago (Harper, 1998).

No longer feeling as comfortable in the company of our fellow citizens, a degree of withdrawal from community and civic life, and a retreat into the relative safety of the home and intimate relations, will be the likely response of some people. And the ways in which the 'search for intimacy' in our private lives can run counter to sociability in the wider society, or public realm, has been widely discussed (see Banfield, 1958; Lasch, 1985; Marcuse, 1964; Sennett, 1977).[3] This may in part explain the results of recent surveys in the UK, which indicate nearly a third of the population have never spent a single evening with a neighbour (Locke and Pascoe, 2000).

Richard Sennett in his classic work *The Fall of Public Man* (1986) presents further evidence of our changing attitudes towards public life and our fellow citizens. This book is effectively a response to David Riesman's much-discussed work, *The Lonely Crowd* (1950). In contrast to Riesman and his co-authors, Sennett maintains 'Western societies are moving from something like an other-directed condition to an inner-directed condition' (ibid., 5). As Sennett notes in the eighteenth century: 'In both London and Paris, strangers meeting in parks or on the streets might without embarrassment speak to each other' (ibid., 86). Indeed, based on his historical research, Sennett maintains that in earlier periods of history there was greater sociability, and warns of the current imbalance between public and private life.[4]

It is not universally accepted that preoccupation with our private lives will invariably be at the expense of the public realm. For example, Ashford and Timms (1993) based on research conducted in Europe, identify a degree of correlation between the amount of trust in the private realm (family and friends) and the amount of public trust (trust towards members of the wider society). The inference from such findings is that enjoying close, supportive and trusting relationships in the private sphere leaves individuals better equipped to cope with public life.

However, at present there is insufficient data to draw such firm conclusions (Misztal, 1996). Nor does the work of Ashford and Timms undermine what is being argued here, as much emphasis has been placed upon identifying and describing the increased dislocation within the private sphere, particularly to family life, in the recent period. In short, not everyone enjoys close, supportive and trusting relationships in their private lives.

Moreover, many households in modern societies no longer contain families, with an increasing number occupied by only one person. In the UK, the Office for National Statistics in a report entitled *Social Trends 27*, predicts more than one in three people will be living on their own in the early decades of this century. It also estimates that the number of people having been through a divorce will double. At the same time the proportion getting married will fall (from 57 per cent in 1992 to 49 per cent in 2020), and fewer children will be produced (Cooper, 1997). For a growing number of people therefore the home is a place where we have few social relationships, and in many cases none at all.

In summary, there are a number of ways in which the insecurity and individualism produced by the processes of late modernity are detrimental to social capital and community engagement. The remainder of this chapter will consider other important developments of our time that may well reinforce this tendency.

The Rise of Consumer Society

In the twentieth century many Western nations became essentially consumer societies. The consumption, as well as production and marketing, of goods and services became a major social and economic activity shaping how people organized their lives. Some writers talk of the emergence of a consumer culture whereby 'the items consumed take on a symbolic and not merely material value', paving the way for the commodification of everyday life (Waters, 1995: 140). As a result it is not just material goods which are commodified; this process extends to non-material items, like ideas, relationships, artistic movements, and so on (ibid.).

Inevitably a number of debates have arisen in relation to the rise of consumer society, ranging from the environmental consequences to its role in the formation of self-identity (see Cross, 1993; Featherstone, 1991; Miller, 1995; Nicholson-Lord, 1994; Shields, 1992a). Some commentators also highlight the positive aspects of a consumer culture, arguing it has enhanced individual choice and led to a greater emphasis upon the rights of the consumer – although these gains are similarly a subject of debate. However, the emergence of a consumer culture will be considered here solely in terms of its consequences for local communities and community life.

A defining characteristic of a consumer society is continual change in the nature and experience of consumption. For instance, a relatively recent development has been the expansion of out-of-town shopping malls and superstores. It has been part of the North American shopping experience for some time, but since the 1980s it has spread to Western Europe, and especially to the UK, which has seen a rapid growth in the number of superstores. Due to economies of scale these stores can offer cheaper goods and products. Inevitably, specialist shops and corner shops in towns, as well as village shops, struggle against such competition, resulting in many of them going out of business. These shops are often important centres of community life serving as sites where local people can meet regularly and form acquaintances, and a sense of community identity can develop.

Rob Shields (1992b) presents a more positive interpretation of shopping malls and superstores, arguing they are also public spaces serving a social purpose, and should not be viewed as just sites of commodity exchange. They are places where people spend time and browse, and where individuals interact as part of a crowd. Furthermore, many people regard their visits to shopping malls as a leisure activity. And some North American suburbs are now constructing shopping malls geared to encouraging community activity and events (Dawson and Lord, 1983). All of which leads Shields to conclude that 'shopping malls have become *de facto* community centres' (1992b, 110).

While Shields provides an insight into the complexity of this particular topic, there are problems with his central contention. This is because people do not tend to live in or around shopping malls and superstores. Consequently, the type of interaction and social communication taking place at these sites is seldom likely to be meaningful. They are purely functional spaces largely devoid of any sense of locality and community. Indeed, the shopping malls and superstores with their purpose-built huge car parks are deliberately designed to draw their customers from as wide a geographical area as possible.

The actual shopping experience at these malls and superstores also affords little opportunity for meaningful social intercourse. The majority of people will drive to them in their private cars, rather than walk or use public transport. While the assistant working at a check-out, and quickly pushing through a constant stream of goods, has little time to converse with customers. Even Shields acknowledges such social exchanges are largely codified: 'pro-forma greetings and salutations, a banal, Goffmanesque interaction between scripted roles of shop assistant and the shopper' (ibid.,102). Moreover, conversation is made more difficult by the fact that many firms encourage their staff, notably in fast-food restaurants, supermarkets and garages, to ask a stock set of questions designed to generate more business. For instance, the employees of McDonald's restaurants are schooled in 'efficiency, calculability, predictability and control' (Ritzer, 1993, 1998).

Another recent development potentially harmful to local community life is the growth of 'home shopping' and home-delivery services. Facilitated by improvements in communications technology, on-line shopping and 'interactive television' is enabling increasing numbers of people to purchase goods and services from the comfort of their own homes. Already well established in the United States and Japan, it is proving popular with consumers in other advanced industrial societies. Unfortunately, this provides another reason for not leaving the home, further reducing the opportunities of meeting and communicating with one's fellow citizens.

This is perhaps reflected in a decline in walking rates in many countries in the West. For example, it is estimated that in Finland the miles walked per person each year is just 120 miles; in France the figure is only slightly higher at 132 miles. Even in Britain, where walking rates are generally higher than in other North European countries, the average person will walk only 227 miles per year. And this figure is steadily declining as the percentage of car journeys increase. Indeed, walking constitutes only 3 per cent of the total distance travelled each week in the UK (Harper, 1998).

Sustaining existing levels of consumption is entailing that we are spending more and more time in the workplace in order to pay for these goods and services. For example, one survey conducted in the late 1980s revealed Americans worked on average one month more per year in 1987, than they did in 1969 (Schor, 1991). A more recent study conducted by the International Labour Organization confirms this pattern: whereas in 1990 Americans worked on average 1,942 hours a year this figure had risen to 1,978 hours in 2001 (Ellison, 2001). All of which means people have less free time to devote to their families and friends, let alone participate in community life.[5]

This view is supported by Gary Cross (1993) who has attempted to analyze why, despite the developments in technology and production methods, we never seem to have either enough money or time?[6] From his study of both the American and European experience, he contends that in the 1920s and 1930s, advanced Western societies opted for consumerism rather than more leisure and a different approach to culture, creating insatiable needs which oblige us to work more than industrialism requires. Thus from this period onwards much of both our working and leisure time has been governed by a consumer culture. We effectively have a 'work-and-spend' culture (Cross, 1993; Schor, 1991).

In a similar vein, Fred Hirsch (1977) considers economic reasons to be undermining social and community life in the contemporary period. It stems from the extension of markets and market principles – the need for efficiency, competition, and so on – into all aspects of everyday life. Like Cross, Hirsch believes in modern affluent society, sociability is increasingly displaced by 'time-absorbing consumption' and, as will be discussed in a moment, 'positional competition' (ibid., 81). These motivations foster an outlook that has a range of social implications. It means there is a constant pressure of time because of the desire to maintain patterns or levels of consumption (Linder, 1970); we have to constantly weigh-up the costs and benefits of our actions. Our behaviour becomes more calculating and conditional: in our decision-making we are more likely to ask ourselves 'what is in it for me?' In turn, human relationships become contingent and transactional. For example, this might mean if we see someone in the street in distress we would walk on the other side of the road (Hirsch, 1977: 79). Similarly, we might ask ourselves what we gain from being friendly towards strangers? We will avoid market researchers and those canvassing for our support because we feel there is nothing directly in it for us.

Hirsch goes on to argue that this 'balancing of personal advantage in social relationships' (ibid., 80) will increase because, as he puts it: '[f]riendliness is time consuming and thereby liable to be economized because of its extravagant absorption of this increasingly scarce output' (ibid., 77).[7] Likewise, Alan Ehrenhalt (2000) detects in the United States that sociability has become 'organized': '[it] consists of planned events that have a beginning and end, and conclude promptly so the participants can move on to their next event in their lives' (ibid., 65). Americans, he maintains, have steadily moved away from leisurely conversations, informality and spontaneity, which can be more demanding of their time. While Will Hutton (1999) considers the spread of consumer society and the extension of market relations into everyday life constitutes an assault against friendship entailing that, as he puts it, 'we are making fewer friends than we did' (1999:193).

There is also the potential within a consumer society for commodities to assume as much significance for people as their relations with others. To substantiate this claim it is necessary to go back to Marx's view of commodity fetishism outlined in *Capital* (McLellan, 1977: 435-43). For Marx, capitalism differed from earlier economic systems in which the system of commodity-exchange was based upon use-value. In contrast, capitalism because it seeks to increase the price of a commodity, is based upon exchange-value. Adorno (1991) developed this notion claiming such is the preoccupation with exchange value within capitalism that social relations have become objectified in terms of money, with the commodity assuming a different use-value. What he means by this is we seek to define ourselves, notably in relation to other people, by the things that we purchase. Thus, to cite Adorno's much-quoted example, we venerate the price we pay for the Toscanini concert, rather than the performance itself.

A consumer culture can also engender social tensions. Baudrillard (1981) maintains consumption is increasingly about style rather than function or, what he terms, 'sign-value'. Similarly, Bourdieu (1984) contends that in our patterns of consumption we are essentially buying symbols not products. People express and construct their identity, and seek status and personal development through the products they purchase (Veblen, 1953). Self-expression will occur through the purchase of a variety of products like cars, clothes, food and holidays (Belk, 1995). The downside of this lifestyle consumption is it can lead to what Hirsch (1977) calls 'positional competition', fostering ostentation, jealousy, rivalry and social emulation.

Thus by manifesting inequalities a consumer culture can be socially divisive. Wanting more than they can afford creates frustration for people, and some will resort to crime to attain these goods (Lansley, 1994). In recent years, this has led to instances in the United States and Britain of people resorting to violence in order to steal trainers – a product increasingly marketed in terms of its sign-value – from those who are wearing them.

There are also implications for the civic community if we view ourselves primarily as consumers. Compared to the citizen, the consumer has no duties and obligations other than to themselves; a state of affairs expressed in the language of rights, and specifically 'consumer rights'. Bauman (1992), in this regard, has argued that capitalism, the real motor behind the consumer culture, has sought to equate individual freedom with consumption. Indeed, being a consumer within a consumer culture can be a highly individualistic experience with much emphasis – encouraged by an advertising industry trying to promote products – upon self-fulfilment and self-improvement.

It is of course important not to exaggerate or overestimate the impact of a consumer society upon social and community life. We all perform many roles during the course of our daily lives, and being a consumer is only one such role – albeit an important one given that it is through shopping that we feed and clothe ourselves. Yet the evidence presented here suggests at the very least the emergence of a consumer society within Western democracies often runs counter to forms of local community involvement. It is an obvious point, but if people are, as writers like Cross and Hirsch maintain, locked into a work-and-spend culture then it leaves them with less time to engage in civic and community activity.

New Technology, Leisure and Work

Another challenge confronting local communities arises from developments in technology, especially in terms of their impact upon work and leisure patterns. Robert Putnam (1995, 2000) has extensively researched this area. In an essay entitled 'The strange death of civic America' (1996), he points to a range of independent sources which indicate that during the last thirty years there has been a dramatic fall in forms of social and civic activity in America. This includes political participation, such as campaigning for a political party, attending public meetings, and so on. But it also includes non-political forms of activity such as the amount of time devoted to clubs and organizations:-

> Membership records of such diverse organisations as parent-teacher associations, the League of Women Voters, the Red Cross, trade unions, and even bowling leagues show that participation in many conventional voluntary associations has declined by about 25 per cent to 50 per cent over the past two to three decades. (Putnam, 1996: 13)

Putnam's important research raises the issue of whether his findings are applicable to other advanced industrial societies. In this regard, the distinctiveness of the United States in comparison with other societies has received much attention in the past, often centring upon debates about 'American exceptionalism'. However, it has been the central claim of this work that the primary processes of late modernity transcend national boundaries and are impacting upon all advanced industrial societies. While making due allowance for the particular distinctiveness of each society, it has been argued the common response of citizens to these processes is likely to be greater individualism and an increasing resort to private-orientated modes of behaviour. For instance, in the UK a recent survey conducted in Basildon, which has come to be regarded as representative of the opinions of the average Briton, found that during the 1990s people had become increasingly individualistic in both their views and activities. This was reflected in the fact that 55 per cent of respondents were not members of any club or society (White, 2001).

Yet there are some recent studies, which would seem to challenge aspects of Putnam's thesis. For example, based on his research of interest group activity in the United States, Robert Wuthnow (1994) contends that 40 per cent of Americans belong to, or are involved with, at least one small group. And they do so for reasons of mutual support and the defence of common interests. It is also the case that different types of civic and political activity have developed in recent years in the United States and other Western democracies, such as the growth in the number of self-help groups – although this can be interpreted as evidence of low levels of social capital.

Nevertheless the extensive nature of the research carried out by Putnam and his colleagues over a number of years, and covering many forms of civic and community behaviour has been widely praised. As one reviewer of his book *Bowling Alone* (2000) has noted, Putnam proves 'to what ought to be the satisfaction of any fair-minded reader' that America has indeed experienced a decline in its stock of social capital (Ehrenhalt, 2000a: 63).

In seeking to explain this trend, Putnam has considered how changes in technology and our leisure time have eroded the civic community. Based on a range of primary research data, most notably from the US national opinion research centre in Chicago, he contends that age is the most important predictor of the degree of civic engagement. More specifically, that older people – those born before 1940 – undertake more civic activity, belong to more associations, vote more often, and so on, than their younger counterparts. This leads Putnam to conclude there must have been new developments confronting the post-war generations 'which rendered them less likely to connect with the community' (ibid., 13). And the key development he cites is the impact television has had in fostering inactivity and a retreat into the private sphere. During the post-war period there has been a dramatic increase in the ownership of television sets, and in the number of hours people spend watching them each day. It is estimated, for example, that the average American citizen now watches television for approximately four hours a day. And if Putnam is correct when the pre-1940 generation pass away there is likely to be even lower levels of civic activity in American society.[8]

In contrast, some commentators consider there is a social and collective dimension to television; that families and nations watch it together and it therefore facilitates a common experience. However, this is probably an outdated view, only ever applicable in the early days of television when there were few channels. This meant people tended to watch the same programmes, which made it possible to discuss them the next day at work. Today, satellite and digital technology enable multi-channel households, resulting in television viewing becoming a more fragmented and individual experience. This is reinforced by the fact that many households own more than one television. It means that, compared to the past, the experience of watching television is less likely to be a family occasion.

The demise of a national television audience has implications for the attempt to promote so-called 'push-button democracy' through the use of electronic communications technology, and in particular interactive television. This is being pursued by the United States and other Western democracies as a result of declining voter turnout and levels of civic engagement in order to encourage their electorates to become more involved in local and national politics. Interactive television can make, so the argument goes, a positive contribution to the strengthening of democracy and civic communities by enabling people to vote on a range of local and national issues (see Black, 1992; Budge, 1993; McLean, 1990). However, the plethora of television channels fragments the viewing audience, making voting more difficult to organize.

And returning to the theme of this chapter, push-button democracy may well be harmful to community life. It reduces the need for individuals to go out into their local communities and campaign for issues, in the form of delivering leaflets and canvassing opinion. Similarly, there is less need for public meetings in town- and village-halls to raise public awareness. All of these forms of local political interaction can be conducted through the medium of interactive television and the setting-up of 'electronic town meetings', where people never actually meet face-to-face (Black, 1992).

Some writers simply dismiss the view that watching television is, or can be, a social experience. For example, Ulrich Beck (1992) considers television destroys conversation and reduces social engagement. It removes 'people from traditionally shaped and bounded contexts of conversation, experience and life' (1992: 132). As Beck puts it: '[e]veryone sits isolated even in the family and gapes at the set'. It leads him to conclude that we are becoming 'isolated mass hermits' (ibid.). Indeed, television with its range of programmes and images, can serve as a substitute for real life; 'individuals can believe that they have had a diversity of experiences from the safety of the armchair' (Tester, 1997: 48).

The increased ownership and use of video-recorders (VCRs) merely reinforces this pattern of behaviour. It means Walter Benjamin's hopes, which he famously expressed in his essay 'The Work of Art in the Age of Mechanical Reproduction', have not been borne out. He considered film, and the experience of going to the cinema, to be a collective and critical experience with political potential. Today, however, while many people still go to the cinema, they do so only occasionally as they are able to watch films and other programmes through the medium of television and videos in the comfort of their own homes. Television has the additional advantage of being substantially cheaper than going to the cinema or theatre (Mulgan, 1989). The spectator is therefore increasingly becoming the private viewer.

The spread of new forms of global communications, such as the Internet and e-mail, provide us with the opportunity to form networks of social relationships beyond our immediate surroundings. In this sense technology enables us to be sociable and to interact with others. However, such relationships can never be fully satisfying as the technology provides for only a restrictive form of communication. Contacting people all over the globe does not constitute the formation of meaningful relationships and friendships. To build such relationships requires us regularly physically meeting other people, spending time with them and gaining shared memories. Indeed, John Gray (1995) considers the virtual community of the Internet to be a form of retreat or escapism from the problems of the real world, and from the effort and responsibility of maintaining proper human relationships. Interestingly, a 1997 study of British office-workers revealed over a third conceded they used e-mail as a way of avoiding direct interactions (Locke and Pascoe, 2000).

Other developments in technology, along with their widespread dissemination, simply entail less opportunity to be sociable. For instance, ever increasing car ownership invariably means fewer people are using trains and buses, which provide greater opportunities for social interaction. Similarly, the growth in private ownership of washing machines means we have less reason to go to laundrettes (Kumar, 1997: 215). Moreover, new technology has paved the way for the emergence of a 'self-service economy', which further restricts social intercourse (Gershuny and Miles, 1983). For example, most petrol stations are self-service. We can also buy books and other goods and services via the Internet without ever meeting a sales assistant. While many financial services are now arranged by telephone or simply by filling-in forms reducing the need for face-to-face contact. In the case of banks, computerization means we can obtain our money from cash-point machines and no longer converse with cashiers. Given this technology can enable companies to reduce staffing levels and thereby save money, the self-service economy looks set to spread.

Person-to-person communication and interaction is therefore becoming less common in many types of business transaction because of developments in technology. Personal service is now considered by many firms to be an unnecessary and expensive way of doing business in the new age. And many companies and banks are shifting to 'direct' marketing and business techniques, such as First Direct. This entails dealing with customers via a telephone service, which means we are less likely to receive visits from sales people (Hewitt, 1998). Indeed, in the UK, the switch to forms of 'direct banking' has led some of the major high street banks to close a number of their local branches. People who know their local bank manager are now a rarity.

The increasingly impersonal nature of contemporary business is attracting much comment. Such a tendency is evident in the practices of Call Centres, which ensure there is little possibility of friendly conversations being struck up between the operator and the consumer. The telephone calls are largely scripted with a computer taking an operator through a series of questions to ask the customer. Both the nature and pace of the conversation is therefore pre-determined. And two factors ensure that the operator sticks to this format and does not indulge in spontaneous friendly banter. Firstly, managers or supervisors can 'listen in anytime to check whether an employee – who will be expected to deal with several hundred clients day – is adopting the correct cheery tone' (Denny, 1998: 18). Secondly, the pay of operators is often performance related: they are therefore under pressure to deal with as many inquiries, or make as many as sales, as possible. All of which is the antithesis of sociability. Yet the growth of call centres in many advanced industrial societies has been spectacular. In the UK, for example, more people work in Call Centres than in traditional industries like coal, steel and vehicle production (Denny, 1998). It is estimated that one worker in 50 is now employed in a Call Centre, and the figure is rising. Moreover, according to the Call Centre Association, half of all existing consumer transaction in the UK is now undertaken through Call Centres.

Overall, recent developments in technology, especially electronic technology, would seem to encourage private-orientated modes of behaviour. As we have seen during the course of this work, the technology now exists to enable us not only to work and shop from home, but we can also be entertained there. All of which reduces the immediate need for people to become involved in their local communities and community life. It might be claimed new forms of labour-saving technology provide us with more time for social and civic engagement. But as has been shown, studies carried out by Robert Putnam and others suggest there is little evidence this is happening; in fact the reverse is the case. While the research of writers like Gary Cross (1993) – mentioned in the previous section – suggest people are simply working longer to pay for these labour-saving devices.

Urban Life under Late Modernity

In assessing the condition of community life in the contemporary period, it is necessary to consider it in relation to the urban environment that more and more of us are living and working in. This will now be examined with particular attention directed at the ways in which urban areas have been affected by the processes of late modernity. It will be argued that aspects of the organization of cities and the nature of city life in advanced industrial societies make it difficult for local communities to function effectively.

To begin with it is clear that the post-Fordist transformation has had a considerable impact upon aspects of urban life. The neighbourhoods and communities within major towns and cities of many advanced industrial societies have been disrupted by the impact of de-industrialization. In the United States and many Western European states the manufacturing sectors in numerous industrial cities have contracted creating large areas of derelict urban space. As urban theorists Robert Beauregard and Anna Haila have observed:-

> Cities like Detroit, Pittsburgh, Chicago, and St Louis in the United States, Liverpool and Manchester in England, Glasgow in Scotland, and Bilbao in Spain experienced blight and dereliction in their once-thriving industrial areas. During the 1980s, for example, Bilbao lost over one-half of its industrial employment and in London manufacturing jobs dropped form approximately 20 per cent of the total to about 10 per cent. (Beauregard and Haila, 2000: 25)

De-industrialization, accompanied by the growth of out-of-town retailing, discussed earlier, has contributed to the decline of city centres with many people simply moving away from them. As Tim Hall (1998) has noted, this development is especially evident in the UK where city centres have, in comparison with continental European countries, historically been dominated by commercial and retail firms, and there is less of a tradition of people living in these areas.

Towns and cities, as a result of de-industrialization, are also less likely to be organized upon the basis of occupation and class. Long-established working class neighbourhoods, once a source of community-orientated and co-operative behaviour, have declined and fragmented. In many cases this process has been completed by what some commentators have termed the 'postmodernization' of cities, which has entailed the gentrification of run-down areas suitable for the affluent to live (see Cooke, 1988; Zukin, 1987, 1988). Many of these industrial cities have also attempted a revival by focusing upon the service sector. However, the workers within this sector are typically commuters and because they do not live close to their place of employment are unlikely to have a strong sense of allegiance to these locations.

Indeed, these urban spaces provide the most vivid manifestation of the human consequences of the post-Fordist epoch. The growing economic inequality and poverty that, as we saw in Chapter 1, is a feature of post-Fordism is evident in the streets and on the pavements of large towns and cities. It is where those who have been left behind or excluded – the underclass of the homeless and the long-term unemployed – tend to congregate.

Peter Marcuse and Ronald van Kempen (2000) consider these economic and social divisions are shaping urban areas. They identify a number of changes to the spatial order of 'globalizing cities' in the recent period – some that are making it more difficult to build inclusive local communities. In particular, ghettos are becoming even more separated from the rest of the city at the same time as exclusionary enclaves for the rich, often physically protected by walls and security checkpoints, are emerging. Marcuse and Van Kempen recognize these developments are primarily confined to the United States – especially the excluded ghetto based upon racial lines – rather than European cities. Nevertheless, they contend there are 'tendencies in that direction' across advanced industrial societies (ibid., 261). Indeed, it is certainly possible to find evidence in the UK of the emergence of exclusionary enclaves with walling and gating becoming a feature of much new urban development.

Marcuse and Van Kempen consider these recent spatial and social formations within cities to be 'strongly related to the processes of globalization' (ibid., 253). However, they recognize the nature of globalization, as we saw in Chapter 3, is unclear and disputed. Yet there is a broad consensus that, at the very least, globalization is contributing to the greater mobility of people within and between societies. In this sense, globalization can be regarded as reinforcing an aspect of city life which runs counter to the fostering of vibrant local communities and that concerns the transient nature of its population. Within the context of an already dynamic environment a high population turnover makes it more difficult to forge meaningful relationships and common ties within neighbourhoods. It thereby reduces the likelihood of people identifying with a particular neighbourhood in urban areas. This trend is reinforced by the demand for workers to be 'flexible' which, as we saw in Chapter 1, is a feature of the post-Fordist epoch. In practice this can mean being prepared to live and work in different locations, often for short periods of time, for their employers. While for those out of work it can entail travelling and relocating to different areas in search of employment.

At any moment a city is occupied by many people who are simply passing through, such as the tourist, the vagrant and the commuter, and consequently have little real sense of attachment and commitment to it and the people living there. Indeed, Zygmunt Bauman (1993, 1996) goes further viewing the tourist and the vagabond or vagrant as harmful to morality. They have no need to intervene in the moral debates of the places they visit, to concern themselves with moral outrages, and they have no moral responsibility or duty towards the local population.

The forces of late modernity shape individual cities in different ways, and it is important to avoid overestimating their influence. In this respect, Robert Beauregard and Anne Haila (2000) stress the continuities with the past that still exist in contemporary cities, particularly in the form of modern or Fordist influences (ibid., 35). Moreover, some writers identify other factors that have had a significant impact upon social and community relations within urban areas. For instance, Jane Jacobs (1961) argues much of the responsibility for the break-up of older urban neighbourhood communities within American cities lies with modernist urban planning, which replaced many of these neighbourhoods with public or planned housing projects. In *The Death and Life of Great American Cities* (1961), she describes the ability of established and dense social networks within these older urban neighbourhoods to reduce crime, notably in terms of its members – especially shopkeepers and traders – watching for criminal and delinquent activity. Local communities are therefore able to contribute to public safety and security – a theme developed in Part II.

Richard Sennett (1986) also criticizes those modernist architects who have designed simply for function. He maintains it has led to the creation of 'dead public space' in our towns and cities: areas that we simply pass through, rather than spaces we value and in which we want to spend time (ibid., 12-16). Ray Oldenburg – as the title of his book *The Great Good Place* (1989) suggests – similarly stresses the importance for community life of places in which its members can communicate and be sociable, such as town squares and cafes. As Oldenburg puts it:-

> The course of urban growth and development in the United States has been hostile to an informal public life; we are failing to provide either suitable or sufficient gathering places necessary for it. (Ehrenhalt, 2000b: 60)

As a result of some of the developments described here, for many people living in cities can be a lonely and alienating experience. The rapid pace of life encourages snatched conversations and casual acquaintances, rather than meaningful encounters and lasting relationships. In this regard, the city more closely resembles *gesellschaft* – the mass society in which people have few meaningful bonds – as opposed to *gemeinschaft* (a close-knit community) in the distinction Ferdinand Tönnies made between types of social relations.

A further development eroding civic and community life within cities, especially in the UK and the United States, has been certain challenges to municipal politics (see Hall, 1998). For example, in the UK since the late 1970s, local governance has been curtailed because of factors like: the increasing centralization of power; a decrease in central government funding to local government; and the greater use of the private sector in social welfare provision, such as housing. This development is a consequence of British domestic politics in the recent period. Yet for ordinary citizens the significance and purpose of municipal politics has been reduced, and this is reflected in declining voter turnout at local elections.

While these developments are not as applicable to continental European cities, nevertheless a case can be made that municipal politics has been undermined in all Western democracies as a result of them becoming consumer societies. Susan Christopherson makes this point in an essay entitled 'The Fortress City: Privatized Spaces, Consumer Citizenship' (1994), which charts how consumerism has altered the nature of the city and city life. In particular, she contends it has eroded the public realm. For example, there is an increasing tendency within cities for many public sites such as parks, churches, schools, libraries and museums, to become privatized places of consumption, notably retailing and office developments. Indeed, Christopherson believes this is a two-way process: that urban development has played a 'critical role' in facilitating consumer culture (ibid., 413).

These changes, Christopherson maintains, reflect the pressure municipal authorities are under to be more self-financing. As well as land and buildings being sold to the private sector, services are often privatized, thereby reducing the scope of democratic governance. For Christopherson, these developments are reflected in changes in the nature of municipal politics. The traditional demands of universal rights to housing and public services are being replaced, and with it notions of social citizenship, by the type of particularist and consumer-rights politics discussed earlier. As she puts it: 'To the consumer-citizen, politics is the practice of selecting from a given array of goods, not questioning and compromising to create a good' (1994: 415).

Umberto Eco would almost certainly concur with the generally negative portrayal of city life presented here. This is because he considers cities are becoming less conducive to sociability. Indeed, in *Travels in Hyperreality* (1987) he writes of the 'medievalisation of the city'. It forms part of his broader contention that there are signs of 'neo-medievalism' within the contemporary period, with the city a key part of this process.[9] For Eco, the city today, like its medieval counterpart, is made-up of micro-societies and ghettos with there often being much tension between the different groups. It is reflected, he observes, in the fact that a white middle-class inhabitant of New York will be wary of getting off the subway at Harlem, and they will not enter Central Park at night (ibid., 79).

Linked to these developments many city-dwellers have an ongoing concern about being victims of crime, especially a fear of violence committed by strangers. Even Raban (1974) who is generally positive about living in a city writes of the randomness of so much urban violence and the unsettling impact it can have upon people. For the inhabitants of cities this can entail a degree of uneasiness about their personal safety, which will work against any desire to be sociable. Neighbourhood crime watch schemes and citizen patrols are therefore as much a reflection of these concerns as an example of community-orientated behaviour.

Eco also points to developments in the contemporary period that depart from his neo-medieval thesis, such as overpopulation and the 'excesses of communication and transportation', which are making cities uninhabitable 'through a paroxysm of activity' (1987: 77). It is resulting in traffic gridlock, air pollution, the accumulation of garbage, and so on. And it is an obvious point, but districts within cities that are unpleasant and unhealthy places in which to live and work do little to facilitate sociability and community life.

However, Michel Maffesoli in *The Time of the Tribes: The Decline of Individualism in Mass Society* (1996), maintains that patterns of group behaviour continue to exist and flourish within cities. More significantly, he sees new forms of group attachment emerging within larger cities, and especially amongst young people, in the form of, for example, youth subcultures. Maffesoli considers these groups to be a form of neo-tribalism and should be regarded as outbursts of sociality.

Yet because these neo-tribes inhabit such a rapidly changing environment as the city, they are inevitably transient in nature, unable to form the basis of lasting associations and communities. As Fukuyama (2000) has observed: '[a] community is not formed every time a group of people happens to interact with one another' (ibid., 14-15).

Many writers on urban living would consider what has been presented thus far as an overly bleak portrayal of city-life. For example, Jonathan Raban in *Soft City* (1974) describes the city in terms of its complexity, vibrancy and diversity. There are also many positive and pleasurable aspects of living in cities and large towns. In comparison with small towns and villages there are more things to do and see, and greater opportunities for gaining work. Moreover, because of the anonymity the city allows us, we are freer to become what we like (Etzioni, 1995: 116-7).

There are also some case studies that suggest sociability and community are an integral feature of cities and city life. In this respect, Herbert Gans (1982) identifies the 'urban villages' which exist within cities as sources of such behaviour. Based on his research, Gans argues these are areas where the inhabitants behave in a cordial manner towards each other. Indeed, many people both knew and conversed with their neighbours, shopkeepers and local leaders.

While Jim Sleeper (1990), based on his study of New York City – Gans concentrated mainly on Boston – stresses the importance of churches, bars and bowling alleys as centres of community activity and interaction. He also identified some evidence of community action in terms of campaigning for local issues. But of course these are only two studies and they may not necessarily be representative of the situation in cities in other advanced industrial societies, and even elsewhere in the United States. Moreover, the research for both studies, especially that of Herbert Gans, was undertaken a number of years ago and may already be out-of-date. In this regard, their findings have to be weighed against the broader processes of late modernity, which it has been claimed here are encouraging greater individualism and a shift towards private-orientated modes of behaviour.

Other examples of community activity within large towns and cities can be detected amongst immigrant communities. These often function to provide protection from hostile outsiders, as well offering support in terms of finding accommodation and jobs, especially for newly arrived migrants (see Dahya, 1974). However, as will be discussed in Chapter 6, this type of community can be exclusive rather than inclusive in nature and orientation, and serve to reduce the need for its members to integrate into the wider society.

Given the competing accounts outlined here, it is difficult to reach a firm conclusion about the condition of community life within urban areas, and especially cities. For Amitai Etzioni, a city is a mixture or hotchpotch of modes of behaviour, that *gemeinschaft* and *gesellschaft* 'exist side by side' (1995: 120). This is undoubtedly true. Conditions will also vary within individual cities as a result of factors like their particular histories, level of economic development and the political parties in control of them. Furthermore, as Marcuse and Van Kempen have noted, the city is not a distinct and unitary entity (2000: 265). Indeed, they contend it is more appropriate to talk of 'layered' cities if we are to reflect the diversity and complexity that constitutes this urban space (ibid.).

Nevertheless, the examples and arguments presented here suggest there are significant obstacles to building community ties within the contemporary city, and that it is perhaps not a natural or conducive arena for civic- and community-orientated behaviour. And as has been shown, this has been exacerbated by the impact of the processes of late modernity. Finally, possibly the most compelling evidence of the condition of city life within advanced industrial societies is that so many people seek to move out of them. As Peter Marcuse and Ronald van Kempen have noted: '[p]opulation movement from central cities to suburbs is a common phenomenon in most developed countries' (2000: 8). The affluent middle classes in particular regard moving to the suburbs and rural areas as enhancing their quality of life.

Conclusion

This chapter has sought to examine the condition of community life within advanced industrial societies, something which is difficult, perhaps impossible, to determine. Yet there are certain necessary prerequisites local communities or neighbourhoods require if they are to function and flourish. Most importantly, social capital is required in the form of shared norms and values, a level of trust, regular contact and sociability between its members, and forms of community and civic activity. The inhabitants of particular communities or neighbourhoods must also feel a sense of attachment to them. However, as we have seen during the course of this chapter these aspects of community life are in some way challenged by the primary processes and developments of the contemporary period. These forces will of course impact upon local communities within individual societies in different ways, dependent upon their particular histories and cultures. But it has been shown that broadly-speaking the processes of late modernity encourage greater individualism, often at the expense of civic and community-orientated behaviour. For this reason, it is appropriate to talk of the erosion of local community life in our time. The implications of this development, and whether we should be concerned about it, are addressed in Part II.

PART II
REBUILDING COMMUNITIES

Introduction

To recap, in Part I it was argued that the primary processes of our late modern age are generating greater individualism. People living in advanced industrial societies are now freer to travel anywhere in the world, less guided by custom and tradition, and some are better able to determine their own life-paths. But there is also increasing insecurity and diminishing social capital and trust in many of these societies, which is evident, for example, in anxiety about crime, precarious relationships, and increasing cynicism, especially towards public and commercial organizations. Indeed, the very freedoms we have gained threaten the forms of common life – such as communities, families, and national cultures and institutions – which facilitate or make possible our individual autonomy. The task of Part II is to address this dilemma.

In Chapter 5, a case is a made for fostering a public-spirited culture as a way of reinvigorating local communities and replenishing social capital. Potential strategies for developing such a culture are outlined, notably a national campaign encouraging people to undertake public-spirited or community-orientated activity for an hour per week. It will be argued that this can serve to counter some of the negative aspects of our age of individualism.

In Chapter 6, it is claimed a public-spirited culture might also start to tackle some of the cultural divisions and tensions plaguing many Western societies. Weak civic communities, as well as conditions of insecurity, have contributed to the rise in what has been termed 'tribalist' patterns of behaviour, such as increased levels of racist violence, the growth of identity politics, and the emergence or revival of ethnic nationalist and separatist movements. While this development reflects a deep-rooted human need to belong to forms of community, it needs to be countered by the building of more inclusive communities and societies.

The aim of Chapter 7 is to construct a philosophical case for developing a public-spirited culture, by considering it in relation to communitarianism and liberalism. It will be maintained it is possible to retain the central ideas of both traditions – the autonomy of liberalism and the community of communitarianism – within a project geared towards facilitating human flourishing. For human flourishing to be a possibility, a prerequisite is that people must have meaningful autonomy, defined as having the freedom to choose from a plurality of options, experiences and life-chances. This is something best achieved or facilitated within vibrant, mutually supportive and inclusive communities. And crucially such communities can be built by developing strategies to encourage public-spirited behaviour.

Fostering a public-spirited culture in the contemporary period entails challenging the formidable processes discussed in Part I. Government would therefore need to be heavily involved in promoting measures to develop such a culture. Defending the principle of this type of government intervention is another important concern of Chapter 7.

In Chapter 8, it will be shown how the educational system has an important role to play in the development of a public-spirited culture. Quite simply, it is more likely that citizens will behave in this way if they have had first-hand experience of undertaking community activity. Consequently, community service should be an established part of the civic education young people receive in schools and colleges.

Chapter 5

Public-spiritedness and Community

Having described the processes encouraging individualistic and private-orientated modes of behaviour in Part I, it will now be argued that devising strategies to foster a more public-spirited culture is an appropriate response to some of the problems engendered by this development. This is because – in the form argued for here – it offers the prospect of building vibrant, inclusive and mutually supportive local communities, which as will be shown can counter some of the negative aspects of living in an age of greater individualism. For this reason, governments need to devote attention and resources to the promotion of public-spiritedness.

As was stated in the Introduction, 'public-spirited' is viewed here in terms of a willingness to engage in community action; of citizens thinking beyond their particular interests and becoming more involved in their communities and societies. And in making the case for fostering a public-spirited culture, a strategy for encouraging community and neighbourly activity is outlined in the first section of this chapter, as well as an indication of its potential benefits. The particular approach advocated here might not gain wide acceptance, but other approaches or schemes might be developed. Indeed, the main purpose of this chapter is to defend the principle of encouraging people to undertake more community and neighbourly activity. This will involve examining likely criticisms of this proposal. In response it will be claimed that some of the consequences of increasing individualism, such as the diminution of social capital, entails that doing nothing is not an option, especially as the economic systems of advanced industrial societies may well be contributing to this development. This point is reinforced in the final section, where it is argued the nature of liberal democracy tends to discourage civic and community engagement, and in a sense can be viewed as indirectly contributing to the individualism of our age.

Fostering a Public-spirited Culture

Any proposal or strategy designed to foster a public-spirited culture would have to be acceptable to ordinary citizens. Ideally, it would place only limited demands upon our time, and generally not encroach upon our individual autonomy. With these points in mind, one approach might be in the form of an ongoing national campaign promoted by government, local authorities, schools and the media to encourage people to be public-spirited for an hour a week by undertaking forms of local community and neighbourly activity. For the sake of convenience – were such a scheme to be implemented – this would likely translate into people doing four hours per month; that is, choosing to do such work all in one morning or an afternoon. Thus this proposal does not significantly encroach upon the free time of citizens. And of course some people might want to devote more time than this to such activity and others already will do, and they should be similarly encouraged. There is also the possibility of being public-spirited at work, rather than in our leisure time. As will be discussed later, an increasing number of companies in advanced industrial societies are setting-up community volunteering schemes.

Furthermore, being only an hour per week would make it easier for women to undertake such activity. This is because numerous surveys indicate that on average women work longer hours than men in many Western societies, especially those balancing careers and family life. Indeed, many feminist writers consider the nature and organization of modern societies, particularly in terms of child rearing practices, prevents women from becoming equal and active citizens (Phillips, 1993: 111).

Government would have to play a major role in setting-up and promoting any national campaign for encouraging community and voluntary activity. This might entail legislating to ensure the adequate monitoring and supervision of schemes, as well as encouraging television companies and other media organizations to broadcast advertisements about the campaign. A government also has the resources to pay for advertising, maintain telephone information help-lines and websites, and generally co-ordinate such a project. It will be argued later in this work, that a democratically elected government has the necessary authority and legitimacy to enable it, within moderation, to try and influence the behaviour of its citizens.

However, it would not be excessively expensive for a government to introduce and maintain such a national campaign. As well as the promotional costs, the major expenditure would be the provision of funding to voluntary associations and community groups organizing locally based projects. Facilitating this type of activity would also necessitate spending money upon both building and maintaining community centres and village halls. Above all it entails working to ensure that people feel safe in their neighbourhoods and able to undertake public-spirited work. This in turn demands that issues such as crime, transport, decent schools and housing, job opportunities and access to shops are tackled. Yet this is what most governments in modern societies already strive to achieve, and therefore does not constitute additional expenditure. Moreover, later in the chapter it will be shown that this proposal could potentially have financial benefits for governments.

To repeat, 'public-spirited' schemes, projects and activities would have to be monitored by government, but this could be carried out in conjunction with local authorities. Indeed, many local or state authorities in Western democracies already have community development programmes, and the promotion of public-spiritedness could be incorporated into such programmes. Furthermore, in countries like the UK where the role of local government has been steadily eroded in recent years, facilitating forms of public-spirited activity would provide it with another function to perform. Thus national or central government would help set-up the overall campaign, but the emphasis would be upon local authorities, and above all local people, devising their own public-spirited initiatives and enterprises. It is after all local people that know most about their communities and neighbourhoods.

As has been indicated, one way in which people can be public-spirited is by working for voluntary organizations. Not only are they already subject to statutory legislation in most advanced industrial societies, the diversity of these organizations enables citizens to undertake a range of activities. They are also experienced in running volunteering schemes, and many of them will be aware of the particular needs and problems of local communities. Indeed, one of the strengths of voluntary organizations is that they often emerge to fill the gaps in state and market welfare provision. And as many voluntary organizations already do much to facilitate community and neighbourly activity, they should be given the means to expand their activities in order to help generate a public-spirited culture. This would entail that the issue of funding, which is an ongoing concern for the voluntary sector in countries like the UK, would need to be addressed (see Sheard, 1995).[1]

There are of course variations within Western democracies in terms of the condition and significance of the voluntary sector. As Pete Alcock (1996) has noted in countries with more limited state welfare provision, such as the United States, the voluntary sector 'is large in both scale and scope' (1996: 98). In comparison, the voluntary sector within the social democratic countries of the European Union is not on the same scale, though it remains important (ibid.). But following on from the theme of Part I, it is increasingly likely that even social democratic governments will in future be looking at a range of ways, including expanding the voluntary sector, for maintaining welfare provision. In the UK, this approach was certainly taken up with enthusiasm by the Conservative government during the 1980s and 1990s. Yet even a strongly social democratic country like Denmark has been expanding its voluntary sector in the recent period (ibid.).

Public-spiritedness could also be displayed through involvement in local community groups and participating in neighbourhood care, transport provision and crime prevention schemes. Alternatively, public-spirited activity could be even more informal, and simply involve helping one's neighbours, particularly the elderly and infirm. This might include shopping for them, doing some gardening, general household chores, or simply social visiting. There would of course be categories of people excluded from this particular strategy, notably paedophiles, rapists, burglars, and others with similar criminal convictions. There would also have to be a series of statutory punishments, ranging from fines to imprisonment, for anyone found using such schemes as a pretext to gaining access to properties for criminal ends. But the advantage of only giving and receiving help from neighbours is that we have more of an idea of the character of the person or persons we are dealing with. Moreover, because this proposal for fostering public-spiritedness is based upon voluntary activity, involving no financial remuneration, the chance for exploitation is reduced.

Nor should it be just the elderly receiving such support. If a culture of public-spiritedness is to emerge then all sections of society should be potential recipients of this help. It is also essential that those undertaking this type of work should similarly come from a wide cross-section of society. Indeed, people who have retired from work will generally have more time to carry out voluntary and community activity. In this regard, in the U.S. the President of the National Retiree Volunteer Coalition, Donna S. Anderson, has argued that retirees are among America's most overlooked resources (Anderson, 1994). While a study conducted amongst retirees in America in 1995 revealed that those who undertook voluntary work for more than ten hours per week scored significantly higher in the 'Purpose In Life' category. They were much less prone to boredom than those who undertook such activity for less than ten hours per week (Weinstein et al., 1995).

More generally, the quality of life within local communities could be enhanced if the public-spiritedness of some citizens was geared to improving the environment. Some time each week or month could be spent by groups of local people coming together to undertake such tasks as helping to repair and restore community amenities (like parks, children's play-grounds, foot-paths and flower-beds), removing graffiti from walls and buildings, and clearing-up litter. Similarly, public-spiritedness might also include joining conservation groups to preserve the countryside, undertaking tasks such as dredging lakes and rivers, planting trees and restoring hedges. This type of activity might also make people more environmentally aware.

There are also opportunities to undertake community volunteering within public services. This is particularly the case in countries like the UK where the public services have often suffered from a lack of funding. In this regard, Elisabeth Hoodless, executive director of the Community Service Volunteers (CSV), argues there needs to be a greater emphasis upon encouraging volunteering outside the charity sector in the UK (Snell, 2000). This would entail, for example, more people becoming special constables, school governors, lay magistrates, and so on. In particular, she highlights how the National Health Service and public libraries would benefit from more volunteers:-

> Half our NHS trusts use no volunteers at all, while the potential for libraries is even greater. Why are we talking about closing libraries? If volunteers were brought in our libraries could run more initiatives such as homework clubs for school children. They could become vibrant places open in the evening and at weekends. (ibid.)

Another opportunity to be public-spirited is provided by the growing number of community volunteering schemes being set-up by businesses in advanced industrial societies. For instance, in the United States, many companies and corporations urge their employees to undertake volunteer programmes of public works activities in the local community, ranging from tree-planting to the construction of public shelters (Caudron, 1994). For the companies such programmes provide opportunities to train employees, build team spirit and company loyalty, and above all enhance their public image (ibid.). Some firms donate old office equipment and furniture to local communities, especially schools; and others make available their facilities to local people. In one scheme – 'the Atlanta Project' – a number of corporations co-ordinated their efforts leading to corporations loaning executives to voluntary organizations, as well as making financial contributions to different projects (Carroll and Horton, 1994).

In the UK, there have been similar schemes and projects, many of which are organized and encouraged by Business in the Community (BITC). This organization, which emerged following the urban riots of the early 1980s, has a membership of some 700 leading companies in Britain, and many companies actively seek to gain the BITC benchmark. There will be a range of reasons for the involvement of companies in BITC, but some companies will have made the connection between profitability and the wellbeing of the communities in which they operate.

For employees, such company volunteering schemes are a way of developing new skills, especially social and communication skills, as well as providing a temporary release from the pressures of their job and the chance to gain a more balanced outlook – many report being refreshed when they return to work. Many volunteers also report that they found community volunteering rewarding, challenging and fun (Dhingra, 2000). And when community projects are organized involving a group of employees from a particular firm, it provides a good way of getting to know work colleagues. Of course for some employees, it is a way of pursuing other career options and finding more fulfilling work.

There is a potential danger with any national campaign of the type advocated here that it is taken over by a government and used for its own political ends (Sheard, 1995). However, the particular campaign for encouraging public-spiritedness outlined in this work is designed to be non-party political. As has been stated its ongoing promotion needs to become tantamount to a function of government: irrespective of which political party was in power the administrative system or permanent civil service would be organized to pursue this policy objective. This would reduce the likelihood of public-spiritedness becoming associated with a single political party. Moreover, many countries in continental Europe have a tradition of coalition government making this scenario even more unlikely. While in those countries with a history of two-party politics – such as the United States and the UK – there is a degree of political consensus emerging over the need for citizens to undertake more civic and community activity. For example, in the UK, the Conservative Party's 'Make a Difference' campaign of the 1980s was followed by New Labour's emphasis upon the 'Giving Age' in the 1990s; both initiatives were geared to encouraging active citizenship. Likewise, in the United States it has been noted that there are certain similarities in the approaches of both the Clinton and Bush administrations towards issues of citizenship, civil society and communitarianism, even though they represent different political parties. For example, one of the first acts of George W. Bush was to give a financial boost to AmeriCorps – a national service programme promoting volunteerism much favoured by his predecessor (Milbank, 2001).

One hour might be considered an insufficient amount of time to undertake any meaningful public-spirited activity. But this would be to misunderstand the real purpose of such a campaign: it is to encourage citizens to think about working for their local communities in the hope that. more will do so and a culture of public-spiritedness might emerge. An hour per week is therefore merely a guideline. Of course, some citizens will never undertake such activity, many only occasionally, and a few people will be cynical about such a project. Yet the aim is to maximize the number of people behaving in this way so that neighbourly and community activity becomes much more prevalent within advanced industrial societies.

However, the effort required to undertake community and neighbourly activity would ensure a public-spirited culture never became so pervasive that people would feel compelled to act in this way. Nor should it be so influential because this would undermine our individual autonomy. Thus 'culture' in its usage here is simply taken to mean accepted conduct or behaviour, and as activity that is widely practised or habitual. But we would retain the freedom to reject or to refuse to participate in such a culture. Ultimately, citizens should be able to decide for themselves whether or not they want to be public-spirited.

The Benefits of a Public-spirited Culture

This proposal for fostering a public-spirited culture would potentially have a number of positive effects. To begin with the proposal outlined here would provide opportunities for people living in a particular neighbourhood or locality to interact and generally get to know each other, thereby helping to reinvigorate local community life. As Frank Furedi observes, '[i]f you do not know very much about your neighbours it is difficult to feel any affinity towards them' (1998: 127). In this respect, Robert MacDonald (1996) in his research of voluntary work in Teeside, found that such activity not only re-created meaningful working lives for people in an area deprived of employment opportunities, it also revived community feeling. Furthermore, greater interaction amongst members of local communities would help to ensure that they live and work in more vibrant and sociable environments. Above all undertaking public-spirited activity would not be a one-way process; it is a way of encouraging reciprocity and therefore provides a basis for building more mutually supportive local communities.

For the recipients of this public-spiritedness, they would receive regular unpaid help from people they are likely to know, either from neighbours or others in their local community. This would go some way to offset the occasionally impersonal nature of such assistance offered by government bodies and other agencies. However, such neighbourliness is not intended to replace the specialised and professional provision of the social services.

The approach outlined here might also begin to tackle some of the common problems facing local communities in modern societies. For example, the emphasis upon good neighbourliness is perhaps a useful way of responding to the increasing number of recorded disputes between neighbours. In the UK, in contrast, successive governments have thus far dealt with this problem by simply passing punitive legislation generally involving fining and/or moving nuisance neighbours.

While another growing problem that could be addressed through public-spirited activity is the anti-social behaviour of some young people. This might be eased if more adults gave up some of their time to organize leisure and educational activities, run sports teams, and so on. In the UK, such schemes have already begun to be adopted. Since its election in 1997 the Labour government has encouraged people, especially those who have retired from work, to volunteer to help children learn in pre-school and after-school clubs (Labour Manifesto, 1997: III).

Encouraging public-spirited behaviour could also potentially provide citizens with some protection from the forces, identified in Part I, fostering insecurity and individualism. This is because the mutually supportive neighbourhoods and local communities such behaviour can help to create, is more likely to produce collective responses to these forces or processes. For instance, public-spirited activity might include groups of people in a local community coming together to set-up neighbourhood crèche provision – again this could be monitored by the local authorities or social service departments. This would provide parents with another source of child-caring arrangements enabling them to be more flexible in the job market and therefore better equipped to deal with the post-Fordist economic conditions outlined in Chapter 1.

Similarly, another form of collective endeavour that could be undertaken by local communities would be an exchange of knowledge and skills amongst its members. This would provide an additional way of equipping individuals for the new economic conditions. Thus those who have particular educational or vocational skills could teach them to neighbours or others in their local community as part of their public-spirited activity. For example, computer experts might run workshops on using computers and word-processors. Or, car mechanics might offer basic advice on car maintenance, and so on. Currently for adults, outside of any training they might receive at work, such provision is primarily through evening classes at schools and colleges. This costs money and only contributes to the building of more inclusive local communities in a limited way.

Greater public-spiritedness might also contribute to tackling some of the particular problems that have become associated with individualism and the retreat into the private realm. For instance, the vibrant and supportive local communities this proposal is designed to build could potentially reduce the contemporary need – described by writers such as Aries (1977, 1987) and Sennett (1986) – to invest heavily in intimate life. More of us would want to participate in and seek support from the type of local communities described here, and this would also provide us with the opportunity of enjoying a wider range of relationships in the form of new acquaintances and friendships. This in turn, albeit in a small way, might take some of the pressure of our personal relationships which, as was discussed in Part I, is increasing as a result of the dominant processes of late modernity.

A more public-spirited culture can also serve as a model for individual conduct. As we saw in Chapter 2, in a post-traditional society many of the institutions and conventions that shaped our behaviour in the past, and provided guidelines for acceptable conduct, have been challenged. What has been proposed here entails a range of institutions – notably government, local authorities, schools, the media and private companies – engaged in a common cause to promote public-spiritedness; that is, people being civil, co-operative and sociable towards each other in their everyday conduct. And this issue of conduct is closely linked to that of social capital, as will now be shown.

As well as helping to regenerate local communities, the fostering of a public-spirited culture can help replenish social capital. The neighbourly and community activity upon which it would be based necessitates sociability and reciprocity out of which higher levels of trust, co-operation and friendliness – that is, forms of social capital – can be generated. Such attitudes, albeit in an attenuated form, might then spread beyond the confines of local communities, so that more individuals reconnect with the rest of their society, become less preoccupied with our private lives, not as wary of strangers, and so on. Local communities can therefore serve as sites or a focus for generating social capital and trust. There can of course be no guarantee that fostering a public-spirited culture will lead to such an outcome. But from what has been outlined thus far it is perhaps possible to see that it might make a positive contribution towards this end.

Finally, there are a number of advantages for governments in encouraging community and neighbourly activity. In particular, it would provide an additional way of meeting the demands of their citizens for social and welfare services. Public-spiritedness is not intended to replace state provision, merely augment it by reviving forms of co-operation and local self-help last seen on a significant scale in parts of Europe during the nineteenth century in response to the hardships produced by industrialization (see Godsden, 1973). This would be attractive to many Western governments, particularly as demographic change and the challenges of globalization (discussed in Chapter 3) mean that they are increasingly looking for improved ways of running their welfare states (Hinrichs, 1985; Tanzi, 2001). For example, Anne-Marie Guillemard (2001) has outlined some of the problems confronting industrial countries, especially in terms of sustaining welfare provision, as a result of an ageing population.[2]

Furthermore, given the greater significance of global forces in the contemporary period, the campaigning and educational role that this proposal demands would provide governments with a way of reconnecting with their citizens and generally reasserting their role in national life. However, the promotion of a public-spirited culture would require subtlety and sophistication. Some citizens, for various reasons, are invariably resistant or hostile to any proposal emanating from government. This is why other institutions and agencies – such as the mass media, schools, private companies and voluntary organizations – would need to be incorporated into organizing and promoting such a project. There would also need to be sensitivity displayed to ensure that existing organic forms of community life are encouraged and not undermined by this form of government intervention.

In summary, national governments – in association with other aforementioned institutions and agencies – need to promote community and neighbourly activity as part of an ongoing campaign. In the UK, New Labour has attempted to promote forms of community volunteering, including Cabinet ministers seeking to set an example by undertaking community work. However, this has attracted relatively little media and popular attention, partly because the Labour government has only intermittently pushed this policy. Thus if there is to be widespread community and neighbourly activity governments need to assign it greater priority and actively promote it. As well as a national campaign, governments might pursue other measures mentioned here such as promoting the voluntary sector and encouraging more companies to set-up community volunteering schemes. In this regard, in Chapter 8, a proposal for incorporating forms of community work and involvement into citizenship education courses within schools and colleges will be outlined.

It might be argued there is nothing currently preventing citizens from undertaking community and neighbourly activity, and generally behaving in a public-spirited manner. This is of course true. Unfortunately, as will be elaborated upon in Chapter 8, there is generally not enough of this type of activity going on to regenerate local communities within advanced industrial societies. It therefore necessitates devising strategies, such as those outlined here, to encourage such behaviour.

A Liberal Critique of Public-spiritedness

Any attempt to foster a public-spirited culture would be likely to attract considerable criticism, especially from liberal political philosophers and theorists. This is because such a project challenges some of the central tenets of liberalism, particularly its emphasis upon individual freedom and privacy. The liberal case against generating public-spiritedness is perhaps best encapsulated in the following quotation from *On Liberty*, in which J.S. Mill declares:-

> There is a limit to the legitimate interference of collective opinion with individual independence: and to find that limit, and maintain it against encroachment, is as indispensable to a good condition of human affairs, as protection against political despotism. (Mill, 1991: 9)

From Mill's perspective, a public-spirited culture would constitute a form of 'collective opinion'. This means it is important to assess the extent to which, if at all, public-spiritedness interferes with individual independence.

In relation to what has been proposed here, many liberals would undoubtedly argue that any attempt to get human beings to act or behave in a particular way entails a degree of coercion. People should have the freedom to decide whether or not to be public-spirited. To deny them this right is to infringe upon their liberty and the principle of self-determination. And if individuals choose by their own volition to act in such a manner, then such actions are of greater worth, and are to be more highly-valued, because they were made voluntarily. As soon as you seek to compel or cajole people into behaving in a certain manner you restrict their freedom of choice. Moreover, because their adherence has been artificially obtained their commitment to such activity is likely to be at best half-hearted and conditional.

These are strong and important arguments. However, in constructing a defence against such criticisms it is first necessary to stress the limited nature of what has been proposed here. To repeat, the particular proposal of an hour per week would not constitute a significant encroachment upon people's time. But more broadly, every person would ultimately retain the freedom to choose whether or not to be public-spirited. Indeed, making such a decision would entail people exercising their individual autonomy.

Furthermore, a case could be made that what has been proposed here enhances individual autonomy. This is a theme developed more fully in Chapter 7, but essentially it centres upon the individual having available to them a plurality of options in order to make autonomy meaningful. In contemporary societies, however, there is often a lack of opportunity and encouragement to undertake community volunteering. Indeed, such activity or behaviour is only ever occasionally discussed in the media or by politicians. Consequently, it simply does not occur to many people in Western democracies to behave in this way. The proposal outlined in this work would seek to address this situation. In so doing, it would make available to citizens a variety of potentially rewarding activities and experiences thereby helping to ensure they have a plurality of options to choose from.

Thus the aim has been to defend the principle of devising strategies to encourage and facilitate community and neighbourly activity in the hope that having undertaken such work and seen for themselves the potential benefits of acting in this manner, people would want to continue to behave in this way. As has been argued, one such benefit would be the building of safer and more inclusive local communities in which to live. There would also be a sense of achievement and self-worth in having contributed to this end. It would therefore not necessarily be the case that the attitudes of citizens towards such activity would be half-hearted and conditional.

In a sense what is being proposed simply replicates the experience of a country like the UK, where since the early 1980s certain structural and ideological developments have resulted in changes in the behaviour of many of its citizens as they adapt to the new conditions. More specifically, the increasing encroachment of the market into all aspects of everyday life has resulted in people employing a variety of coping-strategies. These have ranged from actively joining in with this process – such as buying shares and moving to different regions for work and promotion – to taking-out private pension and health schemes as a safeguard against a diminishing welfare state. Hence, if the conditions and structures within a society are changed to facilitate more co-operative and community-based activity there is the prospect that the behaviour of many citizens will adjust accordingly. In summary, in response to liberal arguments, the objective here is to encourage public-spiritedness by making such behaviour possible, rewarding and productive, rather than to cajole and reform citizens.

It is also the case that encouraging people to behave in a particular manner is far from alien to liberalism. A concern with the right moral outlook, and the desire to inculcate individuals with the correct values and attitudes has long preoccupied many liberal thinkers, notably Matthew Arnold, the historian Thomas Babington Macaulay and J.S. Mill.[3] And the latter argued in *Considerations on Representative Government* that 'the first question in respect to any political institutions is, how far they tend to foster in members of the community the various desirable qualities, moral and intellectual' (Mill, 1991: 226). Mill also believed these qualities could be learned by everyone: 'Genuine private affections, and a sincere interest in the public good, are possible, though in unequal degrees, to every rightly brought-up human being' (ibid., 145). Likewise, many other nineteenth century British liberals regarded the introduction of compulsory state education as vital if the people were to be given the responsibility of voting. Indeed, the Education Act was passed in 1870 during the period that democratic reform was beginning to be implemented in Britain.

Interestingly, J.S. Mill occasionally conceded the importance of public awareness and a commitment to others, including in his defence of liberty:-

> It would be a great misunderstanding of this doctrine to suppose that it is one of selfish indifference, which pretends that human beings have no business with each other's conduct in life, and that they should not concern themselves about the well-doing or well-being of one another, unless their own interest is involved. Instead of any diminution, there is need of a great increase of disinterested exertion to promote the good of others. (Mill, 1991: 84)

Mill was also supportive of Alexis de Tocqueville's assertion in *Democracy in America* that participating in public affairs, even at the lowest level, takes people beyond their own narrow and particularistic concerns.

Liberals would also be likely to criticize this project for ignoring or playing down the importance of the private realm; the sphere in which we are free to be ourselves, as long as we do not harm others. Nancy Rosenblum (1987) has stressed this does not mean a retreat into egoistic forms of behaviour; liberalism she maintains holds a sociable and positive view of the private life:-

> Private life means life in civil society, not some pre-social state of nature or antisocial condition of isolation and detachment... private liberty provides escape from surveillance and interference of public officials, multiplying possibilities for private associations and combinations... Far from inviting apathy, private liberty is supposed to encourage public discussion and the formation of groups that give individuals access to wider social contexts and to government. (Rosenblum, 1987: 61)

However, this is not an entirely accurate representation of the conception of privacy within liberalism. This is because it is possible to detect a persistent hostility towards the encroachment of society upon the freedom of the individual within this tradition. Alexis de Tocqueville in his *Democracy in America* (1835) warned of the threat posed to individualism by mass democracy or 'the tyranny of the majority' as he most famously termed it. J.S. Mill took up this notion, warning of the pressures to conform in modern mass society – 'when society itself is the tyrant' (Mill,

1991: 8) – which both stifled individuality and challenged freedom of expression:-

> ... there needs protection also against the tyranny of the prevailing opinion and feeling; against the tendency of society to impose... its own ideas and practices as rules of conduct on those who dissent from them. (Mill, 1991: 9)

The notion of 'private' therefore for many liberals does not just mean participating in civil society, but a personal retreat from social life.[4] As Will Kymlicka has pointed out: 'modern liberalism is concerned not only to protect the private sphere of social life, but also to carve out a realm *within the private sphere* where individuals can have *privacy*' (Kymlicka, 1990: 258; emphasis in original).   This has led to, as Chantal Mouffe has observed, many liberal writers holding at best a lukewarm view of participation in the public sphere:-

> Ideas of civic activity, public spiritedness and political participation in a community of equals are alien to most liberal thinkers. They consider them as "pre-modern". (Mouffe, 1988: 29)

This is not to ignore or underestimate the human need for privacy. Having our own free time and the chance for solitude is to be valued and cherished.   Freedom from the demands of others and being able to divorce oneself temporarily from the hustle and bustle of contemporary society is almost certainly necessary for our well-being. Moreover, privacy is not just about being alone; there is also the privacy of intimate relationships and friendships.[5]

Yet the call here for public-spiritedness does not run deny or infringe upon the need for privacy. What is intended is a rethinking of attitudes, not a fundamental change in our life-styles, and only because of the potential benefits it would bring to individual citizens and the wider society.

It is also difficult to envisage how the liberal emphasis upon non-interference in our lives addresses the problems arising from the contemporary developments identified in Part I. If social life becomes more insecure and individualistic, and less conducive to sociability and community, this can potentially restrict the very freedom that liberals insist upon. For example, the freedom of movement of citizens is compromised if there are housing estates and parts of towns and cities they avoid due to fears about crime and their personal safety. Tangible evidence of such concerns can be seen in the growth of the personal and home security industry, as well as the spread of closed-circuit television (CCTV) in towns and cities. Likewise, many buildings in both the private and public sector have security guards and stringent entry controls, including the use of passes.   While many of the more prosperous newly-built housing residences are designed with their own security measures such as gates, fences and cameras (Etzioni, 1997a, 1997b).   Thomas Hobbes made the astute observation in the mid-seventeenth century that we judge our fellow citizens and the condition of our own society by our actions:-

> Let him therefore consider with himselfe, when taking a journey, he armes himselfe, and seeks to go well accompanied; when going to sleep, he locks his dores; when even in his house he locks his chests; and this when he knows there bee Lawes, and publike Officers, armed, to revenge all injuries shall bee done him; what opinion he has of his fellow subjects, when he rides armed; of his fellow Citizens, when he locks his dores; and of his children, and servants, when he locks his chests. Does he not there as much accuse mankind by his actions, as I do by my words? (Hobbes, 1985: 186-7)

To turn the liberal argument on its head: why would we want to be free in such societies?   In contrast, the proposal for encouraging public-spiritedness outlined here offers the prospect of enhancing our individual freedom.   This is because it is geared to building more vibrant, inclusive and supportive communities, and thereby providing safer and more pleasant environments in which to work and live.   Certain limited attempts to influence human conduct can therefore be justified. Indeed, this already an established feature of modern societies. As citizens we face a range of restrictions upon our behaviour such as having to go to school, find jobs, pay our debts, obey laws and observe social customs and conventions, all of which in some way encroach upon our autonomy.

Why Doing Nothing is Not an Option

A further reason for developing a public-spirited culture is that the economic and political systems of advanced industrial societies may well contribute to the individualism of our age, especially in terms of damaging social capital and trust, and discouraging civic and community activity. Relying upon a form of self-regulation to take place within these societies, in terms of rectifying the negative aspects of increasing individualism, is therefore not an option.   It requires forms of public policy intervention, such as the proposal outlined here.

The political system of Western societies – liberal democracy – will be examined in the next section. Here the focus is upon the economic system, and more specifically market capitalism.

It is a widely held view that market-based societies require social capital in order to function. Quite simply, there must be sufficient stocks of social capital – in the form of virtues such as honesty, reliability and fairness – for market transactions to take place. For instance, a manufacturer will only supply its products to different retailers if they can reasonably expect to be paid for them.   In this regard, Durkheim emphasized that market relationships were based upon non-market norms and values: 'All in the contract is not contractual' (Hirsch, 1977: 141).   Moreover, when trust exists in market exchange reliance upon litigation is reduced.   As the economist Kenneth Arrow notes:-

> Trust is an important lubricant of a social system. It is extremely efficient; it saves people a lot of trouble to have a fair degree of reliance on other people's word. (Arrow, 1974: 23)

Yet some commentators consider markets and market relations are able to produce trust and social capital. It is claimed the nature of a market society ensures regular contact between, say, a manufacturer and a retailer, and from such trading relationships trust and reciprocity can be built up over time (see Thompson et al., 1991).

Variations of, but nevertheless broad support for, this position can be detected in the work of figures as diverse as Max Weber and Francis Fukuyama.   What links these writers is a shared optimism that modern industrial societies or capitalist economies can sustain themselves.   For Weber, the processes of rationalization and individualization shaping modern society can also be seen at work within markets, which function on the basis of efficiency and impersonality.   An impersonal universalistic trust develops in modern society to facilitate the operation of markets; it replaces the trust of the pre-modern era, which was based upon personal attachments.   It emerges because we rationalize that it is both efficient and in all of our interests (Misztal, 1996: 55).

Fukuyama also identifies rational self-interest at work within markets. He contends it is in our own self-interest to operate in an honest and reliable way in market exchange because it ensures a way of maintaining these business and commercial relationships.   Hence, social capital will be produced 'because it is in the long-term interests of selfish individuals to produce it' (2000: 256).   Consequently, Fukuyama maintains, post-industrial economies will be able to continue because they retain the capacity to generate enough social capital in order to do so:-

> We can be reasonably confident about this because we know that private agents seeking their own selfish ends will tend to produce social capital and the virtues associated with it, like honesty, reliability and reciprocity. (Fukuyama, 2000: 255)

But there are problems with this position. While acting in an honest and reliable way in market exchange might be good for society as a whole, do individuals in their everyday conduct really think and act in terms of these wider concerns? It also ignores the fact that we often behave opportunistically. For example, an individual receiving estimates from different firms to paint their house might take the opportunity to play off the firms against each other in order to reduce the cost. Likewise, a professional football club seeking to sell a player might try to inflate the price by informing the media they have received a lot of interest in him from other clubs in the hope of gaining more lucrative offers. In both cases the individuals and parties on the receiving end of this opportunism will be more wary about future market transactions and suspicious of the motives of others, and the stock of social capital is thereby depleted. It is therefore difficult, as Emile Durkheim (1964) noted, to construct and organize a society based upon rational self-interest and acquisitiveness because such behaviour will frequently run counter to social solidarity (Misztal, 1996: 43).

Furthermore, this conception of markets producing trust underestimates the extent to which certain conditions have to be place before they can properly function. For example, markets require a legal framework in which to operate, something established by the legislature and the judiciary, and enforced by the state through agencies such as the police and civil service (Mulberg, 1995: 127). A framework of this type is needed because we need to have recourse to law in order to redress wrongs committed against us in our market transactions, such as when a retailer refuses to pay a supplier for the goods they have received. There also needs to be a degree of moral consensus that individuals and companies should not renege upon their contracts. In short, for markets to operate smoothly it requires a social and legal infrastructure to be in place, and above all the existence of deliberative institutions. This contrasts with Friedrich Hayek's notion of the market as a form of spontaneous social order, something which could not 'be established by central direction' (Hayek, 1960: 160).

Another reason the notion of the market as generator of trust is in practice problematic is that it ignores the capitalist dimension. While acknowledging there are different models or versions, in essence the economic system of advanced industrial societies is a form of market capitalism. And in certain respects this system of economic organization can be harmful to forms of common life. Of fundamental importance in this regard is that capitalism is geared to profit making – a pursuit which can serve to undermine trust and social capital. For example, people will change suppliers or retailers when they feel they can make more money by using other suppliers or retailers. Relations within capitalist markets therefore become much more a means to an end – that end being profit maximization – often to the neglect of the social consequences or implications.

In the UK, there has been recent evidence of this tendency, with companies increasingly setting-up Call Centres in order to deal with their customers. As was mentioned in Part I, this significantly reduces the prospect of generating social capital because it is more difficult to trust somebody that you cannot meet in person. But it is clearly profitable for firms to behave and organize themselves in this way. For many of them it means they can reduce the number of staff employed in their high street branches.

In contrast, Fukuyama maintains it is in the interest of companies to be reliable, fair and to offer good value and service (2000: 256). These virtues in turn extend into social capital for the wider society even though they are produced out of self-interest. For Fukuyama, it does not matter whether these virtues stem from self-interest or are genuinely held, the effect for society is the same:-

> Individuals who believe that honesty is the best policy (i.e., that honesty has a selfish value) end up acting not that differently from those who believe that honesty should be valued for its own sake. (Fukuyama, 2000: 256)

However, contrary to Fukuyama, the motives behind our behaviour are important. When the virtues he identifies are not genuinely held – merely a marketing and promotion exercise – it is just as likely to produce cynicism as social capital within the wider society. Although of course the motives behind our behaviour are invariably complex, and rarely will our actions be the product of a single motive (see O'Neill, 1992).[6]

There is also considerable evidence within advanced industrial societies that capitalism is better at generating economic inequality than social capital, particularly when there is only minimal regulation by government. And as was pointed out in the Introduction to this work, in various ways inequality can act as an obstacle to community and co-operation. For instance, when there are wide disparities in wealth and income within a society it becomes difficult to instil into people the idea that they have common interests with their fellow citizens.

Thus capitalism can operate to undermine the very conditions it requires to exist. There is also an environmental aspect to this issue in the sense that the pursuit of profit can lead, and some would argue is leading, to the destruction of the planet. But this matter lies beyond the scope of this work and will not be examined here.

In this debate much rests upon how one interprets capitalism. Nevertheless it is possible to regard the Fukuyama-Weber position as an optimistic reading of how the economic systems of modern societies function. Indeed, it is more likely that other agencies, such as families, local communities, charities, and even government, generate more social capital and trust than market capitalism. Likewise, as Edmund Burke would surely have observed, custom, tradition and religion perform a similar role. As Fred Hirsch points out, some of the social virtues found in religion such as truth and obligation 'are now seen to play a central role in the functioning of an individualistic, contractual economy' (1977: 141). But he also notes 'the individualistic, rationalistic base of the market undermined the unseen religious support' (ibid., 143). Yet Fukuyama, because of his emphasis upon self-interest producing social capital, is less convinced by such arguments: 'God, religion, and age-old tradition are helpful to this process but not necessary' (Fukuyama, 2000: 255).

In summary, it would be unwise to rely upon the economic system of advanced industrial societies to rectify the negative aspects of increasing individualism. Moreover, there is a strong possibility that market capitalism has contributed to this development. As Fred Hirsch contends:-

> The social morality that has served as an active understructure for economic individualism has been a legacy of the precapitalist and preindustrial past. This legacy has diminished with time and with the corrosive contact of the active capitalist values – and more generally with the greater anonymity and greater mobility of industrial society. The system has thereby lost outside support that was previously taken for granted by the individual. (Hirsch, 1977: 117)

Forms of active intervention are therefore required – such as the proposal outlined here for fostering a public-spirited culture – in order to rebuild communities and replenish social capital. In the final section of this chapter it will be argued that the nature of the political systems within these societies reinforces this position.

Liberal Democracy and the Lack of Civic Engagement

There has been much discussion about the strengths and weaknesses of liberal democracy.[7] However, the concern of this final section is to consider liberal democracy in relation to the broader themes of this work. In this regard, while acknowledging its many positive aspects, it will be shown that liberal democracy often produces low levels of participation in civic and community life, and weak attitudes of public-spiritedness and responsibility – the type of behaviour and attitudes needed to build mutually supportive and inclusive communities. The dominant mode of governance within Western societies may therefore have been indirectly contributing to – or at the very least reinforcing – the individualism of our age.

Liberal democracy in advanced industrial societies essentially means representative democracy. However, an oft-heard criticism of representative systems of democracy is that ordinary citizens have little real influence upon the decisions made by governments.[8] By delegating power to their elected representatives the majority of the population are largely excluded from the decision-making process. And there is evidence that Western electorates have been aware of this state of affairs for some time. For instance, in the UK a survey undertaken in the late 1970s revealed almost half of the respondents did not think they had any 'influence on government', and only a third thought that their political system 'works for the interest of most people most of the time' (Abercrombie, 1980: 140-8).

Lack of accountability is another charge raised against representative democracy. A government having to seek re-election every five years or so ensures only a very limited form of accountability. This is reflected in the fact that governments are prepared to introduce legislation when there is a lack of enthusiasm for it, and even widespread opposition. Again the UK provides numerous examples of this practice, from the unpopular 'poll tax' implemented by the Conservative Government in the 1980s to the Labour Government setting-up the Welsh Assembly – despite only one in four people in Wales voting for it in a referendum held in September 1997. Defenders of representative democracy would point out that having presented their election manifestos to the voters, elected governments have a mandate to rule. However, this view mistakenly assumes that electorates read and are fully conversant with the manifestos of the different parties. It also ignores the realities of electoral politics in modern democracies, with governments often formed from coalitions or elected by a minority of the vote.

The governments in many representative democracies do not reflect the nature of the population of their respective societies. Ethnic minorities and women are especially under-represented in many of these systems. In the case of women, Vicky Randall (1987) has charted their under-representation at all levels of political office in liberal democratic systems throughout the world. Women elected to national governments make up only between 2 and 12 per cent of the elected representatives. The only exception being the Nordic countries where there is a greater proportion of women representatives, and in the UK which following the general election of 1997 saw a substantial rise in the number of women MPs. However, the British Parliament scores less well in terms of the proportion of MPs from ethnic minority groups. Twelve non-white MPs gained seats in the House of Commons in the general election of 2001; there should have been nearer fifty to reflect the population as a whole.

Representative democracy is also criticized for offering limited choice to voters as a result of the desire of major political parties to capture the middle ground in order to be elected. There is also a widespread perception that some electoral systems, notably the so-called 'first-past-the post' voting system employed in countries like the UK, are simply unfair and distort rather than reflect the wishes and interests of the electorate.

In summary, the nature of representative democratic systems entails many citizens consider government is far removed and unaccountable, and consequently feel unable to shape their own societies in any meaningful sense. On balance such attitudes are likely to discourage interest and involvement in civic and political affairs. Instead, people will understandably concentrate upon the private realm devoting attention to their personal lives, which they perceive as having more control over. This may in part explain the signs of voter apathy and general disengagement – especially among young people – from the political process in many Western democracies. Interestingly, much of the debate surrounding this issue concentrates upon image and presentation, stressing the need for political parties and their leaders to do more to attract voters. Rarely is there any discussion that this development might be due to greater individualism in the contemporary period.

Popular detachment from the political process appears to take many forms. In Europe, there is consistently a low turnout for local and European elections. While in the United States only half of the electorate usually bothers to vote in the presidential elections, even less in congressional contests. And in the UK, voter turnout fell dramatically at the 2001 general election to around 58 per cent. There is also evidence of a decrease in party political activity in some countries. In the UK, the major political parties have been confronted with a declining membership for a number of years. Moreover, the majority of voters in Western democracies now have less commitment to any political party; a process termed 'partisan de-alignment' by political scientists. For example, the proportion of voters identifying strongly with one of the two main parties in the UK fell from 40 per cent in 1964 to 19 per cent in 1979 (Jones and Kavanagh, 1983). And while 1 in 12 voters in the mid-1960s expressed no 'party identification', this figure had increased to roughly 1 in 6 by the 1980s (Sarlvik and Crewe, 1983).

Numerous reasons have been postulated to account for the perceived diminution of interest in mainstream political parties and processes in many modern societies, but the lack of a substantive input into the political system on the part of citizens must be considered a significant contributory factor.[9] It has resulted in civic and political activity – such as attending meetings, joining political parties, canvassing, and so on – becoming the preserve of a dedicated minority.

Low levels of popular involvement in civic and political life under liberal democracy can also in part be traced to its historical and philosophical origins. A key factor in this regard is the predominance of liberalism over democracy within the concept of liberal democracy, and the fact that, as both liberals and critics contend, the individual – who exists prior to society – lies at the heart of liberal thought (Parekh, 1993). Although democracy with its Athenian roots preceded liberalism this is of little significance in accounting for the contemporary form of liberal democracy. This is because democracy, and democratic systems of any scale, effectively disappeared from the West between the Ancient Greeks and the nineteenth century. It is for this reason that commentators like Anthony Arblaster (1984) believe liberalism – which emerged in parts of Europe from roughly the seventeenth century onwards – determined the nature of liberal-democracy. Thus democracy was defined and shaped within the parameters established by liberalism. In particular, figures like Alexis de Tocqueville and J.S. Mill with their wariness of majority rule were to influence the form that liberal democracy came to take. As Bhikhu Parekh has argued:-

> Liberal democracy is basically a liberalized or liberally constituted democracy... Liberalism is its absolute premise and foundation and penetrates and shapes its democratic character. (Parekh, 1993: 157)

The consequence of this historical development is that contemporary liberal democracy is both centred upon the individual and does little to encourage active political participation. This is evident in one of its fundamental principles: that every citizen has the right to vote. While this is a valuable political right it produces a minimalist conception of politics in that it makes it unnecessary for citizens to participate fully in civic and public life. The individual is able to remain detached from such matters, reconnecting with the rest of society only at election times, and in most liberal democracies voting is not compulsory.

The reforms needed to improve liberal democracy, and whether more participatory forms of democracy are feasible in complex modern societies, has been much debated (see Barber, 1984; Gould, 1988; Hirst, 1994; Pateman, 1970). However, such an analysis lies beyond the scope of this work. The aim here has been to demonstrate that the dominant system of governance in Western societies can in certain respects be viewed as reinforcing the processes identified in Part I that are leading to greater individualism. Liberal democracy, for the reasons outlined, does little to encourage involvement in civic and community affairs. It places limited demands upon citizens in terms of civic obligations and responsibilities. They can rely upon their elected representative to undertake such work leaving them free to concentrate upon their personal lives.

However, this will not lead to the building of more inclusive and mutually supportive communities and societies. If we want to achieve this, and thereby address the problems created by excessive individualism (such as low levels of trust, co-operation and sociability) then specific measures need to be developed. Hence the call here to foster a public-spirited culture. Doing nothing, and simply leaving these challenges to the formal mechanisms of liberal democracy, is not an option.

It is also the case that people who are active in their local communities are more likely to be interested in civic and political life. There may be a number of reasons for this correlation. But one commonsensical explanation is that a citizen engaged in community volunteering would see for themselves the difficulties confronting their communities in terms of, for example, shortages of resources and lack of amenities, and the way of addressing these problems is by becoming more politically active.

Other forms of community activity, such as membership of local clubs and societies, can produce a similar outcome. This was something Robert Putnam (1994) found in his study of civic participation in Italy. Involvement in such groups was a way of developing negotiating skills, learning about political processes, and generally fostering political awareness. Moreover, those regions in Italy – such as Emilia-Romagna – with flourishing group activity also tended to have a higher readership of local newspapers, good turnouts in referendums and greater levels of political activism. And as might be expected, Putnam found a correlation between high levels of civic participation and good governance.

Thus the proposal outlined here for fostering a public-spirited culture might help to revive civic and political life within advanced industrial societies. This is because it is geared to encouraging us to think and act beyond our private existence, especially the contemporary emphasis upon working and consuming. More specifically, involvement in our local communities can pave the way for more participatory forms of politics. Further arguments for encouraging public-spirited behaviour will be outlined in the next chapter.

Conclusion

In summary, fostering a public-spirited culture – in which an active role would be played national governments – is an appropriate response to dealing with some of the negative aspects of increasing individualism. However, citizens should retain the freedom to choose whether or not to act in such manner, and this principle has been embodied in what has been presented here. Apart from the national campaign to encourage public-spiritedness, citizens would be under no pressure to undertake public-spirited activity. Indeed, it would be very difficult to determine whether or not a person is behaving in this way.

Chapter 6

The Retreat into Tribalism

In this chapter, further reasons are advanced for fostering a public-spirited culture. This is based upon an examination of what appears to be another major global trend of our time: the retreat into 'tribalist' patterns of behaviour. The definition of 'tribalism' employed here is taken from Mathew Horsman and Andrew Marshall's *After the Nation-State: Citizens, Tribalism and the New World Disorder* (1994). They consider it to be the retreat by individuals into communities defined by '... similarities of religion, culture, ethnicity, or some other shared experience. The retreat is driven by fear and confusion, and fed by the reassuring "sameness" of others in the group' (1994: x).

It will be claimed that in response to the processes of late modernity, rather than pursuing or just pursuing individualistic strategies some people are retreating to their particular 'tribe' or tribes. This is evident in the reinvigoration of ethnic, racial and national identities, in the forms of exclusion and discrimination operating against minorities and immigrant groups, in the vitality of many separatist or independence movements and in the rise of religious fundamentalism. Furthermore, it may also be evident in the activities of some new social movements, such as environmental and ecological groups.

The chapter will examine three aspects of this issue. Firstly, the 'retreat into tribalism' is outlined in more detail. 'Tribalism' is a conveniently shorthand term employed to describe a range of developments. Secondly, the growth of identity politics – which it is claimed in certain respects constitutes a form of tribalism – and its implications for modern societies is considered. Lastly, 'tribalism' is assessed in relation to a public-spirited culture. It is argued that the latter can begin to tackle some of the worst excesses of the former.

The Return to the Tribe

There are many possible reasons for significant numbers of people resorting to tribalist patterns of behaviour, and it will be very much dependent upon particular circumstances, local conditions, and so on.

Indeed, numerous interpretations have emerged to explain this phenomenon. They range from the role of the mass media in exacerbating ethnic, racial and nationalist tensions (Ahmed, 1995) to the impact of the end of the Cold War which has given a free rein to the forces of ethnic nationalism and racism (Glenny, 1993). However, any plausible explanation must take account of the key developments in the contemporary period.

Insecurity and the Dissipation of the Social

As has been shown, the primary processes of the contemporary period – globalization, post-Fordism and detraditionalization – have helped to create an 'age of uncertainty'. The fixed identities and forms of collective solidarity of the past are increasingly absent, entailing that social life is more fragmented and insecure. While the predominant response has been a resort to individualistic strategies and life-styles, these conditions can also be viewed as contributing to the retreat into tribalist patterns of behaviour. The search for security and stability has led some people to try and rediscover old certainties and patterns of collective behaviour in the form of ethnic, racial and national identities.[1] This tendency is succinctly encapsulated in Zygmunt Bauman's declaration that '[t]he dissipation of the social rebounds in the consolidation of the tribal. As identities go, privatization means tribalization' (1996: 57).

There is considerable support for Bauman's contention. For example, Alberto Melucci (1989) contends that as the basis for group membership, such as class, erode within increasingly complex, individualistic and differentiated societies, ethnic identity has considerable appeal. Above all it offers forms of solidarity which are rooted in 'language, a culture and an ancient history' (ibid., 92). Likewise, Ulrich Beck and Elizabeth Beck-Gernsheim (1996) see a retreat into ethnic identity stemming from the 'precarious freedoms' we are confronted with as a result of this process of individualization. They raise the question of what is 'to integrate highly individualized societies?' (ibid., 43). And they consider the rebirth of nationalism and ethnic conflicts in Europe to be one response to this dilemma. It constitutes a tried-and-trusted means of dealing with challenges and difficult conditions: a turning inwards for protection – and the reassurance of sameness – while turning against those perceived as 'outsiders' (ibid.).

Another writer who would concur with this position is Michel Wieviorka (1994). He has sought to identify the reasons for the recent rise of racist activity in Europe, and especially in France. The particular aspect of the 'age of uncertainty' that Wieviorka concentrates upon is post-industrialism or post-Fordism; something he regards as a major socio-economic transformation, or as he puts it, *une grande mutation*. As we saw in Chapter 1, one of the consequences of post-Fordism is a shift towards greater reliance upon personal initiative and enterprise and away from collective action, and for the individual in a number of ways to become isolated from his or her work colleagues. And there will be some people who are simply marginalized from mainstream society through such processes. As Wieviorka notes: '[t]hose who are "out", or fear to be, have a feeling of injustice and loss of previous social identity' (ibid., 179). For Wieviorka, the individual is able to find new forms of collective behaviour and group identities by turning to race and ethnicity; it enables them to once again feel part of a group. Ethnic revival and even forms of racist activity therefore permit a degree of reorganization of society and an escape from isolated individualism.

Wilhelm Heitmeyer (1993) takes a similar position with regards to the rise of racism and racial violence in Germany, a phenomenon mainly perpetrated by young people. He considers this to be a result of the process of individualization which modern societies like Germany have undergone. The concomitant decline in social and communal life means social status and social identity are no longer 'givens', but have to be achieved through personal effort with a great risk of failure. In response, some young Germans are defining their identity in terms of race and nationality; they find some sense of belonging in close-knit racial groups. And for some such membership requires involvement in racist violence as a way of proving and demonstrating their identity. As Heitmeyer puts it: '[w]hen natural social membership and acceptance disintegrate to such an extent that the only certainty of being German remains, then violence is given a direction' (ibid., 27). The fact that the growth of the extreme right and the increased incidents of racial violence have predominantly been in the former GDR reinforces his claim about the influence of individualization. This region has undergone massive economic restructuring in the transformation to a market society, removing the security once provided by the state in the form of jobs and public housing, and provoking widespread uncertainty.

The primary way an ethnic or national group is able to offer the individual some protection and stability is by acting as a form of community. It provides the chance to combine with others of similar outlook and background, and to gain reassurance and feeling of security from this group solidarity. Moreover, identifying with what one perceives as one's community has the added advantage over retreating into individualism and the private realm, of not generating feelings of isolation and loneliness. The reassertion of ethnic and national identities may therefore reflect a human need for community and a sense of connection with others. This point will be returned to and developed in the next chapter.

The notion of an ethnic group or nation functioning as a form of community has been a source of debate, particularly in terms of the latter performing this role. In this respect, Benedict Anderson's historical analysis of the psychological appeal of the nation is relevant. He considers the nation to be an 'imagined community' because as he puts it:-

> ... the members of even the smallest nation will never know most of their fellow-members, meet them, or even hear of them, yet in the minds of each lives the image of their communion. (Anderson, 1983: 6)

It is a community because despite the tensions and inequalities which inevitably exist within it, 'the nation is always conceived as a deep, horizontal comradeship' (ibid., 7). Furthermore, because the nation is an *imagined* community does not mean that attitudes towards it are somehow not genuine or deeply felt. Without this fellow-feeling, Anderson argues, how else can we explain why people are prepared to kill and die for their nations?

Anthony Giddens (1990) has also emphasized the psychological appeal of nationalism, particularly its ability to satisfy a need for a sense of identity. He considers this to be especially necessary under modern conditions in which processes like globalization have led to the 'disembedding' of experience of a specific time and space. And this returns us to the central claim of this chapter: the turn to ethnic, national and local identities, as well as other tribalist forms, should in part be viewed as a response to the new conditions.

Globalization, Hybridization and the Other

A further way in which globalization might be reinforcing 'tribal' identities is through ensuring we encounter 'the Other' upon almost a daily basis. The greater movement of peoples across the globe for all sorts of business, cultural and other reasons entails we all engage with more frequently than in the past, those of different cultures and societies. This creates the opportunity for cultural hybridity, multiculturalism and cosmopolitanism and with it the fragmentation of older identities. It forces people to think about 'who they are'; as Stuart Hall (1996) maintains, identity is forged in the relationship between us and 'the Other'. Yet some people inevitably seek to resist the processes ushered in by globalization and try to hold on to old certainties in the form of national identities and national traditions.

This point is taken-up by Anthony Smith (1995) who points to the continuing strength of what he terms *ethnie* – the ethnic core of nations – which will confront any movement towards a global culture and cosmopolitanism. For Smith, *ethnie* are pre-modern in origin, are bound-up with memories and myths, and remain deeply ingrained within the popular consciousness in many regions of the world. Surveying this debate, Mary Kaldor (1996) considers the contest between cosmopolitanism and nationalism will do much to shape the twenty-first century.

Some writers have raised the possibility that the cultural integration produced by globalization might lead to competition and even clashes between different cultures (Featherstone, 1991; Huntington, 1996). There may already be evidence of this development within Europe. In a number of European countries there is concern and on-going debates about the likely impact of globalization and immigration upon their respective nation's culture. Indeed, refugees and asylum-seekers, and how to deal with them, has become a key political issue in many European states. In response many national governments have sought to assuage the fears of domestic populations over the security of their jobs and access to welfare states. They have largely done this, in conjunction with the European Union, by tightening immigration controls, restricting the movement of 'non-Europeans' within Europe, and generally building what has been termed 'Fortress Europe' (Fekete and Webber, 1994).

The extreme right in Europe has sought to exploit these concerns. For example, the Republican Party in Germany and the National Front in France have emphasized cultural separatism and the right of people to their own national identity and culture within their own country. While the rise to power of Joerg Haider's Freedom Party (FPO) in Austria was to a significant extent based upon its anti-immigration agenda. The country is one of the richest in the world per capita, and its level of unemployment is among the lowest in Europe. Yet the Freedom Party tapped into a long-standing fear of mass immigration, particularly given the prospect of eastern countries joining the European Union (Batha, 2000). In a 1997 poll, 42 per cent of Austrians admitted to some degree of racism and xenophobia, compared with a European Union average of 33 per cent (Batha, 2000).

There have been other forms of reaction to aspects of globalization in the contemporary period. It has contributed to the rise of strong religious identities throughout the world, such as Islamist movements, Jewish fundamentalism in Israel, Christian evangelicalism in the United States, and a militant Hindu revivalism in India. The attempt to maintain the basic teachings and traditions of these religions by many of their respective followers has been viewed as partly a reaction against the homogeneity and sameness of globalization and global consumerism.[2] In this respect, writers like Fred Halliday (1996) and John Esposito (1992) consider the Islamist revival of recent years to be largely a defensive movement against spreading Western culture and secularism.

Similar forms of resistance to globalization are evident in the endeavours of many national governments to protect aspects of national life, such as their language, customs and cultural industries. This can be seen in the campaign by the French government to preserve the French language, as well as the attempt to limit the number of American films that can be shown in France in order to protect its indigenous film industry. While the Canadian government has sought to limit the extent to which US culture industries can hold a stake in Canadian media and telecommunication industries (Held, 1999: 371). In the UK, there are regular scare-stories about the threat to the national way of life, ranging from the possible demise of the pound to the threat to the British sausage. Although in Britain animosity is directed primarily against the European Union reflecting a lack of awareness that its formation is in part a response to the new global conditions.

A further way in which globalization might be contributing to 'tribalist' patterns of behaviour concerns the challenges it poses to the nation-state. As was discussed in Chapter 3, globalization and its associated neo-liberal ideologies, is entailing that increasingly, in a range of ways, the citizens of many advanced industrial societies can no longer be as reliant upon their respective states and governments. Moreover, substantive economic and political decision-making is increasingly taken by non-state institutions and organizations; a process over which ordinary citizens have no direct influence. In response to these developments some people are rejecting formal state processes, turning their back on national politics and political parties, and taking matters into their own hands by seeking local solutions (Miles, 1994; Starr, 2000). This can range from protests and illegal actions by environmentalists, road protestors and squatters to those carrying out racist activity. Rather than simply accepting and identifying with a particular nation-state, it involves a rethinking by people of what they consider to be their community.

These changing attitudes are perhaps reflected in the growth of identity politics – discussed in the next section – and in the difficulty that some nation-states are having in containing ethnic nationalist demands for autonomy and separatism. For example, within Europe since the early 1990s there has been a trend towards the formation of more ethnically homogenous and exclusive states, evident in the break-up of the former Soviet Union and Yugoslavia, and in the division of Czechoslovakia in

1993 into separate Czech and Slovak states. While Russians living in Estonia and Latvia have faced pressure from nationalists to restrict their civic rights; a move which runs counter to the Enlightenment principle of universal citizenship upon which the nation-state has been constructed within Europe. And separatist or independence movements remain, or have become, a significant force in the domestic politics of countries like Belgium and Spain; and within the UK, Scotland and Wales now enjoy greater autonomy as a result of devolution. John Newhouse contends Europe's rising regionalism rather than the European Union constitutes 'the larger threat to the authority of the nation-state' (1998: 36). These developments lead Horsman and Marshall (1994) to question the future viability of the nation-state in its present form. 'Exit the nation-state, enter the tribes' is Zygmunt Bauman's description of this state of affairs (1993: 141).

Another aspect of our globalized, post-industrial age contributing to ethnic mobilization has been the developments in electronic media and communications technology. This has greatly facilitated the work of informal or non-state networks and organizations. It enables ethnic communities and nationalist groups to disseminate their message, paving the way for the establishment of world-wide support networks, especially amongst emigrant and diaspora populations who are able to maintain contacts with their 'homeland' (Richmond, 1984; Schlesinger, 1991). And far-right groups are increasingly using the Internet to spread their message. For example, an annual report by Germany's intelligence agency on extremist threats, published in April 2000, warned that far-right German groups had set-up some three hundred web sites (BBC World Service, April 4, 2000).

It would seem therefore that in a variety of ways the primary processes of late modernity might also be contributing to the reinvigoration of ethnic, national and racial identities. There is an ongoing interaction between local and global models of identity, and aspects of this interaction would appear to be provoking particularistic and parochial responses. To repeat, it is only some people who could be said to be acting in this way, hence the regional variations. Indeed, as has been mentioned, we are also witnessing the emergence of what might be termed the 'new cosmopolitans'. These are invariably professional or business people, educated and well-travelled with global connections and interests, some of whom will have a weak or waning sense of their own national identity and its importance. The greater geographical mobility that is a feature of globalization, and the increased contact with different cultures this entails, might also engender insight, shared understanding and tolerance.

The retreat in this 'age of uncertainty' into 'tribalist' identities and patterns of behaviour is therefore not necessarily a permanent condition. Such identities are constantly reformulated in the interaction between the global and the local. Moreover, the forces of globalization also work to deny the establishment of coherent and unified identities and cultures, whether they be national, racial, social or ethnic. Above all identities are not fixed and immutable; they can and do change. As Stuart Hall (1990) has argued, it is more appropriate to consider identity-formation as an ongoing process. Individuals also possess multiple identities and this will shape their behaviour in different ways. In this sense they are not just dominated or defined by, what has been termed here, their 'tribalist' identities. Nevertheless the current adoption of tribalist forms, which includes ethnic nationalism and racist violence, is a cause for concern. How we can begin to counter such a development is addressed in the final section of this chapter.

The Politics of Identity

The drift into tribalist patterns of behaviour is also reflected in the rise of identity politics in modern societies. This is the increasing tendency for people to identify strongly with a particular group or groups in society, whether this is to do with religion, colour, culture, gender or sexuality. Above all it has entailed organizing, campaigning and constructing political demands based upon such allegiances and identities. It will be regarded here as a type of tribalism because it accords with Horsman and Marshall's definition of the retreat by individuals into communities defined by some form of shared experience. As will be shown, this retreat often leads to a concern with one's particular identity or tribe rather than the community or society as a whole; an unwillingness to openly engage with other groups; and an insistence upon the essential rightness of one's own particular identity or group. These are the characteristics of the tribe.

The factors behind the rise of identity politics, and the form it has taken, will obviously vary from country to country. For example, there are differences in the experience of Europe and the United States concerning this development. In the case of the former, it is the decline of class in terms of its role in shaping and organizing social life, which has facilitated the rise of identity politics.[3] This challenge to class, as we saw in Chapter 1, can to a significant extent be traced to the developments associated with post-Fordism or post-industrialism.

In contrast, class has not played such a central role in shaping American society. This is evident in the lack of both an organized, militant and politically effective socialist movement and in the fact that egalitarianism has never been 'in the forefront of political debate' (Aronwitz, 1992: 67). Instead, it has been claimed, the heightened importance of identity politics within America has much to do with disillusionment with assimilation (Shain, 1995). While Richard Merelman (1994) views identity politics and the recent instances of cultural conflict in the United States as highlighting the decline of white ideological hegemony. For Merelman, this development paves the way for more competition between different groups, and for greater resistance by minorities to the power of the dominant group.

A more general explanation for the turn to identity politics is provided by Francis Fukuyama (1992) who links it to the importance for human beings of 'recognition'. Drawing heavily upon the work of Hegel, Fukuyama contends 'Men [*sic*] seek not just material comfort, but respect or recognition' (ibid.,152). This is reflected, he maintains, in the fact that many of today's most contentious issues, such as abortion, sexual harassment, and racism, are fundamentally conflicts over recognition and dignity. With regards to the first two issues, Fukuyama sees them as ultimately a struggle by women for status, respect and a sense of self-worth. The issue of racism in America, he contends, must be viewed in the same way because 'in the eyes of many whites, a black is... "an invisible man", not actively hated but unseen as a fellow human being' (ibid.,176). For Fukuyama, these are, employing the vocabulary of Plato and Socrates, thymotic issues: they are based upon 'the desire for recognition'. While Fukuyama may overstate his case – in particular playing down the economic aspect of these disputes – the desire for equal recognition is a strong motivation behind identity politics, and has been a campaigning issue for many such groups.

However, because it often resembles a form of tribalism, the politics of identity has created numerous problems for modern societies. The United States, in particular, has suffered from a virulent form of identity politics. It has led one commentator, Lewis Lapham, to write an article entitled 'Who and What Is American?' (1992). In part this stems from America being an immigrant society, and that many groups of immigrants have sought to maintain their identity in what was supposed to be a 'melting pot' society. This has led to numerous cultural clashes. For example, Orthodox Jews in Crown Heights, New York, have tried in the past to close certain streets where they live in order to observe the Sabbath. The problem with this assertion of cultural identity is it infringes upon the freedom of others; and in this particular case has had a harmful impact upon relations with local black Americans.

John O'Sullivan (1996) argues the American experience of identity politics has led to a decline in toleration for others. It has inhibited the development of shared norms and values in society and multiplied the potential for social conflict to the point where everyday life in America is a constant, low-intensity cultural war. Identity politics has also harmed the democratic process because it has led to particular groups voting as a block to further their own interests, rather than in terms of a consideration of the wider community. As a consequence, it has made framing legislation much more difficult. This is reinforced by the fact that identity politics is invariably articulated in the language of rights. As we have seen this can lead to entrenched positions and unwillingness to compromise, and even fanaticism and violence. It is also an approach guaranteed to ignore the complexity of particular issues.

Social and political life conducted in this way can produce enclaves in which those who do not belong, those who are not of a particular identity, are excluded. Indeed, those excluded can often be vilified as the enemy. It can also lead to calls for separatism. For instance, some gay and lesbian activists advocate such a policy in their promotion of a 'Queer Nation'; while some feminists ('political lesbians') advocate keeping apart from men.[4] This can lead to the 'ghettoization' of society, making sociability more difficult and thereby eroding the quality of social life for everyone. It can also hinder the development of a civic community and culture. Above all this form of identity politics neglects the extent to which people possess multiple identities, as well as the degree of common and shared interests that exists between us all (Etzioni, 1997b: 205).

The politics of identity has often coalesced around debates over multiculturalism, even though there is often a lack of consensus over its definition and what it entails. Many proponents of multiculturalism view it as a celebration of difference and diversity, and a means of promoting cultural pluralism. In this regard, Linda Frye Burnham (1994) contends multiculturalism means all cultures honouring and working with each other. Bhikhu Parekh (2000) also notes that multiculturalism is also frequently perceived to be about (usually nonwhite) minorities, and this he argues is incorrect:-

> Multiculturalism is about the proper terms of relationship between different cultural communities. The norms governing their respective claims, including the principles of justice, cannot be derived from one culture alone but through an open and equal dialogue between them. (Parekh, 2000: 13)

Unfortunately, as its critics point out, the promotion and implementation of what might be termed multicultural policies has often led to tensions developing between different communities and groups (Etzioni, 1995; Fukuyama, 1995). For example, in America there are ongoing disputes over the content of education curricula in schools, colleges and universities. This debate has often become polarized between supporters of multiculturalism and those concerned to promote an overarching American identity and civic culture. The former emphasize the right of young people to learn about their own particular ethnic or cultural background, with some arguing that this American identity and civic culture is essentially dominated by white Europeans. Indeed, Molefi Kete Asante, a leading advocate of multiculturalism, contends that because the United States is a country of immigrants, each with their own particular culture, '[t]here is no common American culture' (Chavez, 1996: 41).

These debates have fuelled a number of disputes and demonstrations. For instance, in May 1993 a group of Mexican-American students caused $500,000 worth of damage when they stormed a faculty building at UCLA in protest that the school's Chicano studies programme had not been elevated to full department status (Chavez, 1996).[5] This and other instances of such conflict has led Linda Chavez (1996) to declare that multiculturalism is driving Americans apart. While one educational commentator, Ellen K.Coughlin, has posed the question: 'Is the story of America that of a common culture or of many different, perhaps irreconcilable ones?' (Etzioni, 1995:148).

In defence of identity politics, two points need to be made. Firstly, it is the case that in many modern societies various groups or sections of society, such as blacks, homosexuals and women, have suffered, and continue to suffer, various forms of discrimination and, to return to Fukuyama's point, from a lack of recognition. Identity politics offers both group solidarity, and is therefore a source of support and protection, and a chance to campaign against such forms of injustice. Secondly, the danger of acting and thinking in terms of the community or society as a whole, which is what is being advocated in this work and by many of the critics of identity politics, is that diversity and difference are subsumed under a single dominant ideological hegemony. That assimilation inevitably entails domination for some.[6] In contrast, identity politics, and in particular multiculturalism, is potentially able to challenge the hegemonic position of a single cultural group.

These two issues – that of discrimination/non-recognition and cultural domination – need to be addressed, both in terms of what is just and unjust, and because it might reduce the necessity of resorting to entrenched positions which is a feature of some forms of identity politics. The particular contribution a public-spirited culture might make will now be considered.

Tribalism and Public-Spiritedness

Having outlined some of the different forms of 'tribalism' in the contemporary period, it is now possible to consider the role a public-spirited culture might play in curbing such attitudes and behaviour. From the outset, however, it should be recognized that what can be achieved is largely dependent upon the nature of the particular society in which it would be introduced or developed. For example, in societies where there is a history of conflict – such as in Northern Ireland – the impact of projects encouraging public-spiritedness would be negligible, and in any case are unlikely to be implemented.

The primary way in which a public-spirited culture might challenge tribalist attitudes is that it can work to prevent the conditions provoking them as a result of the vibrant, mutually supportive and inclusive local communities it is designed to create, and the trust and social capital it can generate. This might take the following forms.

Firstly, as we have seen in this chapter, the turn to ethnic, cultural and national groups has in part come about because of insecurity and diminishing forms of common life within our age of individualism. The transition to post-Fordism has disrupted communities, and with the popularity of market ideologies amongst many Western governments ensuring they are doing little to arrest this development, it means ethnic and national groups are one of the few remaining meaningful sources of collective identity and support in the contemporary period. In this regard, a public-spirited culture, as argued for here, seeks to rebuild local communities which in turn would offer alternative sources of support, solidarity and collective behaviour thereby reducing the need for individuals to turn to 'tribalist' groups.

Secondly, as we have also seen in this chapter, tribalism is more likely to thrive when people feel marginalized from mainstream society, often because they perform no meaningful role within it. They may well be drawn to groups that are exclusive and even extremist in nature because they offer an alternative form of reassurance and specifically a sense of belonging and purpose. The public-spirited culture promoted in this work addresses this tendency because it is based upon inclusiveness. All members of society – with the exception of certain categories of criminals mentioned in Chapter 5 – would be encouraged to undertake and participate in forms of neighbourly and community-orientated activity irrespective of class, wealth, ethnicity, race, gender, religion and sexuality. It affords the opportunity to interact with fellow citizens, as well as the chance to learn new skills and perform more meaningful and productive roles within society.

Obviously the form of inclusiveness offered by the fostering of a public-spirited culture is of a limited kind – essentially the chance to feel more part of a society or local community by becoming engaged or involved in a common undertaking. This does not address the prevalence of forms of social exclusion within many Western democracies, for which there are many causes requiring a range of policy initiatives (see Byrne, 1999).

Thirdly, as well as working to erode forms of marginalization, public-spiritedness might also help to counter the tendency or desire, mentioned earlier, for separatism within identity politics, and thereby avoid the 'ghettoization' of society. This is because it addresses an integral feature of identity politics: the desire for recognition. By undertaking some form of public-spirited activity for a neighbour or other member of the local community an individual is recognising the existence of those they are helping; publicly acknowledging that they are a person deserving of support and assistance irrespective of their ethnic group, race, religion, gender or sexuality. It would mean that those belonging to minority groups are considered part of the wider community and no longer, as Fukuyama claims many black Americans feel, 'invisible'.

This contrasts sharply with a recent suggestion in the UK that people of different ethnic and cultural backgrounds should be forced to live together. Gurbux Singh, the former chairman of the commission for racial equality (CRE), contends white and ethnic communities must be forced to integrate through public policies, notably housing and education, to avoid further trouble. He believes such measures are necessary to avoid the racial disturbances which took place in a number of towns and cities in the north of England during the summer of 2001 (Ashley and Hetherington, 2002).

But there are problems with such an approach. To begin with you cannot force people to live in a certain area. Moreover, the element of compulsion in this approach would be likely to increase hostility between the different ethnic and cultural groups. While public policy should discourage segregation, in order to gain shared understanding and mutual respect it has to be a gradual and subtle process.

In this regard, the fostering of a public-spirited culture might be able to make a contribution. Ongoing schemes to encourage community and neighbourly activity, where all sections of society are urged to become involved, will enable people from different ethnic and cultural groups to interact over time. This gradual approach would be more likely to produce a positive outcome because it allows time for understanding, civility, trust and reciprocity to be generated. Indeed, it might make the arguments of those exploiting such tensions less convincing. For example, religious and cultural leaders who stress the hostility of other groups and argue for separatism and non-assimilation, such as the late Rabbi Meir Kahane,

Malcolm X and the Nation of Islam's Louis Farrakhan, might find it more difficult to make their case (Klein, 1994). Thus implementing national programmes to encourage forms of public-spirited activity could potentially counter some of the misperceptions and mistrust upon which racism, intolerance and cultural conflict depend and breed.

However, in this particular respect there would be limits to what a public-spirited culture might achieve. This is because – and this applies to any proposal seeking to break down ethnic and cultural division – it is dependent upon the participation of all groups within a society, and people venturing out from their particular enclaves. In some cases this would be difficult. For instance, some Muslims, Orthodox Jews and those of other faiths living in Western democracies view a degree of separatism as a way of maintaining their cultural identity in secular societies. Interestingly, Gurbux Singh – while noting that public policy in areas such as housing has led to segregation – urges minority communities in the UK to become more actively engaged in the wider society as a way of breaking down ethnic and cultural division. He understands their desire to, as he puts it, 'create little Punjab', but they must 'open out, realise they are living in Britain... and embrace the wider community' (Ashley and Hetherington, 2002: 1).

This is an increasingly important area for Western democracies as they become more culturally and ethnically heterogeneous – the size of minority communities will increase with refugee and asylum-seeking populations. When it is not properly addressed it can lead to tensions, and even conflict. This point is borne out by the recent experience of the UK. The Cantle Report, which investigated the 'race' riots in northern towns and cities during the summer of 2001, concluded that white and black people are leading 'parallel lives' (Grice, 2001). It stressed the need to promote cohesion based on mutual knowledge and meaningful contact between different cultural groups.

In response to the riots, the Cantle Report, tensions after September 11th, and ongoing debates about how to deal with refugees and asylum seekers, the UK government has outlined a range of measures. These include proposals that new immigrants will have to take citizenship classes (and tests) and English lessons, as well as the introduction of a ceremony with a new loyalty oath, before they can become British citizens.

However, these measures – which in many ways replicate the approaches adopted in the United States and Canada – are essentially a one-off induction course, and do not address some of the problem areas identified by the Cantle Report. For instance, in terms of mutual knowledge, there is nothing in these proposals to ensure that Britons learn about why immigrants have fled their countries. But above all, in contrast to what has been proposed in this work, they do not ensure or facilitate any communication and interaction between the immigrant and indigenous populations.

Another advantage of what has been proposed here is that the limited nature of the project for encouraging public-spiritedness entails little or no infringement upon cultural diversity. This is a charge often raised against communitarianism. More specifically, it is claimed it denies heterogeneity in the pursuit of social cohesion and close-knit communities. Critics argue this can restrict cultural pluralism, and often leads to domination by the strongest 'community' or group at the expense of minorities. The response of communitarians is that their project merely seeks to overcome cultural divisions within modern societies by balancing unity with diversity and building a 'community of communities' (Etzioni, 1997; Tam, 1998). As Etzioni puts it: 'The concept of a *community of communities* (or diversity within unity) captures the image of a mosaic held together by a solid frame' (ibid., 197). For communitarians, this project is essential if the fragmentation and break-up of societies like America is to be avoided.

Whether such charges against communitarianism are valid is not the primary concern of this work. The aim has been merely to demonstrate that such a case cannot be made against the programme for encouraging public-spiritedness argued for here. And, to repeat, such claims are inapplicable because of the more limited nature and scope of this particular project. It is confined simply to trying to build more mutually supportive and inclusive local communities in order to make them better places in which to live. Above all it does not seek to exclude or subsume particular ways of life or cultural traditions, merely to counter those forms of tribalist behaviour that can foster intolerance and conflict.

Finally, by challenging forms of marginalization, and encouraging inclusiveness and mutual support, a public-spirited culture might help to revive or reinforce the principle of universal citizenship, which as we have seen is often undermined by the retreat into tribalism. In particular, the degree of interaction and active participation developing such a culture would require could help to generate shared values and a sense of common purpose.

Conclusion

In summary, the processes creating an 'age of uncertainty' should also be considered an important factor behind the growth of forms of 'tribalism' in many Western democracies. Furthermore, the fostering of a public-spirited culture, in the manner argued for here, has the potential to counter some of the conditions producing such attitudes and behaviour. This therefore constitutes a further reason for devising and implementing such a project. But of course properly tackling ethnic and cultural division would require a range of policy measures, such as establishing forums for political dialogue, countering racism and racial discrimination, ending forms of social exclusion, and so on.   As with the other areas addressed in this work, encouraging public-spiritedness is not intended as a panacea for all contemporary ills, merely that this might make a positive, albeit limited, contribution to tackling some of them.

Chapter 7

Communitarianism, Liberalism and Public-spiritedness

In Chapter 5, it was argued that government would need to play a pivotal role in the implementation and co-ordination of schemes designed to encourage public-spiritedness. This means, contrary to the position of many liberal theorists and libertarians, government and the agencies and institutions of the state cannot be neutral. Defending this position, and more broadly the principle of government intervention into the lives of its citizens, is the first task of this chapter.

However, the main aim is to continue making the case for fostering a public-spirited culture, considering it in relation to communitarianism and liberalism, which have distinctive positions on the issues addressed by this proposal. These issues include the relationship between the state and the individual, as well as the importance of community and social cohesion. Indeed, the debate between liberals and communitarians was in part provoked by concerns about how to deal with the growing social divisions and fragmentation affecting many Western societies. For communitarians, the explanation for these developments lies largely with the form of liberal individualism, which emerged in some of these societies during the 1980s. Liberals counter by warning of the dangers of communitarianism, citing the threat it poses to our rights and individual freedom. The intention is to avoid the polarization surrounding this debate, and to draw upon the strengths of each tradition.[1]

Any discussion of communitarianism and liberalism is made more difficult by the fact that there are a number of approaches within each tradition. For example, some commentators locate communitarianism within the tradition of civic republicanism with its onus upon civic virtue; others do not even consider communitarian ideas constitute a distinct political theory, merely offering insights into some of the shortcomings of liberalism.[2] While within liberalism can be found both liberal neutralists and social liberals. As the intention here is merely to focus upon key themes within both traditions, inevitably this diversity of opinion and approach is not given sufficient attention. Nevertheless, as has been stated, the primary aim is to forward the discussion on public-spiritedness, and considering it in relation to communitarianism and liberalism provides a further way of outlining what it might entail.

The second and third sections of this chapter form the main defence of both government intervention and the promotion of public-spiritedness. It will be argued these can be justified because they potentially contribute to 'human flourishing'. In order to justify this position, what constitutes human flourishing, and why it is something we should strive for, is outlined in the second section. While there might be an infinite number of ways that people lead flourishing lives, the intention is to identify common themes without which human flourishing would be unlikely. Having identified important constitutive elements of human flourishing, the third section will consider the conditions and environment needed to enable people to flourish, drawing upon central themes within both liberalism and communitarianism. This will include outlining how a public-spirited culture, promoted by government, could also contribute to creating the appropriate conditions for human flourishing.

Some Problems with Neutrality

Neutrality is an important theme within liberalism. A number of different forms or types of neutrality have emerged, notably in the work of F.A. Hayek (1960), Robert Nozick (1974), Bruce Ackerman (1980) and Ronald Dworkin (1978).[3] However, broadly-speaking it entails government must remain neutral when confronted with different conceptions of the good. Neutrality, it is argued, ensures equal respect and concern is shown to the different groups and communities that make-up our complex modern societies. This necessitates government refrain from encouraging citizens to pursue a particular conception of the good, which means avoiding actively supporting some forms of activity at the expense of others, and leaving it to individuals to determine what is valuable in life. Instead, government should confine itself simply to establishing 'neutral' rules and procedures that ensure pluralism and diversity.

Writers who advocate neutrality are generally wary of government intervention in the affairs of individuals. Hayek (1944) maintained that attempts by government to regulate aspects of our lives puts us on 'the road to serfdom'. More specifically, whenever government pursues notions of social justice and egalitarianism it inevitably requires an ever-increasing use of coercion in economic and social life, and can lead to totalitarianism. Indeed, behind such intervention there is an implicit assumption the conception of the good being promoted by government is superior to alternatives.

For writers like Hayek, a government is able to enforce its will and ignore opposition or alternatives because it has the power to do so in the form of the backing of the state. But can we trust government to make the right judgements? And what are we to do if a government is corrupt? This has led writers, such as Bruce Ackerman (1980), to argue for neutrality on the grounds that it is able to constrain the potential abuse of power. To avoid such dangers, many contemporary liberal theorists contend government should refrain from pursuing policies such as egalitarianism, and confine itself to protecting the rights and liberties of its citizens (Mulhall and Swift, 1992: 258).

However, there are a number of flaws in the liberal position on neutrality. To begin with, the contention that power inevitably becomes the primary determinant of the good – and for this reason government should remain neutral – does not apply in all cases. In democratic systems, governments face regular elections and if the conception of the good life they espouse is not acceptable to the majority of the population they will be replaced. Thus democracy facilitates competing conceptions of the good and helps to prevent domination by a single conception.

There are also numerous counter-examples to Hayek's correlation between government intervention and the loss of individual freedom. In this regard, countries with a tradition of *laissez-faire* government do not necessarily have a good record in terms of respecting the rights and liberties of its citizens. For instance, in the United States there have been a number of claims made about government involvement in human rights abuses, such as the McCarthy witch-hunts and the treatment of prisoners – both American and more recently Taliban and al-Qaida. In contrast, the countries of Scandinavia – which are characterized by social democratic governance and extensive welfare states – generally have a better record on human rights, as well as providing greater equality of opportunity.

Moreover, in emphasizing the threat that government intervention poses to individual freedom, there is a tendency amongst neutralist liberals to produce one-sided accounts which largely neglect its positive consequences. For instance, achieving universal literacy may well require government undertaking certain interventionist measures, such as increasing forms of taxation, which encroach upon personal liberty, but this has to be balanced against the benefits it would bring to individuals and society.

Neutrality, of course, is not a neutral concept. As Brian Barry (1990) has noted, even the idea of neutrality is impossible: it is a product of what those with 'liberal attitudes' favour. And in relation to this point, communitarians have often noted a tendency for the liberal theorist 'to think of himself or herself as essentially tradition-free' (Mulhall and Swift, 1992: 291).

More significantly, neutrality is simply impracticable. Governments are making decisions, and thereby expressing preferences, all the time. For example, when a government decides to subsidize the arts, such as theatre and art galleries, and chooses to tax gambling and smoking, it is making value-judgements about which activities it considers more desirable for its citizens to pursue. As Stephen Mulhall and Adam Swift (1992) have observed, governments are continually encouraging their citizens to act and behave in particular ways. For example, legislation on racial discrimination and racist violence is intended to influence attitudes and patterns of behaviour in society. All of which forms part of a wider charge against recent liberal theory that it is too abstract and fails to take account of social and political realities or contexts (see Bellamy, 1992).

In summary, there are a number of weaknesses in the liberal conception of neutrality. As will be seen later in this chapter, a more substantive case against neutrality can be made on the grounds that it runs counter to human flourishing.

The Value and Nature of Human Flourishing

A normative account of human flourishing will now be outlined and defended. It is Aristotle who provides perhaps the most famous and well-developed conception of human flourishing. His account will be discussed, and some of his insights incorporated, as part of an attempt to construct a workable model for the contemporary period. In this respect, it will be argued there are some important elements to human flourishing. Firstly, it should contribute to a sense of well-being. Secondly, it is based upon the principle of association or, to the use Aristotelian term, friendship. And, thirdly, it is bound up with the use of, and extension of, our particular creative powers or abilities. While there are, as was stated in the introduction to this chapter, innumerable ways in which people might lead flourishing lives, it will be claimed that without one or all of these elements it is difficult to envisage how this might be achieved.

A Sense of Well-being

Integral to the Aristotelian conception of human flourishing is *eudaimonia*, regarded as a positive and desirable condition. This term or concept has been variously interpreted, but is often viewed as a sense of well-being and this is how it will be understood here. Thus we should be able to pursue our lives – though preferably our activities would be valid and worthwhile – so that we experience or might attain a sense of well-being. While what might constitute a sense of well-being will be analyzed in a moment, it is of course ultimately a subjective experience. The point being made here is simply that the majority of people would want to 'flourish' in this manner.

The proviso that it would be preferable if our activities were valid and worthwhile, and how this impacts upon the autonomy of the individual, is explained in the next section. But for now it should be noted there is a considerable difference between a life that feels good, or is perceived as good by an individual, and one that is good. As Aristotle declared, 'it is impossible for those who do not do good actions to do well' (1981: 393). Hence value-judgements must be made with regards to our activities and lifestyles because without them it can lead to problems, as well as spurious conceptions of human flourishing. For instance, a drug pusher who sells a large amount of drugs would in their own terms be flourishing: he or she has chosen an activity to pursue and is doing very well at it. The dominant norms and values of society must therefore also influence the nature of human flourishing.

There are different ways of producing a sense of well-being. Flourishing should not just mean being successful in terms of winning, coming first, or financial prosperity. If this were the case then very few people would attain a sense of well-being; either because there are only so many who can win gold medals, or, because not everyone is able to earn a lot of money. Even the notion of seeking to excel is problematical because it can bring unhappiness and dissatisfaction if we fail to achieve such standards. This differs from Aristotle's conception of flourishing, which was often linked to the achievement of excellence.

Human flourishing, therefore, must have an internal dimension – a point returned to later – and should not just rely upon external recognition and trappings. It should be based upon an inner satisfaction, of an activity well done to the best of one's ability, irrespective of how it compares with the performance of others, both past and present. For this reason, satisfaction or enjoyment from the activity one has pursued must be viewed as an important ingredient of human flourishing.

In relation to the internal and external dimension to human flourishing, Aristotle distinguishes between what he terms internal (or 'the soul' as he puts it) goods and external goods (such as money, property, power, status), placing a higher value on the former:-

> External goods, being like a collection of tools each useful for some purpose, have a limit: one can have too many of them, and that is bound to be of no benefit, or even a positive injury, to their possessors. It is quite otherwise with the goods of the soul: the more there is of each the more useful each will be (if

indeed one ought to apply to these the term 'useful', as well as 'admirable').
(Aristotle, 1981: 392)

Aristotle is quite clear why he makes such a distinction: external goods are simply a result of fortune or a 'coincidence of events' (ibid., 393), and by themselves do not make the individual more just or more enlightened. In contrast, internal goods are based upon the virtues: the individual flourishes 'because of himself and what he is by his own nature' (ibid.).

All of this has important implications for the contemporary period in which, as a result of environmental degradation and waste, coupled with continuing demographic and lifestyle pressures upon the earth's resources, we are now confronted with the urgent need to rethink current forms of behaviour. In particular, the economic pressures of the market mean environmental concerns are frequently relegated or sidelined. Human flourishing has therefore to be based upon sensitivity towards the environment, ensuring that our activities do not harm it. If they do, then they cannot be defined as 'human flourishing'. This is because by damaging the environment, it is not only harming our own sense of well-being, by creating more unhealthy and unpleasant conditions in which to live; it is also restricting the flourishing of others including future generations.

Writers like Golding (1972) and Passmore (1980) deny we have a responsibility towards future generations, our moral obligation is simply to our contemporaries. While both writers offer sophisticated arguments to defend this position, it ignores the attachment that many of us feel to the future. For example, young people in our societies will want to avoid the later years of their lives being blighted by a poor and unhealthy physical environment. Moreover, many of us will be parents and therefore profoundly concerned about the state of the planet for our children's sake.

To an extent our behaviour is also governed by awareness that future generations can harm us. While we are alive the younger generations can call us to account for actions and potentially punish us. And when we are dead, and unable to defend ourselves, our reputation can be damaged.[4]

Furthermore, our commitment to the future is revealed by our actions. For instance, why do we plant trees when it is unlikely that we will be alive to see them when they grow to full maturity? Why do we have children? And why do we buy houses? Similarly, why is the international community implementing measures to prevent ozone depletion? Such actions and measures, at all levels, are in part influenced by a consideration for the well-being of future generations.

In practical terms, sensitivity towards the environment means a reorientation away from external goods, such as the fast car and the latest consumer products, and towards internal goods: devoting more time to our friends, families, communities, reading, learning foreign languages, and so on. At a public level, this might entail putting pressure on government to prioritize internal goods in its decision-making.   This could include campaigning for a range of measures: from the protection of the countryside to child-care provision. But again the idea emerges of human flourishing having to be a valid and worthwhile activity. How this relates to public-spiritedness will be established in third section of this chapter.

Finally, both for Aristotle and in its usage here, a sense of well-being is not regarded as simply happiness or pleasure. As Bernard Williams has pointed out in *Ethics and the Limits of Philosophy* (1985), *eudaimonia* is not the same as the modern conception of happiness which is transitory, rather it refers to 'the shape of one's whole life' (ibid., 34). It is also questionable whether any experience can be reduced to a single mental state. For example, an author completing a book will feel many things ranging from pleasure or happiness at a sense of accomplishment to relief and weariness. While some writers might feel disappointment or a sense of emptiness that the work is finished, others might be dissatisfied with the end product.

It is for this reason that hedonism has been criticized. The pursuit of such an aim would be to ignore or deny very human emotions like unhappiness and anger. Experiencing a range of emotions and feelings is what contributes to a rounded life and outlook. J.S. Mill recognised the importance of this when he described happiness in his essay *Utilitarianism* as:-

> ... not a life of rapture; but moments of such, in an existence made up of few and transitory pains, many and various pleasures, with a decided predominance of the active over the passive, and having as the foundation of the whole, not to expect more from life than it is capable of bestowing. A life thus composed, to those who have been fortunate enough to obtain it, has always appeared worthy of the name of happiness. (Mill, 1991: 144)

A similar theme is taken-up by Robert Nozick. In *Anarchy, State, and Utopia* (1974), Nozick argues that if neuro-psychologists produced a machine capable of injecting us with a constant supply of drugs which put us in a permanent pleasurable state, it is likely very few people would take advantage of this opportunity.

Association

Association or friendship must also be considered an important element in human flourishing. Indeed, Aristotle discuses it extensively in the

Nichomachean Ethics (1953). But before discussing the particular role performed by association, it is necessary to outline what Aristotle meant by the virtues. The reason for this is that friendship for him was one of the primary virtues.

For Aristotle, the chief ingredient in *eudaimonia* is virtue, and how we achieve it – the virtues we will need – was an ongoing concern.[5] The individual, like the state, cannot prosper unless they do good actions, and they cannot do this unless they have virtue. Virtues are not a means to a particular *telos*; they are the qualities of character or disposition that allows the individual to lead a full and active life (MacIntyre, 1981: 149). These qualities of character include, for Aristotle, courage, self-control, modesty, self-respect, and truthfulness, to name but a few. Well-being therefore comes from action based upon, or in accordance with, virtue:-

> ... to each individual it is the activity in accordance with his own disposition that is most desirable, and therefore to the good man virtuous activity is most desirable. (1953: bk.10, ch.6)

But there is an element of intuition with Aristotle's virtues. He often assumes that an individual will act in accordance with these virtues without always establishing solid moral reasons for doing so. For example, an individual will act courageously simply because it is a virtue without knowing the purpose for acting in such a way. In contrast, the aim in this work has been to make the case for people acting in a more public-spirited manner, notably in terms of the benefits it can bring both to the individual and society.

Aristotle goes on to argue that whereas our faculties of sense are with us from birth, moral virtues, such as our sense of justice and self-control, have to be learnt and gained through practice, like training to become builders and instrumentalists (*Ethics*, bk.2, ch.1). And whether we become good or bad builders and instrumentalists, and just or unjust people, 'depends on the way we behave in our dealings with other people' (ibid.). Aristotle sums these points up in the phrase: 'like activities produce like dispositions' (ibid.). This is essentially the claim of this work: for people to think in a more public-spirited manner it is necessary to get them to undertake public-spirited activity.

Returning to the second constituent element of human flourishing – association or friendship – it will now be explained why it should be viewed in this way. Again Aristotle can help us out. Friendship or friendliness, as he often terms it, is a virtue and an essential component of a flourishing life. As he notes in *Nicomachean Ethics* (1953): 'Nobody would choose to live without friends even if he had all the other good things' (1953: 258). Friends are necessary for happiness: 'the happy man needs friends' (ibid., 304). We value, according to Aristotle, our affiliation with others; without these relationships, these feelings of affection, our existence is incomplete. In particular, he regards the bonds of true friendship as forming the basis of the bond between citizens which constitutes a *polis*.[6] This is therefore not an ordinary friendship between two people. It is what Aristotle means in *The Politics* when he says no citizen belongs to himself, rather everyone is attached to each other, affiliated as part of the state:-

> And it is not right... that any of the citizens should think that he belongs to himself; he must regard all citizens as belonging to the state, for each is a part of the state; and the responsibility for each part naturally has regard to the responsibility for the whole. (Aristotle, 1981: 452)

This is an important aspect of Aristotle's work. It also serves to counter claims that his conception of human flourishing centres upon the individual being preoccupied with their own *eudaimonia*, with little thought for the fate of others (see Ross, 1995). Aristotle's stress upon the importance of friendship, and the role it can play in the construction of the *polis*, is an effective refutation of such claims.

There are, of course, problems with this notion of friendship or association. How is it possible in modern societies containing large and diverse populations, to have enough friends and associates to constitute a political community? Indeed, Alasdair MacIntyre considers this would have been problematic even during Aristotle's time: the Athenian city-state contained many thousands of people and forming such relationships would have been impracticable (1981: 156). Although in defence of Aristotle, the Greek word for friendship has a wider meaning than in English, being viewed as any mutual sympathy between two human beings. Yet this is still insufficient to cover all the relationships within a city-state.

The Aristotelian conception of the political community would also seem to be - inappropriate in the contemporary period with the drift into individualism and private-orientated modes of behaviour. Such common feelings that do exist often our expressed in terms of patriotism and nationalism, and these tend to exclude rather than include. The nearest we come to the Aristotelian model is in institutions like hospitals, schools and universities where there is often a common sense of purpose amongst the people working within them – although in the UK this is increasingly being eroded by market-driven reforms. But at the level of the polity there is little conception of community, nor common feelings. Friendship, as MacIntyre has observed, is solely confined to the private realm (1981: 156).

In summary, having established association or friendship – a sense of attachment to others – must be considered an important element in human flourishing, contemporary conditions often seem to work against such relationships, as well as making it difficult to generate mutual sympathy between citizens. How this might be addressed, and this aspect of human flourishing facilitated, will be explored in the third section of this chapter.

Creativity

The third element of human flourishing involves the use of our creative abilities. Specifically, it is about people being able to develop their particular talents and capabilities, and having the opportunity to be inventive and imaginative. Agnes Heller in *Beyond Justice* has described this process of developing endowments into talents as 'the construction of the self' (1977: 312). For Marx, creating things and being creative is what distinguishes human beings from animals. Whereas animals are essentially concerned with their own survival, and their activity is geared towards this end, we have the capacity to exist beyond these limits. We are able to create the beautiful and not just the functional. As Marx declared in the *Economic and Philosophical Manuscripts*:-

> The animal only fashions according to the standards and needs of the species it belongs to, whereas man knows how to produce according to the measure of every species and knows everywhere how to apply its inherent standard to the object; thus man also fashions things according to the laws of beauty. (Marx, 1977: 82)

Thus for Marx creativity is central to our species-being. But he considered the system of private property and the division of labour it generates denies us our species-life. This is because the division of labour so integral to capitalism produces widespread alienation. As Marx put it:-

> ... when alienated labour tears from man the object of his production, it also tears from his species-life, the real objectivity of his species and turns the advantage he has over animals into a disadvantage in that his organic body, nature, is torn from him. (Marx, 1977: 82-3)

More specifically, under capitalism and the system of wage-labour, workers do not own what they produce as this belongs to those who own the forces of production. It also means they have no control over the production process. This is reinforced by the division of labour whereby roles and tasks are distinct and specific, something which is reflected in the division between intellectual and material labour such as that between a manager and a factory worker (1977: 168). For the individual worker, this system effectively alienates them from their own labour: 'he does not belong to himself in his labour but to someone else' (ibid., 80). And with the expression of their creativity denied to them, labour for the worker simply becomes a means to an end: a way of earning an income to enable them to survive.

It is not the intention here to assess the validity of Marx's claims about capitalism. Of relevance to this discussion is the impact being unable to use our creative abilities can have upon us. Marx contends that alienated labour means the worker:-

> ... does not confirm himself in his work, he denies himself, feels miserable instead of happy, deploys no free physical and intellectual energy, but mortifies his body and ruins his mind. (Marx, 1977: 80)

For Marx, the only way of restoring to human beings their labour, and hence their creative abilities, is by replacing the existing mode of production with communism where there will be the free development of individuals (ibid., 190-1). Under the latter, as he famously argues in *The German Ideology*, the division of labour is abolished and we are able to undertake a range of productive and creative activities, thereby making use of all of our skills and talents:-

> ... in communist society, where nobody was one exclusive sphere of activity but each can be accomplished in any branch he wishes, society regulates the general production and thus makes it possible for me to do one thing today and another tomorrow, to hunt in the morning, fish in the afternoon, rear cattle in the evening, criticize after dinner, just as I have a mind, without ever becoming hunter, fisherman, cowherd, or critic. (Marx, 1977: 169)

Despite the considerable appeal of Marx's vision, it raises a number of issues. To begin with how would such a society function and be organized? For instance, considerable training is needed to gain the skills and experience required for jobs such as doctors and engineers. We would surely not wish people to rotate these roles. Hence some form of division of labour is necessary for the efficient organization and smooth running of society.

Furthermore, there seems little prospect of a communist society being established in the foreseeable future. To wait for, and place faith in, the emergence of communism does not contribute in any practical sense to the improvement of conditions for workers in the contemporary period. We need therefore when considering ways of facilitating individual creativity, as with all the other points raised here in relation to human flourishing, to remain within the bounds of possibility.

Given these doubts, perhaps Marx's most significant contribution to this area lies with his vivid descriptions of the human condition when we are denied the free expression of our creative abilities. It runs counter, in the language of Aristotle, to our sense of well-being. Moreover, this theme is not just the preserve of Marxism. Adam Smith, for example, though an advocate of the division of labour, discusses in the *Wealth of Nations* his concerns about the impact upon workers of repetitive factory work (Smith, 1976: V, i, 61). While J.S. Mill in *On Liberty* stresses the importance of individuals being able to develop their capacities and abilities to be 'the best thing they can be' (Mill, 1991: 71).

There is therefore a degree of consensus over the importance of creativity to human flourishing. However, as we saw in Part I, contemporary modes of work and leisure do not allow many of us to be creative. For a lot of people there is basic lack of time and opportunity to be creative when confronted with increased pressures in the workplace and being caught-up in a 'work-and-spend' culture. Action is therefore needed to remedy this state of affairs. With the overthrow of global capitalism unlikely in the near future, we must therefore look for alternative ways of facilitating creativity.

Government, Human Flourishing and Public-spiritedness

Having set-out what might constitute human flourishing and the value of attaining it, the focus will now be upon identifying the conditions and environment best-suited to facilitate this end. While there will be many factors involved in enabling people to flourish, the position taken here is this is made easier by the existence of three inter-related conditions or concepts: autonomy, pluralism and community. It will also be claimed autonomy and pluralism are dependent upon community in order to function. Furthermore, community would be better able to facilitate autonomy and pluralism through the fostering of a public-spirited culture, promoted in large part by government. This therefore constitutes the second part of the defence of government intervening in the affairs of its citizens.

Autonomy

Autonomy is a central theme within liberalism. The aim here will be to demonstrate that attaching certain conditions to the concept of autonomy, while seemingly a contradiction in terms, can in fact enhance the life of the individual.

There are many different interpretations of autonomy (see Richard Lindley, 1986). However, Joseph Raz has developed a particularly useful and convincing conception of autonomy in his book *The Morality of Freedom* (1986). Raz argues, displaying his liberal credentials, that a good life must be an autonomous life: a person's well-being depends on them being the maker or author of their own destiny. In terms of this work, autonomy can be considered a prerequisite of human flourishing in that it facilitates the constitutive elements identified in the previous section. For instance, when we have degree of autonomy we are able to choose the activities we feel are conducive to our well-being. It also enables us to decide how we are to exercise our creative abilities and talents, as well as providing us with the freedom to form friendships and other intimate relationships.

However, Raz adds a proviso, arguing that individual freedom is insufficient by itself. Autonomy should not mean the freedom to fritter away our lives, or commit evil or criminal acts. For Raz, 'a person's well-being depends on the value of his goals and pursuits' (1986: 298). This can be irrespective of the value an individual attaches to these goals and pursuits simply because their views may be mistaken. As Raz notes, '[s]atisfaction of goals based on false reasons does not contribute to one's well-being' (1986: 301). It would mean a person is not leading a flourishing life, and they should be informed of this fact. This can be achieved in two ways: firstly, though Raz does not address this point, through the moral approval or disapproval of others in society towards our actions; and, secondly, as will be discussed in more detail in a moment, through government attempting to influence our behaviour.

Raz makes this point about the pursuit of valuable and valueless activities, by using the examples of a livestock farmer and a gambler:-

> A person who spends all his time gambling has, other things being equal, less successful a life, even if he is a successful gambler, than a livestock farmer busily minding his farm... The reason is that they engage in what they do because they believe it to be a valuable, worthwhile activity (perhaps but not necessarily because of its value to others). They care about what they do on that basis. To the extent that their valuation is mistaken it affects the success of their life. (Raz, 1986: 298-9)

Vegetarians might question the particular comparison that Raz makes, but this misses the point. Raz is merely establishing that we can make comparisons; we can tell or reach a consensus about who is, and who is not, leading a flourishing life. This is because our goals and ambitions as well as our values are in large part shaped by the societies in which we live. For example, there would be little dispute that a drug addict does not lead a fulfilling and autonomous life, even from most drug addicts. Indeed, all those engaged in an addictive activity, such as drugs, gambling and alcohol have lost a degree of autonomy because their freedom of choice is restricted.

Any notion therefore that we each have a unique perception of what constitutes valid and worthwhile activity, and which bears little relation to the dominant norms and values within society, cannot be sustained. We are all to varying degrees aware of these norms and values and they inform our moral outlook: even the criminal is aware when he or she has conflicted with them and broken the law. Furthermore, as Bernard Williams (1985) has noted, in educating children we seek to instil these values and give them a sense of right and wrong. There are few parents who knowingly seek to disadvantage their children by excluding them from the ethical codes of conduct in society and presenting them with alternative guidelines (Williams, 1985: 48).

To repeat, each of us is influenced by the societies in which we live. Moreover, though some liberal theorists would disagree, society exists prior to the individual.[7] We are born into societies with established cultural norms and values, and growing up in them inevitably shapes our behaviour and therefore the nature of our autonomy. Even our self-perception and identity emerges from interaction with others in society, and how they view us (Sandel, 1992). While Alasdair MacIntyre (1981) contends the liberal emphasis upon casual association between individuals on the basis of rational calculation, ignores the fact that we are emotionally involved with other people, such as friends and family members. Through such relationships our outlook, aims and values will be determined. Consequently, if we isolate ourselves the only good we could be capable of imagining would be imbued with self-interest. As MacIntyre has observed:-

> To cut oneself off from shared activity in which one has initially to learn obediently as an apprentice learns, to isolate oneself from the communities which find their point and purpose in such activities, will be to debar oneself from finding any good outside of oneself. (MacIntyre, 1981: 258)

This degree of isolation is of course impossible. Even the behaviour of Robinson Crusoe on his desert island, and specifically his industriousness and his racism, was a product of his interaction with others in the society in which he was raised (Doyal and Gough, 1991: 60).

To recap, individual autonomy must be considered an important prerequisite of human flourishing, but this autonomy is inevitably constrained by our social environment. Our actions and decisions are shaped by the fact that we are social beings; they are not simply a series of transactions and contractual exchanges. Autonomy, therefore, has more substance and meaning when we recognize that we are not disengaged from our surroundings.

Having established it is possible to determine who is leading a flourishing life, government can play an important role in informing and advising of such matters. A democratically elected government can express the sentiments of its citizens, as well as being able to receive expert advice from various quarters.[8]   Government is therefore uniquely capable of helping us to use our autonomy wisely; to steer us away from the pursuit of activities which are not valid and worthwhile whether this be through forms of taxation, moral pronouncements, legislation, or, the provision of information to help us make informed decisions.

Libertarians and many liberal theorists conceive of autonomy as people being free to make their own decisions. Often regarded as one of the founding fathers of liberalism, John Stuart Mill maintained in *On Liberty* that the only justification for government intervening in the affairs of an individual was 'to prevent harm to others. His own good, either physical or moral, is not a sufficient warrant' (Mill, 1991: 14). Even if we make the wrong decisions we can nevertheless learn from our mistakes.

There is some appeal to this position. Yet it could result in people harming themselves. Moreover, contrary to Mill, there is no such thing as pure self-regarding conduct: all our decisions and actions in some way have an impact upon others. When we inflict harm upon ourselves it affects our family, friends and associates. In this regard, libertarians are simply mistaken when they defend the right of the individual to take potentially addictive drugs by arguing that such matters should not be the concern of government. The legitimacy of government intervention lies in the impact such activity can have upon others. And in fairness to Mill, elsewhere in *On Liberty* he concedes there can be:-

> ... good reasons for remonstrating with him, or reasoning with him, or persuading him, or entreating him, but not for compelling him, or visiting him with any evil in case he do otherwise. (ibid.)

Mill is acknowledging here that government can seek to influence the behaviour of the individual. And this is in essence the position of this work: government should be able to encourage its citizens to act more public-spiritedly. As Joseph Raz has argued, government must aim to enable 'individuals to pursue valid conceptions of the good and to discourage evil or empty ones' (1986: 133).

It might be thought the emphasis here upon distinguishing valid and worthwhile activity, and defending forms of government intervention in our lives, destroys any notion of autonomy. Yet what is being proposed does not deny the individual the freedom to pursue activity which might be widely regarded as inappropriate and pointless, and to ignore the urgings of government. Should some people choose to spend their time gambling, and do nothing for their local communities, then this has to be accepted. People cannot be made to attend an opera when they would rather watch a football match. This is why the arguments and proposals formulated during the course of this work have been merely to encourage, rather than compel, people to undertake public-spirited activity.

By re-examining the standard liberal conception of autonomy – which is what has been attempted here – it is possible to make a case for government influencing the behaviour of its citizens. Having established this point, such intervention – given the potential benefits outlined in Chapters 5 and 6 – could take the form of measures designed to encourage citizens to behave more public-spiritedly.

Pluralism

Another prerequisite of human flourishing is pluralism. Joseph Raz contends any plausible conception of the good life should not just be based upon autonomy, it must also include a multiplicity or plurality of options being available to the individual if their autonomy is to be of any real value. There is little point in a person being autonomous if their life-chances are limited. Pluralism in practice means being able to enjoy a broad range of associations and relationships, and to have a variety of opportunities to use our creative abilities – all of which can contribute to our sense of well-being. Indeed, Raz's advocacy of a multiplicity of options being available to us, is what distinguishes him from many other liberals.

How can we best ensure that the life-chances of citizens are not limited? Again government, through the institutions and mechanisms of the state, can play an important role in this regard. It is in the position to implement policies – such as the provision of adequate health care, decent schools and housing, and the promotion of family life in all its legitimate diversity – to ensure all citizens have the opportunity or potential to flourish. From this starting point, government can also work to ensure a plurality of meaningful options are available, such as reasonable employment prospects, the possibility of higher education for all its citizens, and effective training and re-training schemes. Furthermore, government has the capacity to facilitate our creativity. As Lionel Jospin's government in France demonstrated, it is possible to pass legislation to reduce the working week and thereby provide people with more leisure time to use their talents and abilities.

Government also has the capacity to curb developments and forces hindering the attainment of *eudaimonia*. In this sense some aspects of a market society might be said to run counter to human flourishing. For example, free market capitalism often entails some people relocating to different regions in search of work, and thereby disrupting family and community life. This therefore undermines an important constitutive element of human flourishing – the need for association. In this particular case, government can regulate aspects of the market economy, as well as invest in run-down regions, to reduce the necessity of people having to move in order to gain employment. Such intervention is another way in which government can help to ensure its citizens have a plurality of options available to them.

Thus as well as being able to inform and influence us, a case can also be made for government intervening in the lives of its citizens on the grounds of establishing the conditions for human flourishing. As Raz puts it:-

> The autonomy principle permits and even requires governments to create morally valuable opportunities, and to eliminate repugnant ones. (Raz, 186: 417)

And Raz believes it is important that these opportunities exercise 'the capacities human beings have an innate drive to exercise' (ibid., 375). This constitutes a significant challenge to the liberal principle of neutrality and provides justification for a range of government interventions, including addressing the plight of the poorest members of society. After all, to use David McLellan's paraphrase of the Marxist position, 'it was no use having the right of access to the Grill Room at the Ritz if you couldn't afford the bill' (1983: 145).

Liberal theorists have often challenged the role of government as provider of opportunities. For example, it is argued that if activities such as ballet and opera do not receive wide public support, why should government intervene to protect them? Indeed, maintaining such pursuits through financial subsidies infringes upon the liberty of the majority of non-ballet and non-opera goers who have to finance these pursuits through taxation. Moreover, in the UK, some politicians have stated that if ballet and opera were to decline, it would not greatly concern the majority of British people.

However, such criticisms ignore the importance of human flourishing. If ballet and opera bring enjoyment to some people and enriches their lives, it is therefore contributing to their sense of well-being. And without intervention from government it is likely these activities or leisure pursuits would simply become the preserve of the wealthy, and possibly disappear altogether in some countries. The state should therefore try to ensure such opportunities are available to all. To repeat, autonomy only becomes meaningful for the citizen when he or she has a plurality of options and life-chances.

Community

The Need for Community Community must also be considered a necessary condition for human flourishing. Elizabeth Frazer (1999) has correctly noted there is a lack of analysis of the concept of community, and few attempts are made to define it, both within communitarian writing 'and in political theory more generally' (1999: 46). However, in part this is surely because community is very much a subjective experience: we each decide for ourselves what constitutes a form of community for us, whether it is based upon our workplace, neighbourhood, religion, nation-state, and so on. And because people belong to multiple communities, and will have varying degrees of attachment to each of them, this further complicates the issue.

One way of demonstrating that community is a necessary condition for human flourishing is by highlighting the way in which it helps meet a deep human need for a sense of belonging and connection with others. That we have such needs is evident from numerous anthropological and sociological studies. Brief mention of one sociological study should be sufficient to illustrate this point. It is a piece of research undertaken in the United States by Arthur Kornhaber and Kenneth Woodward entitled *Grandparents/ Grandchildren: The Vital Connection* (1980).

Kornhaber and Woodward studied the impact contemporary developments, such as rising levels of divorce, were having upon the relationship between grandparents and their grandchildren. They found from undertaking a series of in-depth interviews with different groups of grandparents and grandchildren that where there was little or no contact between them, mutual feelings of loss, deprivation and unhappiness developed. As Agnes Heller (1987) has observed there is great emotional intensity in personal attachments, and in identifying with another person or persons it in turn makes us full members of the human race: 'being bound to one human being, I am fully bound to the human race' (1987: 319).

The way in which community fulfils this human need for a sense of belonging and connection with others is that individuals belong to particular and organic communities: their lives and relationships are real and concrete. Thus community is not an abstract principle but a lived and vital human experience. For communitarians, community must therefore be considered a human need. This entails we must protect and maintain established communities, and seek to build new communities (see Etzioni, 1995a).

Liberal theorists, in contrast, focus upon the individual as an autonomous being, often tending to play down this need for community (see for example Gauthier, 1992). With the starting point of much liberal thought being the free person, a primary aim for liberals is to identify the abstract or universal rules of morality that transcend particular communities and which the individual may adhere to. The emphasis is therefore upon the universal, rather than the particular. Indeed, for many liberals a preoccupation with the latter can lead to a moral relativism, whereby moral and ethical principles are simply confined to a particular community making it impossible to make judgements about other communities. How would it possible, for instance, to condemn human rights abuses in another society? What would be the grounds for denouncing the actions of a Hitler or a Saddam Hussein?

Communitarians such as Michael Walzer (1992) counter the charge of moral relativism by challenging the notion that morality can be based on abstract universal principles; rather the values people hold, if they are to be meaningful, must be rooted in, and emerge from, their particular communities. This debate is very much influenced by the work of Hegel who distinguished between the ethical principles rooted in a particular community, what he termed *Sittlichkeit,* and the universal rules or principles of morality (*Moralität*). Interestingly, Hegel sided with the former arguing that the strongest bonds were in these types of community, and crucially they were the only arena in which genuine moral autonomy could be achieved. Thus for Hegel, *Sittlichkeit* was the higher form of morality. What Hegel means by this is similar to the Christian notion of brotherly love which must first be directed to one's neighbour, rather than humankind in general (Selznick, 1995).

However, the pertinent point for this discussion is Hegel's contention about the strength of the bonds within communities, and the sense of attachment people can feel towards their particular community. This has been evident throughout history in the number of people who have risked their lives in defence of what they perceive as *their* community.

Yet communities can also be a breeding ground for chauvinism and intolerance. Tension and antagonism can develop both within a community as well as between different communities, and given the strength of allegiance some people feel towards their particular community this can often be difficult to defuse. The events in the Balkans during the 1990s demonstrate this point only too well. At the time some of the atrocities committed during this period were reported as being partly motivated by the desire to revenge massacres carried out by, for example, the Croat Ustaše and the Serbian Chetniks during the Second World War. Indeed, such behaviour has led some commentators to stress the urgency of promoting internationalism, as embodied in liberalism rather than communitarianism. But this view does not undermine the central point being made here: the importance of forms of community to human beings.

As well as the charge of intolerance, it is often claimed an emphasis upon community and the common good – which is central to the communitarian project – can suppress important aspects of human behaviour, such as autonomy and eccentricity. While pressures to conform can stifle diversity and minority opinion. Michael Sandel has responded to these claims by noting that 'intolerance flourishes most where forms of life are dislocated, roots unsettled, traditions undone' (1984: 17), and these are conditions which can emerge when there is a lack of community and community life. Furthermore, intolerance and chauvinism need not be a recurring feature of communities and community life. As was hopefully demonstrated in Chapter 6, it is not beyond the capacity of human beings to develop more inclusive communities, which might in turn serve to curb 'tribalist' attitudes and behaviour.

Another reason community is significant to people is the role it plays in our self-formation. We grow up in different communities, they profoundly influence our lives and this is the reason they exert such a hold over us. For communitarians like Charles Taylor (1992), a community not only includes a common language, but also evolves a common culture. Communities therefore shape our outlook and are more than just forms of association. As Hegel maintained we are first and foremost historically conditioned, rather than free and rational agents. Hence our allegiance to community is in most cases not conditional, a weighing-up of the potential advantages and disadvantages, in the manner described by social contract theorists like Thomas Hobbes (1985) and John Locke (1990). Often it is not even a matter of choice.

In contrast, the social contract tradition of liberalism maintains human beings choose to construct a society for the fulfilment of certain individual ends. Society or community is viewed essentially in instrumental terms. This has contributed, as Charles Taylor (1992) has noted, to the prioritization of the individual and their rights over society, as well as ensuring the citizen has minimal obligations and duties.

However, there are certain flaws in the social contract thesis. In particular, how is it possible for the individual to make a contract when they are born into a society or community already in existence? John Locke tries to resolve this dilemma in his *Two Treatises of Government*, by distinguishing between our express and tacit consent. More specifically, he argues we give our tacit consent to society, and its laws and mode of governance, by choosing to live in it and enjoy its benefits (see Locke, 1990: 177-8).

But his case is unconvincing. As Edmund Burke has observed in his *Reflections on the Revolution in France* (1986), the social contract is beyond our experience and individual capacities to construct: we are not just talking here about 'a partnership agreement in a trade of pepper and coffee' (ibid., 194). Rather it is a 'partnership not only between those who are living, but between those who are living, those who are dead, and those who are about to born' (ibid., 194-5).

A final defence of community can be made in terms of it facilitating self-sufficiency. Communitarians maintain that self-sufficiency, even our personal survival, is better ensured within the community than outside of communal life. Co-operation amongst people enables the production of sufficient material 'goods' – such as houses, clothes, food – which enables individuals to flourish and lead lives which are not concerned with everyday survival. Aristotle, from whom many communitarians draw inspiration, was perhaps one of the first people to make this point. He argued that self-sufficiency, or *autarkeia* as he termed it, was only possible within the *polis*: it could not be attained in isolation. Indeed, he goes so far as to claim in *The Politics* that anyone who was not part of the polis was either a beast or a god:-

> Any one who by his nature and not simply by ill-luck has no state is either too bad or too good, either subhuman or superhuman... Whatever is incapable of participating in the association which we call the state, a dumb animal for example, and equally whatever is perfectly self-sufficient and has no need (e.g., a god), is not part of the state at all. (Aristotle: 1981, 59-61)

In summary, it has been argued that for reasons of self-constitution and self-sufficiency, as well as providing a sense of belonging and connection with others, there is a basic human need for community. Communities are an essential component of human life. Having made this point, it is now possible to describe a further way in which community is a necessary condition for human flourishing. This will entail highlighting the particular ways in which local communities can operate in this manner. It will also be shown that a public-spirited culture might aid local communities in facilitating human flourishing.

Community, human flourishing and public-spiritedness In demonstrating the relationship between community and human flourishing, it needs to be reiterated that communities do not exist in the abstract. They are the environment or arena in which autonomy and pluralism function; more specifically, it is within communities and societies that each of us make decisions on how to lead our lives thereby exercising our autonomy through pursuing a plurality of options. Communities therefore shape the nature of our autonomy and pluralism. And given it has been argued here that autonomy and pluralism are prerequisites of human flourishing, communities must be considered an important determinant of whether we can be creative, form associations and friendships and generally attain a sense of well-being.

Put another way, highly individualistic societies – where there is a lack of community life and concomitantly low levels of trust and sociability – are likely to restrict autonomy and pluralism thereby making human flourishing more difficult to achieve. For example, how can individuals flourish if they do not feel completely safe or secure in the society and communities in which they live? Inevitably, the range of options and activities that the individual can pursue are restricted under such conditions. Moreover, where there is a dearth of social capital in the form of sociability, trust and shared values, it will serve to inhibit the formation of friendships and other relationships. In this regard, Frank Furedi has argued that '[i]ndividual insecurity and social isolation are what helps stimulate the image of a world of risky strangers' (1997: 125). Indeed, there has been much discussion about how these 'insecure times' are making us more cautious and less trusting of others (see Franklin, 1998; Vail et al., 1999). We take greater account of the risk involved, whether this is to do with our personal relationships, our financial affairs or the food that we eat. As Furedi puts it: 'who can you trust?' (1997: 125).

Thus for autonomy and pluralism to exist and operate – and therefore for human flourishing to be a possibility – it requires a compatible environment. It will now be argued that a public-spirited culture can contribute to the building of such an environment.

As was shown in Chapter 5, the fostering of public-spiritedness can potentially help build more vibrant, mutually supportive and inclusive local communities. It is in this sense that a public-spirited culture might facilitate human flourishing because such communities are likely to be conducive to this end in a number of ways.

To begin with, as was discussed in Chapter 6, by seeking to involve all sections of society in public-spirited activity there is the prospect of fostering inclusiveness, and reducing forms of intolerance and discrimination. Western democracies are increasingly culturally diverse, and becoming more so. A more public-spirited culture – in the form argued for in this work – does not infringe upon this pluralism, but simply seeks to promote greater interaction and communication between different ethnic and cultural groups. It is only by working and co-operating together within the context of local communities that shared understandings and greater insight into cultural difference might emerge. Moreover, such communities and societies are likely to be more stable and less marked by cultural tensions – a setting conducive both to autonomy and pluralism.

While in individualistic societies, as we saw in Part I, where common bonds are weak and there is fear of violence and crime, people will feel constrained in what they can do. Autonomy and pluralism are restricted when, for example, people seek to avoid visiting certain areas or neighbourhoods because of concerns for their personal safety. Likewise, because a high level of private-orientated behaviour is invariably a feature of individualistic societies, organizing social and collective activities is made more difficult. Robert Putnam's discovery of the decline of bowling leagues and other forms of associative life in America lends support to this view. A public-spirited culture, on the other hand, seeks to build common bonds and to foster sociability and group endeavours; it would therefore expand the range of activities and meaningful pursuits a person could undertake.

The reciprocity and mutual support a public-spirited culture is intended to generate can also facilitate human flourishing in that it would provide a form of collective security in our 'age of uncertainty'. As we saw in Chapter 5, public-spiritedness offers a way of countering some of the negative aspects of contemporary processes. For example, it provides a way of meeting the demands for labour flexibility in a post-Fordist era through schemes to establish neighbourhood crèches and the exchange of educational and vocational skills. The latter would also afford people an opportunity to explore their potential by enabling them to acquire new skills outside of a formal educational setting. Thus it is the type of local communities that more community- and neighbourly-orientated activity could help to build, which would pave the way for meaningful autonomy and pluralism, and thereby facilitate human flourishing.

Moreover, actually behaving in a public-spirited manner can enable us to flourish in a number of ways. Notably in terms of achieving a sense of well-being, the first constituent element of human flourishing identified here, which it was argued needs to be based upon valuable activity. This is because through being public-spirited we can gain a sense of inner satisfaction and achievement from helping others, which will contribute to our sense of well-being. Such behaviour is also valuable in terms of the benefits it brings to the recipients of our efforts. This even applies to conservation and environmental work, which would benefit both current and future generations, as well as enabling us to feel better about ourselves that we had contributed in some way to improving the condition of the environment in which we live.

Association, the second constituent element of human flourishing identified here, can also be facilitated through public-spirited activity. For example, the various schemes outlined in Chapter 5 – such as helping one's neighbours, working for voluntary associations, running neighbourhood crèches, and so on – are all based upon people interacting and co-operating together within local communities. This therefore provides an opportunity to make the acquaintance of new people, as well as to strengthen existing contacts and associations. Furthermore, this interaction and co-operation might help to foster mutual sympathy between citizens, which Aristotle viewed as forming the basis of a state or *polis*. This is because, to reiterate a point made in Chapter 5, neighbourly and community activity can serve to generate social capital and trust for the wider society, thereby strengthening social cohesion.

As for creativity, the third constituent element of human flourishing, a public-spirited culture would not be able to counter what Marx maintained was the alienation we feel in our active life under capitalism. This according to Marx would require the overthrow of capitalism, and it has been the aim here to promote what is practicable.

However, behaving in a public-spirited manner does allow for a degree of creativity, albeit in a limited sense. To begin with an individual deciding to be public-spirited for their neighbourhood or local community can choose what form their efforts will take. They are in control of their own actions and their labour belongs to nobody but themselves, which stems directly from the lack of a financial or profit-making motive involved in public-spiritedness. Furthermore, what has been proposed here also allows scope for the citizen to use their initiative and be creative in the type of activity they choose to do. It can range from dredging lakes to painting murals, and they would not have to confine themselves to one particular task. Indeed, being able to undertake a range of activities entails there is no division of labour and that we are able to make use of all our skills and talents. This would also provide people with the opportunity to take-up different types of activity from their working lives. For instance, a teacher might want to repair local amenities in order to use their manual skills, and so on.

In summary, as well as being a necessary and vital part of human life, community – especially in the form of local communities – can help us to flourish in various ways. This has significant political implications because it places pressure upon governments to try and maintain local communities. In contrast, for example, to the approach adopted by the Conservative Party in the UK during the 1980s – a period which saw the decimation of many local communities following the decline of traditional industries – the onus should be upon government preserving and reinvigorating communities. As Michael Sandel has observed, government should be geared towards enacting 'laws regulating plant closings, to protect their communities from the disruptive effects of capital mobility and sudden industrial change' (1984:17). In this regard, the argument of this work has been that government should also look at ways of promoting a public-spirited culture as a means of rebuilding local communities, through such measures as devoting more resources to voluntary associations and local community groups.

Conclusion

There have been two aspects to this chapter. One aim has been to establish the principle that contrary to the position held by libertarians and many liberal theorists, government can and should intervene in a range of ways in the affairs of its citizens, both to influence their behaviour and to shape the society in which they live. This case has been made in order to justify the type of national campaign for encouraging public-spiritedness outlined earlier in this work, which would entail government playing an important role. However, this is not tantamount to large-scale government or state intervention in social life. If it were, it would erode the very autonomy, which it has been claimed here people require in order to lead fulfilling lives.

The other purpose of this chapter has been to consider the project for fostering public-spiritedness, argued for in this work, in relation to liberalism and communitarianism. It has been shown that it is possible to retain the central ideas of both traditions – the autonomy of liberalism and the community of communitarianism – within a project geared towards facilitating human flourishing. Indeed, autonomy and community, as well as pluralism, are prerequisites to achieving this end. Moreover, as has hopefully been demonstrated, a public-spirited culture might play a positive role in enabling more citizens to have meaningful autonomy within a vibrant community, and therefore could contribute to human flourishing.

Chapter 8

Citizenship – A Modest Proposal

A case will be now made for community volunteering or service being an integral part of the civic education young people receive in schools and colleges. It will be claimed this is necessary in order to foster a public-spirited culture. This proposal should therefore be viewed as paving the way for the schemes for facilitating public-spiritedness outlined in Chapter 5. In this regard, there is also the prospect that young people getting involved in community work might ignite the interests of their parents.

The second half of the chapter will examine a range of potential criticisms of this proposal. This will include a consideration of the contention that if you take the voluntary dimension out of community volunteering it undermines the whole notion of volunteering.

Citizenship and Public-spiritedness

A Modest Proposal

It would be easier to encourage people to undertake forms of neighbourly and community activity if they have had experience of such work, and preferably if they have become accustomed to behaving in this way at a young age. Thus to get people thinking and acting in a public-spirited manner it is proposed they should undertake community volunteering or service as part of their civic education. Civic or citizenship education is of course already a part of the curriculum throughout Europe and in the United States, Canada and Australia. And the incorporation of this proposal into existing civic education programmes might be made easier if guidance in the running of community service projects were included in teacher training courses.[1]

Such a proposal need not, and probably should not, apply to all those of school age. Indeed if it were, as well as creating organizational and supervisory difficulties, there would probably be too many children and not enough good works to be undertaken. Instead such a scheme might be concentrated upon students aged between 15 and 18. Community service would therefore be confined to those students coming to an end of their secondary school education, and those going on to further education. Influencing the behaviour of this age-range is especially important because it is the stage at which they become adult members of society. Moreover, children any younger than this age would require considerable supervision, and in terms of community activity there would be a limit to what they could undertake and achieve.

As for devising and creating suitable volunteering schemes, as well as supervising them, this could be undertaken by schools and colleges in conjunction with local authorities and local voluntary organizations. It would require central government providing the necessary financial resources to implement this scheme, especially in terms of ensuring there is sufficient staff within schools and colleges. Yet this proposal would cost relatively little to fund, as young people would be providing their labour free of charge, and the work they undertake for their communities might reduce government expenditure in some areas.

In terms of the type of volunteering schemes which might be devised, organizations like the Institute for Voluntary Research in the UK have researched this area and produced guidelines on what young people seek from voluntary work. These include a variety of activities; providing good experiences; incentives in terms of public recognition and awards; and fun (Guardian Education, 2002). And the activities young people might undertake within their local communities could range from conservation and environmental work, such as rebuilding hedges and cleaning-up canals and rivers, to helping the homeless, the sick, and the elderly. Community service might also involve an element of self-interest for young people. For example, decorating and maintaining areas where they are likely to congregate and socialize, such as youth centres and skateboard parks.

Alternatively, and perhaps preferably, young people could simply be asked what they would like to do. This approach would allow them to use their initiative and creativity, and as a consequence be more likely to retain their interest. It might include involvement in website design or exhibiting art they had produced in libraries or other public places. The only proviso would be that their choice of activity should in some way contribute positively to their local communities.

As for the amount of time young people should spend doing community volunteering, this should be left to the schools and colleges to determine. This will largely be dependent upon staff availability and expertise. But the particular needs and requirements of the communities in which the schools and colleges are located will also be an influence. This approach differs from the one advocated by a 1998 government-sponsored report in the UK by Bernard Crick, which suggested that 5 per cent of the curriculum be devoted to community service. To repeat, it is only being argued here that community volunteering should be an established part of the civic education young people receive, which would entail they undertake such activity on a reasonably regular basis. In practical terms, this might mean, as with the proposal outlined in Chapter 5, spending a morning or an afternoon upon such activity, but whether this was once a month, or even once a term or semester, would be for the schools and colleges to decide.

Some teachers might argue there is not enough room on the school timetable to include community volunteering. This is probably the case in the UK, where the rather prescriptive National Curriculum dominates the school day. The implementation of this proposal – at least in the UK – would therefore require some debate about the type of education young people receive and experience, especially in terms of determining the balance between their academic and personal/ social development. Yet as Richard Pring (2000) has observed, there should be an ongoing debate about the aims and purpose of education. Indeed, the National Curriculum is regularly criticized for being overly preoccupied with academic performance and attainment. And there is awareness within the UK Government that education should be more broadly interpreted. As David Blunkett, the former Education Secretary, acknowledged in a speech given at Liverpool Town Hall in March 1999:-

> Education is not just about preparing people for work. It is fundamental to the development of responsible citizens able to play their part in society... (BBC News Online, 'Making pupils better citizens', 8/3/99)

However, the intention here is not discuss in detail the British experience, merely to defend the principle of including community service in the civic education young people receive in schools and colleges.

While it would mean additional responsibility for schools and colleges, community volunteering could enable them to build and strengthen ties with their local communities. It might also reinforce or revive the values of co-operation, community and caring within schools, which can often be relegated by the exam-orientated – and hence often individualistic – nature of the educational system. In this regard, community volunteering offers the chance for young people to work in teams and engage in multiple tasks on some projects, which would require the ability to co-operate and compromise. And in general this scheme would provide an opportunity for schools and colleges to focus upon the personal and social development of their students.

As well as enhancing the quality of community life, community service can make an important contribution to the civic education of young people. To begin with there is the prospect that they will become more aware of their role and responsibilities in their communities through undertaking such activities. Forms of community work and involvement might also provide them with an insight into the extent to which people are interdependent and benefit from co-operative behaviour; that we are not isolated individuals whose actions have no consequences for others. While regular contact with those they are helping would enable them to get to know people outside of their peer group. It might also help to bridge the generation gap; the oft-heard complaint of many senior citizens that young people show no respect for them would have less merit.

Furthermore, a number of academic commentators have described the ways in which community service schemes can instil social values in young people (e.g., Delve, Mintz and Stewart, 1990). And in terms of fostering a public-spirited culture, by having had the experience, and often enjoyment, of undertaking community service at school can help to ensure new generations of volunteers continue to emerge.

The Benefits for Young People

For young people, undertaking community work would be beneficial in a number of ways. For a start, it would simply give them a break from their studies. Having time allocated for activity that has nothing to do with exams, as well as a chance to work with their friends on different tasks and projects, would be welcomed by many students. But as well as giving them the chance to get out of school or college for a while, more importantly this would provide them with the opportunity for new experiences. For example, they might come into regular contact with a range of people from alcoholics and drug addicts to the disabled and infirm, which they otherwise might not interact with (Baer, 1995). Numerous academic commentators have stressed the way in which community service schemes provide a broader and invaluable experiential education (see Kendall, 1990; Williams, 1980) and 'authentic learning experiences' (Shneider, 1994). And this type of interaction would in turn contribute to the building of more vibrant local communities.

Another benefit for young people from this proposal is that involvement in a variety of tasks and activities within their local community would serve as a good introduction into the world of work. They could experience a range of jobs thereby enabling them to make more informed choices when it comes to choosing their own career paths. It would also provide them with an opportunity to develop new skills, thereby enhancing their prospects of gaining employment when they leave school or college. Of equal importance, many young people would gain a sense of satisfaction from helping others as a result of undertaking community work.

Thus overall this proposal would provide young people with a significant learning experience, serving to broaden their outlook, and hopefully making them think about being public-spirited when they leave school or college. It should therefore be viewed as an important part of their civic education. Indeed, it is questionable whether citizenship can just be learnt from books, and written about in the classroom. Citizenship, and certainly if we seek to encourage active citizens, requires a practical dimension, and in particular a degree of involvement in local communities.

Precedent and Contemporary Practice

In case this proposal is thought impracticable, it should be noted that community service schemes for young people already exist in some countries. For example, in the United States, students are expected to select and undertake a community service project for a few hours a month as part of their civic education (Hirsch and Goldsmith, 1996). And in the Steirer Case of 1994, in which two students challenged the right of their school to require them to perform community service work, the Court of Appeals for the Third Circuit affirmed the constitutionality of mandatory community service programmes for students in public schools (Bittner, 1994).

Moreover, as was mentioned in Chapter 5, President Clinton introduced in September 1994 a new national service programme for student volunteers known as 'AmeriCorps' (Wofford, Waldman and Bandow, 1996). This scheme awards students a sum of money – in 2002 the figure was $4,725 (£3,308) a year – which can be used for education and training costs if they complete a year of volunteering. The scheme has proved successful with approximately 300,000 people taking part in AmeriCorps between 1994 and 2001 (Stroud, 2002). There has also been discussion about introducing a similar scheme in the UK, whereby young people who volunteered for community service during their 'gap year' would have their university fees paid (Garner and Cassidy, 2002). The advantage of this approach – if employed in conjunction with what has been proposed here – is that it would be a way of building on the volunteering young people had already undertaken in schools and colleges, as well as increasing access to higher education.

There are also non-military national service programmes in countries throughout the world, such as Canada, Germany, Turkey and Israel. While these programmes are different from what has been proposed here, nevertheless they do involve forms of community service.

In France, military service for eighteen year-olds, which dates back to the Revolution of 1789, was abolished in 1997 and replaced by a 'citizens rendezvous'. This is a voluntary non-military service lasting for a week, which is intended to be an intensive introduction into republican civic values. Any young people wanting to do more may then volunteer for another nine months of national service. Yet the problem with this approach is there is little incentive to undertake the extra nine months stint.

It is also questionable how much can be learnt within a single week. A psychological study conducted by Richard Stevick and John Addelman (1995) of a private liberal arts college in America revealed that short-term volunteer experience – the participants undertook only eight weeks, or 21 hours, of community service – does not lead to individuals developing notable altruistic feelings. In contrast, the proposal outlined here is for regular community work to be undertaken over a longer period of time and up to four years for some students. There is therefore the possibility this work will become viewed as routine and unexceptional. This in turn would help to normalize behaving in a public-spirited manner within the wider society.

In the UK, community service is very much on the political agenda, and has been for a number of years. This is evident in the Labour Party's 1997 Election Manifesto, *Because Britain Deserve Better*, which states:-

An independent and creative voluntary sector, committed to voluntary activity as an expression of citizenship, is central to our vision of a stakeholder society. We are committed to developing plans for a national citizens' service programme, to tap the enthusiasm and commitment of the many young people who want to make voluntary contributions in service of their communities. ('Labour Manifesto', *The Times*, 4/4/97, p.IV)

This statement of intent – and an influential 1998 Crick Report *Education for Citizenship and the Teaching of Democracy in Schools* mentioned earlier – culminated in citizenship being added to the National Curriculum for 11- to 16-year-olds from September 2002 and it will include a community service element. As yet, there has not been much detail about the implementation of community service. Although it appears it would entail young people doing some community work outside of the school day, and thereby as part of their homework (Phillips, 2001). If this is the case, the problem with this approach is that young people generally do not like doing homework. It is likely therefore that community volunteering will come to be regarded as a burdensome task. There is also an issue of who will supervise the students outside of school hours.

In contrast, it has been argued here that community service needs to take place within school hours. This would also serve to demonstrate the importance that is attached to it. As Peter Hayes, acting director of education at Community Service Volunteers (CSV), has noted, capturing the interest of young people entails volunteering becoming part of the ethos of schools, and not appearing as if it has been bolted on to ensure they undertake 'worthy' activities (McCurry, 2001). However, to repeat, there is a lack of detail about the community service element of the new National Curriculum at this stage. And overall this is a bold and welcome initiative.

Finally, in preparation for the changes being introduced in September 2002, many secondary schools in England and Wales have begun introducing community volunteering. Although much of this has been focused within schools in the form of, for example, mentoring and anti-bullying schemes. This is also a welcome and positive development. However, if more vibrant, mutually supportive and inclusive local communities are to emerge, a balance needs to be struck between the amount of volunteering taking place within schools and colleges, and that going on in the wider community.

In summary, a proposal for fostering public-spiritedness in young people has been outlined. As well as highlighting its potential benefits, the feasibility of this project has also been stressed. Not only are similar models already in operation in some countries, but in general it would be relatively easy and cheap to implement and administer. Some possible criticisms of this proposal will now be considered.

A Critique of Community Work for Young People

One likely criticism of this proposal is it runs the risk of being used by government as a never-ending source of cheap labour. In particular, young people might simply be used as a substitute for public service workers. The leaders of trade unions would almost certainly argue that such a scheme would lead to large-scale redundancies in the public sector. Indeed, in the UK, when the Chancellor Gordon Brown announced a £300 million boost for community volunteering in January 2001, leaders of the public services union, Unison, made exactly this forecast (Wintour, 2001).

Yet for a number of reasons this need not happen with what has been proposed here. To begin with most people employed in the public sector have considerable work experience, and many are well trained and highly skilled, and could not be replaced by young people helping out occasionally in their community. Furthermore, in the towns and cities of most modern societies there is invariably an abundance of things that can be done to improve the quality of life within them: renovating property, scrubbing-out graffiti, picking-up litter, helping run shelters for the homeless, and so on. This is work which local government and councils often struggle to tackle because of the financial constraints many of them labour under. Moreover, some of the activities proposed here for young people to undertake offer an inexhaustible supply of work. For example, in the case of conservation and environmental work, and in terms of helping the elderly, sick and homeless the amount of work needing to be done is not finite. These areas place ongoing demands upon local government in terms of the human and financial resources needed to deal with them. Thus there is plenty of work for young people to do, and no legitimate reason for making public service workers redundant because of this proposal.

Another criticism often raised against any proposal to improve community life is that effectively these are responses to the inadequacies of the state to perform this role. If this is the case then, so the argument goes, the project is fundamentally flawed in that it relies for its implementation upon this inefficient state. This is an interesting criticism but does not really apply here for two reasons.

Firstly, the main agencies implementing this proposal would be schools and colleges. As they are located within particular communities they would be in the best position to consult local opinion in order to determine the type of community activity that was needed. They would also be aware of the limits and capabilities of individual students, and could help to ensure they did not undertake work for which they are not suited. The state, in contrast, would only need to play a relatively minor role in promoting and monitoring this scheme. This scheme would therefore operate at a local and particular, rather than a national and state, level. As was argued with the proposal outlined in Chapter 5, this is the most effective way of reviving local communities.

Secondly, as has been outlined, much of the community work young people would carry out under this proposal could complement the functions performed by the state, and in particular cover those areas within local communities where there are gaps in state provision. As a recent editorial in *The Guardian* newspaper, published in the UK, noted:-

> Policy makers – from the left and right – recognised years ago that no matter how much is invested in the welfare state, there would still be a huge shortfall in meeting everybody's needs. (*The Guardian*, 12/1/01)

And of course this proposal for young people forms part of a wider attempt to foster a public-spirited culture, which would generate mutuality within society in order to compensate for what many perceive as a retreating state in our late modern age.

This proposal might also be criticized for introducing an element of compulsion into the development of a public-spirited culture. Requiring young people to undertake a voluntary work component as part of their citizenship education – indeed even requiring them to undertake citizenship education – would be construed by some as infringing upon their autonomy. In fact this argument has formed the basis for a number of direct challenges to community service schemes. For example, in the United States, the conservative Institute for Justice has filed several lawsuits in a number of federal states to prevent schools from making their students undertake community service, likening it to a form of slavery (Hirsch and Goldsmith, 1996). Some critics have argued that getting young people to behave in this way intrudes upon parental authority (Bullock, 1996); others have claimed it wastes limited funds which should be spent on the teaching of more valuable basic skills in schools (Martin, 1996).

One way to respond to any suggestion that this proposal constitutes an infringement upon individual freedom would be to point J.S. Mill's position on this issue, which he outlines in *On Liberty* (1991). In this essay, he asserts that government may legitimately intervene in the lives of children and young people when it is for their own benefit and protection. For Mill, they come under the category of 'those who are still in a state to require being taken care of by others' (ibid., 14). Similarly, T.H. Marshall in his seminal essay, 'Citizenship and Social Class' (1996), contends that the education of children is so that they can attain citizenship. As he puts it, education 'is trying to stimulate the growth of citizens in the making' (ibid., 16).

However, this particular line is not completely satisfactory in that it seems to deny children and young people certain rights and equal status with adults. Thus while a start has been made the defence of the element of compulsion within this proposal needs to be further developed.

In considering this issue it is also important to note the extent to which we are already compelled to do a range things within modern societies, ranging from having to wear seat-belts in cars to paying taxes. Even a liberal like J.S. Mill acknowledged that an element of compulsion may well be necessary in a free society:-

> There are also many positive acts for the benefit of others, which he may rightfully be compelled to perform; such as, to give evidence in a court of justice; to bear his fair share in the common defence, or in any other joint work necessary to the interests of the society of which he enjoys the protection... (Mill, 1991: 15)

With regards to education, attendance at school for children has also generally been compulsory within most Western democracies. Nor should this be viewed as infringement upon individual freedom, for as T.H. Marshall (1996) has observed 'civil rights are designed for use by reasonable and intelligent persons, who have learned to read and write. Education is a necessary prerequisite of civil freedom' (ibid.,16). And as was made clear earlier in this chapter, forms of community work can provide young people with an invaluable experiential education, and therefore should be viewed as better preparing them to exercise their civil freedom.

As well as having to attend school, young people in Western democracies are also compelled to learn certain subjects (such as Maths, English, Science and a foreign language). Indeed, in the UK the National Curriculum not only specifies the subjects to be taught in schools, but also lays down guidelines on the content, pedagogical practice and the educational standards to be attained. Thus there is already a great deal of compulsion operating within the educational systems of modern societies because it is perceived to be beneficial for young people and the wider society.

A degree of compulsion can therefore be acceptable when it has beneficial consequences, and does not inflict unnecessary harm or constraint upon those being required to behave in a certain way. And this proposal would not impose excessive demands upon young people. As argued for here, community volunteering would be incorporated into the school day, and therefore not infringe upon their free time. Moreover, as was outlined earlier, forms of community activity would in a range of ways be potentially beneficial for young people. But most importantly, when young people reach adulthood – while they would be encouraged to continue to act in this manner under the proposal outlined in Chapter 5 – they would be able to make an informed but ultimately autonomous decision about whether or not they wanted to be public-spirited. J.S. Mill adopts a similar approach in *On Liberty*:-

> Nobody denies that people should be taught and trained in youth, as to know and benefit by the ascertained results of human experience. But it is the privilege and proper condition of a human being, arrived at the maturity of his faculties, to use and interpret experience in his own way. (Mill, 1991: 64)

Some Problems with Voluntarism

Another substantive criticism against this proposal is that if you take the voluntary dimension out of community volunteering it undermines the whole idea of volunteering and being public-spirited. Thus citizens – young and old alike – should offer their services on a voluntary basis, rather than being required or compelled to provide them. This position is fine in principle, but as will now be shown does not take sufficient account of the everyday realities of life within advanced industrial societies.

Voluntarism is Insufficient by Itself

Relying upon people of their own free will to take-up volunteering and other forms of public-spirited activity with little or no encouragement, as is the case in most Western democracies, entails that large numbers of people do not act in this way. For example, based upon an analysis of research conducted in the United States, Richard B. Freeman (1997) concluded that many people volunteer only when requested to do so. They considered themselves to be morally obliged to offer their services when asked, but would just as rather let someone else undertake such activity.

In accounting for such attitudes, J.S. Mill noted there is a natural indolence in people, and that once patterns of behaviour become established it is difficult to change them:-

> It is a common error of Socialists to overlook the natural indolence of mankind; their tendency to be passive, to be the slaves of habit, to persist indefinitely in a course once chosen. Let them once attain any state of existence which they consider tolerable and they will thenceforth stagnate; will not exert themselves to improve, and by letting their faculties rust, lose even the energy required to preserve them from deterioration. (Mill, 1965: 795)

This has relevance for the contemporary period. If we are witnessing a drift into more individualistic and private-orientated modes of behaviour within advanced industrial societies, Mill's arguments suggest that many people will do little to alter this lifestyle. Thus unless people are encouraged to be more public-spirited, including in the form of the educational experience defended in this chapter, then many people will simply not behave in this manner.

Moreover, relying upon voluntarism can never ensure that people will continue to volunteer their services. That is, those people willing to volunteer might only do so once or at best occasionally. Japan provides a recent and vivid demonstration of this point. There was as an upsurge in volunteering among young people following the Kobe earthquake of January 1995. However, there were insufficient mechanisms and policies geared to maintaining this level of activity, and it subsequently declined when the schools and colleges re-opened (Nakata, 1995).

In contrast, it has been argued here that a public-spirited culture needs to be fostered as part of an ongoing national campaign, and resources should be provided to facilitate community and neighbourly activity, as well as incorporating such behaviour into citizenship education programmes.

Voluntarism and Late Modernity

Relying upon people to volunteer their time and services is also unlikely to be able to counter the formidable processes of late modernity, which as we saw in Part I are undermining local community life. This is because there is generally not enough of this type of activity going on within advanced industrial societies. Indeed, the drift into individualism and more private-orientated lifestyles means such community-orientated behaviour is probably less likely in the future. And there may already be some indications of this tendency in certain countries.

For instance, in the United States there is attitudinal evidence of a growing interest among young Americans, especially amongst college students, in attaining financial success, and therefore of gaining well-paid, high-status jobs. Crucially, this is often at the expense of participating in their communities and concern for the position of the disadvantaged in their society (see Dey, Astin and Korn, 1991; Stevick and Addelamn, 1995). As one American commentator, Abigail McCarthy, puts it: 'we have become a nation of nonjoiners' (1996: 8). She argues this is especially the case in what she terms the 'urban sprawl' (ibid., 9); a similar point was made in Chapter 4 of this work with regards to the difficulties of sustaining neighbourhoods and local communities in urban areas.

Thus despite its history of association the United States, as Fukuyama (1995) has noted, is starting to conform to the popular perception of it as a highly individualistic society. There has been a decline in those social institutions and structures which are dependent upon community and voluntary activity by citizens such as 'neighbourhoods, churches, unions, clubs, and charities' (ibid., 11). For Fukuyama, this is contributing to the erosion of trust and sociability in American society.

Likewise, in the UK, the 1997 National Survey on Volunteering revealed that slightly less people were volunteering with a noticeable decline in participation by young people (Davis Smith, 1998). The proportion of 18 to 24 year olds doing voluntary work within the UK fell from 55 per cent in 1991 to 43 per cent in 1997, a decrease of 1.4 million (Bright, 1998). Furthermore, there is evidence to suggest that fewer young people are willing to undertake voluntary work abroad. The Voluntary Service Overseas (VSO) – a Government-funded organization that places people in development projects abroad – has recently reported a rapid decline in young British recruits wanting to work in the developing world (ibid.).

However, statistics and surveys on volunteering are notoriously difficult to interpret. In contrast to the evidence just outlined, figures from the National Centre for Volunteering in 2000 suggest nearly 22 million people in the UK of working age volunteer (Palmer, 2000). Yet Malcolm Dean (2001) rightly instructs caution when dealing with surveys on volunteering:-

> Be wary of volunteer surveys. If there were 22m active and regular volunteers, there would not be a problem. But there aren't. Ask the voluntary sector. Right across the board shortages are being recorded. Both new and well-established organisations – such as the Samaritans are suffering. (Dean, 2001: 5)

It is a view supported by a recent editorial in *The Guardian* newspaper, which notes of the situation in the UK: 'There are 185,000 registered charities and another 200,000 voluntary and neighbourhood groups, almost all of which could do with more volunteers' (*The Guardian*, 2001).

What are we to make of this range of statistical data? It might be wise not to rely upon it completely and instead to employ common sense. In this regard, in societies like the UK and the United States, where people are generally working longer hours – and there is increased pressure upon young people to pass exams and get jobs – it seems logical to assume this will have a detrimental impact upon levels of volunteering. Consequently, measures will have to be taken – such as those outlined in this work – to maintain even existing levels of volunteering; simply relying upon voluntarism will not be sufficient in the contemporary period.

Voluntarism and Building Communities

It is also unlikely that simply hoping people will be public-spirited and take-up volunteering can provide the basis for building vibrant, inclusive and mutually supportive local communities, which it has been shown here are needed to counter the negative aspects of increasing individualism. Building such communities would require more people becoming regularly involved in community and neighbourly activity than is currently the case. Yet some of the reasons for this lack of community involvement are understandable. Quite naturally, we will have a closer attachment to some people, such as family and friends, than to others. And many people will feel that as long as they have helped and shown consideration to this inner circle, they have demonstrated their fellow feeling and compassion, and therefore have little or no obligation to other members of their community.

Thus without encouragement or incentives there will always be some people who will undertake a considerable amount of volunteering, and others that will do little or nothing at all. This is evident in the United States, where even though it has been estimated there are around 90 million volunteers, volunteering is not being undertaken evenly across the social spectrum (Clark, 1996). For instance, Peter Drucker (1993), who has written extensively on volunteerism in the United States, notes the bulk of the volunteers in America are:-

> ... husbands and wives in the professional, two-earner family, people in their thirties and forties, well-educated, affluent, busy. They enjoy their jobs. But they feel the need to do something where 'we make a difference', to use the phrase one hears again and again – whether that means running a Bible class in the local church; teaching Black children the multiplication table; or visiting old people back home from a long stay in hospital and helping them with their rehabilitation exercises. (Drucker, 1993: 159)

The aim of building vibrant, mutually supportive local communities is what really distinguishes the fostering of a public-spirited culture, as argued for this work, with voluntarism. With the latter any volunteering that takes place is invariably not geared towards such a specific end or goal. Although of course this does not in any way undermine the value of such behaviour.

The Issue of Motives

The issue of motives is often raised in relation to voluntary work, especially in terms of whether such behaviour is based upon genuine altruism. In this regard, it is often suggested that when an individual decides of their own free will to undertake volunteering it is of greater worth or value than if they have been urged or encouraged to behave in this way. By inference, volunteering is robbed of any meaning or value if it is not freely undertaken.

There is some merit to this contention. However, it is also the case that the motives of those people who voluntarily volunteer will not always be of the noblest kind. Indeed, in some instances this is understandable. For example, in the UK and the United States, an increasing number of workers have been getting involved in company volunteering schemes and choosing to help their local communities. Yet they may in part be motivated by the fact that some companies are taking greater notice of community experience when appraising the performance of their employees.

Likewise, many students take-up volunteering in order to enhance their employment prospects. In the UK, for instance, schemes set-up by the Prince's Trust and the Community Service Volunteers (CSV) are in part designed with this end in mind. Similarly, in the United States, a significant motivation for the students on the AmeriCorps programme might well be that this form of volunteering provides them with the financial means to enter higher education.

Thus those who choose to volunteer will not necessarily be driven by a strong sense of altruism. This is revealed in a study of volunteering in Canada carried out by Francois Vaillancourt (1994). Using data from a 1987 Canadian national survey of volunteer work, Vaillancourt found that it is individuals whose career or family is likely to benefit who are more likely to undertake volunteering.

For most of us therefore it is likely there will be a range of motives behind our decision to take-up volunteering and public-spirited activity. Consequently, regarding this issue, we should perhaps be less concerned with motives, and more interested in outcomes. And if such behaviour can help to build more vibrant, inclusive and mutually supportive local communities, then this should be regarded as a positive development. Thus if encouragement and incentives have to be employed in order to encourage community-orientated behaviour, and so that people may get into the habit of it, then this has to be accepted. Moreover, given the greater individualism of our age such an approach is probably unavoidable.

Conclusion

In summary, it has been argued in this chapter that in order to get people thinking and behaving in a more public-spirited manner this needs to be part of the education they receive in schools and colleges. More specifically, it is proposed young people between the ages of 15-18 should undertake community service as part of their civic education. In defending this position, it was stressed this proposal did not unfairly infringe upon the autonomy of young people. As adult citizens they can decide for themselves whether they wish to continue such activity, but crucially having experienced community volunteering at school will enable them to make more informed decisions. Moreover, simply relying upon people to come forward and take-up community volunteering, without this type of experience and encouragement, would not provide the basis for rebuilding local communities.

Finally, and briefly, it is necessary to address the broader issue of whether schools and colleges should even be involved in teaching citizenship. For example, some commentators consider children should be allowed to be children, without the responsibilities of citizenship (a theme discussed by Herman van Gunsteren, 1996).

This is a difficult issue to deal with, and much depends upon one's particular perspective of the role of education. The position taken here is that within modern societies the educational system has always played an important role in socialization and the transmission of the dominant norms and values, and learning about citizenship is simply part of this process. Emile Durkheim (1961) went further viewing schools and education as a means of ensuring the continuation of society. While Robert Putnam (2000) rightly contends education is a powerful predictor of many forms of social participation. Similarly, Francis Fukuyama (1999) argues one of the most important sources or generators of social capital in contemporary societies is the educational system. Furthermore, in a post-traditional era in which the authority of other agencies of socialization, like the family, occupational group and the church has been challenged, it is likely that schools and colleges will have to play a more prominent role in this process. And as has been shown here, community service can make a positive contribution to the performance of this role.

Conclusion

In this book some of the major developments of our age, such as globalization, post-Fordism and detraditionalization, have been examined. It has been argued these processes are fostering greater insecurity, which is in turn producing more individualistic and private-orientated forms of behaviour generally to the detriment of local community life within advanced industrial societies.

How we should respond to such developments has been the other major task of this work. In this respect, the case has been made for devising strategies to foster a public-spirited culture, as a way of reviving local communities, and in which an important role would be played by national governments. Specific proposals for facilitating the emergence of such a culture have been set out during the course of this work. In Chapter 5, the potential benefits of a national campaign to promote community and neighbourly activity were highlighted. Likewise, in Chapter 8 it was claimed that developing a public-spirited culture requires community activity and involvement must be an integral part of civic education programmes taught in schools and colleges. The potential benefits of such approaches in terms of both building more inclusive societies and human flourishing were outlined in chapters 6 and 7, respectively.

It might be considered that fostering a public-spirited culture is an inadequate response to the powerful forces of late modernity. Yet it has been shown here how such a culture could in a number of respects begin to counter some of the worst excesses of these processes. Firstly, it encourages mutual assistance and support as a response to contemporary patterns of insecurity. This contrasts with the, in many ways understandable, tendency of people to retreat into forms of identity politics (Chapter 6) or into the private realm, both of which can be detrimental to community life and social capital.

Secondly, a public-spirited culture can help to create vibrant and inclusive local communities or neighbourhoods, and hence more desirable places in which to live and work. There can be no guarantee this would be the outcome from developing such a culture, but it has hopefully been demonstrated that it could a make a positive contribution towards this end. It might also repair some of the damage inflicted upon many communities in recent years by a combination of globalization, post-industrialism and market ideologies.

Thirdly, as was argued in Chapter 5, in helping to revive local communities, a public-spirited culture can also serve to replenish social capital. The community and neighbourly activity upon which this revival or rebuilding would be based necessitates reciprocity and sociability out of which higher levels of trust, co-operation and friendliness – that is, forms of social capital – can be generated. It was also claimed such attitudes, albeit in an attenuated form, might then extend to the wider society. In this sense local communities or neighbourhoods could function as arenas for the generation of social capital.

Fourthly, a public-spirited culture also touches upon the problem of individual conduct. In a post-traditional era in which many of the conventions and institutions that provided guidelines for acceptable behaviour have been challenged, it reasserts a conception of what is appropriate conduct in society emphasizing reciprocity and public-spiritedness.

However, in order to enjoy some of these potential benefits, there needs to be a rethinking of the role of government. It has been one of the central themes of this work that encouraging community and neighbourly activity must become a more significant part or feature of contemporary modes of democratic governance.

Yet as was stressed in Chapter 5, a public-spirited culture could never be so preponderant that people would feel compelled to act in this way – the greater individualism of our time, as well as the demands of family, friends and work, can help ensure this was the case. Nor should it be so influential because this would undermine the autonomy which enables us to lead flourishing lives (Chapter 7). Indeed, it has been made clear throughout this work, citizens must decide for themselves whether or not to be public-spirited. This avoids the Blairite emphasis upon responsibilities and duty, which the UK Chancellor Gordon Brown has picked-up on in his call for a new culture of 'civic patriotism' (Norton, 2000).

As was made clear in the Introduction, it will take more than just a culture of public-spiritedness to rebuild local communities and revive community life. This needs to be complemented by other more established forms of public policy, such as ensuring within districts and regions that there are job opportunities, adequate transport systems and decent local shops and housing. It has merely been claimed that fostering a public-spirited culture can contribute to this objective, and would be a productive way of addressing the negative aspects of increasing individualism within advanced industrial societies.

Fukuyama and Spontaneous Order

As was stated in the Introduction, this book is based on my DPhil thesis, which was completed in 1997. Since then the literature on the areas covered in this work has continued to expand. In this respect, a significant publication has been Francis Fukuyama's *The Great Disruption: Human nature and the reconstitution of social order* (2000). Fukuyama deals with many of themes tackled here, but his conclusion is considerably more optimistic. He accepts social dislocation has taken place on a wide-scale within advanced industrial societies – or, as he might put it – those societies which have undergone the 'great disruption'. Yet he claims to identify new forms of social connectedness in our postindustrial social order. There are essentially three main elements to Fukuyama's thesis.

Firstly, he places considerable faith in human nature. His discussion of human biology and psychology, leads him to stress our 'innate human capacities for reconstituting social order' (ibid., 282):-

> Human beings by nature are social creatures with certain built-in, natural capabilities for solving problems of social coooperation and inventing moral rules to constrain individual choice. They will, without much prompting, create order spontaneously simply by pursuing their daily individual ends and interacting with other people. (ibid., 231)

For Fukuyama, we are also rational creatures and therefore recognize the need for social and cultural or moral rules. This means both nature and rationality, he maintains, 'ultimately support the development of the ordinary virtues like honesty, reliability, and reciprocity that constitute the basis for social capital' (ibid., 273). And this for Fukuyama, is how spontaneous order can emerge.

Secondly, he believes there is now evidence of social order being reconstituted, entailing we have passed through the 'great disruption'. In defence of this claim he cites a range of data from decreasing crime figures to signs that divorce rates are levelling out in many advanced industrial nations. Curiously, he also sees hopeful signs in the revival of certain moral conservative groups in the United States, and the popularity of conservative radio call-in shows hosted by figures like Dr. Laura Schlessinger.

Thirdly, he contends the nature of a post-industrial economy is leading to new opportunities for co-operation and sociability, out of which trust and social capital can be generated. For example, Fukuyama sees such attitudes and habits developing amongst high-tech workers in industry and business because the nature of their work encourages such practices.

However, there are a number of problems with Fukuyama's thesis. Firstly, his claims about human nature, and specifically human biology and psychology, are both bold and contentious. Human nature is a notoriously difficult and slippery 'thing' or concept to pin down. It is also much contested and rarely politically neutral being used to support particular theories, causes and arguments (see Forbes and Smith, 1983). For example, Thomas Hobbes in *Leviathan* employed a form of psychology and human biology to argue people were naturally aggressive, asocial and competitive, and this in turn became the justification for his views on the nature of the state.

Secondly, and more closely related to the themes of this work, the statistical data Fukuyama cites as evidence of the reconstitution of social order, is not entirely convincing. There might be a range of factors at work here that have little or nothing to do with the revival of social order. For instance, declining crime rates may simply be the result of more efficient policing methods. Furthermore, such statistics can at best only provide a snapshot of what is taking place within advanced industrial societies. As Fukuyama himself points out 'indices of social order have increased and decreased over time' (2000: 264). It is for this reason that this work has not simply relied upon statistical evidence, but has sought to identify the fundamental or defining processes of our age.

As for the revived fortunes of moral conservatism, this might be a temporary development. Indeed, the revival could be interpreted as revealing the strength of the individualism of our age, and a desire to recapture a past that has been lost, rather than a new social order (Lichterman, 2001). Moreover, the popularity of moral conservatism appears to be largely confined to the United States; there is little evidence of it within Europe. For instance, in the UK, the Conservative Party's 'back-to-basics' campaign of the early 1990s failed to capture the enthusiasm and imagination of the British people even before the activities of certain Conservative politicians made a mockery of it.

Thirdly, contrary to Fukuyama, the primary processes of late modernity are leading to increased insecurity, greater individualism and diminishing stocks of social capital. This at least has been the claim of this work. Moreover, globalization, post-Fordism or post-industrialism and detraditionalization show no signs of waning. This means there is little prospect for the emergence of new forms of cooperation and a reconstituted social order. And as we saw in Chapter 1, a feature of the shift to a post-Fordist or post-industrial economy is that most people are not part of the core of high-tech workers, and can as a result suffer various forms of exclusion to the detriment of social capital.

We therefore cannot rely upon the emergence of a spontaneous social order to address the negative aspects of living in our late modern age – and in fairness to Fukuyama he does acknowledge its limitations. Hence the need to devise strategies for fostering a public-spirited culture, or other forms of public policy intervention. As Fukuyama concedes towards the end of his thought-provoking work:-

Social order will not simply be reconstituted through the decentralized interactions of individuals and communities; it will also need to be constructed through public policy. (Fukuyama, 2000: 274)

The Prospects for a Public-spirited Culture

The type of public-spirited behaviour proposed in this book should not be regarded as unusual and unlikely ever to happen. The practice of people devoting time to community activity and voluntary groups is well established in advanced industrial societies, even in societies as seemingly diverse as Japan and the United States. In the case of the former, Fukuyama contends 'Japanese society supports a dense network of voluntary organizations' (1995: 53), a significant number of which are what the Japanese call *iemoto* groups. These groups – which people can freely join and are not based on kinship – have emerged largely to support and sustain traditional arts and crafts.

There is also a history of association in the United States. Based on his travels in the 1830s, Alexis de Tocqueville in *Democracy in America* famously observed that forming and joining groups and associations to tackle common problems or address particular needs, was part of the American way of life. He reported that communities were intersected by, and indeed made-up of, networks of these different groups and associations. It has been claimed that Tocqueville's portrayal is not based upon detailed and wide-ranging research, and this in turn leads him to overestimate the role and importance of associations in American society (see Deakin, 2001). However, Robert Putnam's thorough investigation of community life in America essentially concurs with the long history view, emphasizing the 'boom' in association building in the late nineteenth century: 'In the last decades of the nineteenth century Americans created and joined an unprecedented number of voluntary associations' (Putnam, 2000: 383). But crucially, as has been discussed in this work, writers like Putnam and Fukuyama have noted American society is now losing its habit of association and becoming more individualistic.

In the UK, which is also becoming an increasingly individualistic society, there are numerous charities, as well as organizations dedicated to preserving old buildings, heritage sites and the countryside to which many people freely devote their time. There are also a number of established voluntary work schemes for young people, such as those set-up by the Prince's Trust and the Community Service Volunteers (CSV). More recently, there has been the TimeBank initiative that enables citizens to register their interests and skills, and the activities they would like to volunteer for. It establishes a national data base in which people 'bank' the time they have available for volunteering, thereby providing charities, voluntary and community groups with the opportunity to seek out appropriate volunteers (Dean, 2001).

These are commendable and much needed schemes, which need to be supported. At its launch in 2000 Time Bank recruited 18,000 volunteers (ibid.). But these schemes need to be reinforced by an ongoing national campaign to encourage community and neighbourly activity, promoted by a range of institutions and agencies, especially government, if larger numbers of people are to participate and a public-spirited culture to emerge.

There are also examples of the type of national campaign to promote public-spiritedness argued for in this work. In some advanced industrial societies governments have sponsored generic campaigns designed to produce widespread participation in community and civic life amongst its citizens. For instance, in the UK, this has taken the form of the Good Neighbour Campaign in the late 1970s, the Make a Difference initiative in the 1980s and the New Labour emphasis upon the 'Giving Age' in the 1990s (Davis Smith, 2001).

Moreover, the promotion of particular projects with specific policy objectives, ranging from Aids-awareness campaigns to encouraging people to report those they suspect of drinking and driving, is an established part of democratic governance. In the UK, another example of this more targeted approach has been the 'Neighbourhood Watch Scheme' pushed by government, the police and other agencies since the 1980s as way of tackling the problem of rising crime. It has enjoyed considerable success with thousands of neighbourhoods adopting this scheme.

The fostering of a public-spirited culture, and the role this could play in rebuilding local communities, would potentially have broad appeal. There is growing recognition within Western democracies of the need to develop the sort of ideas and proposals outlined in this work. In the UK, the New Labour government is very much orientated towards addressing the problems of local communities. While in the United States, President Clinton organized a major summit to find ways to promote volunteerism in America (April 27-29, 1997). Such was the importance that Clinton attached to this objective, the summit was non-partisan and headed by a

Republican, Colin Powell, and attended by former Presidents – George Bush, Jimmy Carter and Gerald Ford (Gergen, 1997).

More recently, in his State of the Union address, presented early in 2002, President George W. Bush sought to build on programmes introduced by Clinton. In particular, Bush proposed to expand the number of volunteers by 200,000, arguing for a 50 per cent increase in funding for AmeriCorps (Stroud, 2002). What is perhaps most significant is that Democrats, as well as Republicans, support such measures.

Likewise, in the UK, a similar cross-party consensus seems to be emerging over such matters. The Home Secretary, David Blunkett, has argued that 'volunteering is an essential building block to create a more inclusive society' (Stroud, 2000). This marks a considerable departure from the more statist approach towards social problems pursued by 'Old Labour'. Similarly, the Conservative Party appears to be moving away from Thatcherite policy in this area. The shadow home secretary, Oliver Letwin, has stressed the importance of developing a 'neighbourly society' (Travis, 2002).

However, in reality the prospects of a public-spirited culture – or something approximating it – emerging within advanced industrial societies is difficult, perhaps impossible, to determine. As has been shown, the dominant processes of the contemporary period run counter to such behaviour. And much would depend upon the particular conditions and circumstances within each society. Factors such as the nature of the national culture, the type of political system, the relationship between the state and citizen, and so on, would all have an influence. But the aim of this work here has been simply to raise arguments for fostering such a culture. Having completed this book I am now off to undertake some public-spirited activity for my local community...

Notes

Introduction

1. The reason for making this point is that I do not believe these policy issues have received sufficient attention in some recent writing on community and social capital (e.g., Putnam, 2000).

Chapter 1: Post-Fordism and Individualism

1. Some commentators prefer to use the term post-industrialism to describe these developments. For example, Krishan Kumar (1995) considers post-Fordism, along with post-modernity and the idea of the information society, to be three varieties of post-industrial theory. In contrast, Stuart Hall considers post-Fordism to be 'a broader term suggesting a whole new epoch...' (1989: 117), than post-industrialism. This debate and lack of consensus over terms inevitably leads to a degree of conceptual slippage – a tendency undoubtedly replicated here. However, irrespective of such debates, the primary purpose of this chapter is simply to convey how recent developments within the workplace have impacted upon wider society.
2. There is considerable debate over the reasons for the decline or crisis of Fordism. For example, see Aglietta (1979), Boyer (1986), Lipietz (1986), and Piore and Sabel (1994).
3. For an informed critique of the deindustrialization thesis, especially in relation to its applicability to the United States, see Joel I. Nelson, *Post-Industrial Capitalism: Exploring Economic Inequality in America* (1995).
4. There is some debate about the nature and pace of these changes. See, for example, Tom Forester (1988), Krishan Kumar (1995: 156-8) and Ian Miles (1998a, 1988b). A further development in this debate is the creation of a 'televillage' on the outskirts of Crickhowell in mid-Wales in the UK. This is a village where people as result of the new technology are able to both live and work (Fisher, 1995). A similar scheme has been set-up in Telluride, Colorado (Hannon, 1995).
5. André Gorz (1982) considers we are witnessing the demise of the working class and with it the prospects for collective action along such lines. Although Scott Lash and John Urry have questioned this development arguing that within modern societies 'capitalist social relations continue to exist' (1987: 7). Similarly, Goran Therbon (1984) contends capitalism is still 'organized' and that associated structures and institutions, such as the welfare state, class relations and labour organizations remain intact.
6. For an informative discussion of the core-periphery division, see David Harvey, *The Condition of Postmodernity* (1989), chapter 9.

7. In particular, Japan has been identified as a society closely following this pattern. For Robin Murray (1989b), Japan provides the most complete example of a fully developed sub-contract and franchise economy, whereby on 'the one hand, there is a central core accounting for a third of the workforce (with the celebrated corporate welfare systems, high skill levels and jobs for life). On the other, there is a peripheral sub-contract and sweated economy, casualised, low-paid, weakly organised, and restricted to a grossly inadequate public welfare system' (ibid., 58).

8. However, this view is rejected by Chris Harman (1996) who, as well as raising counter-arguments and -evidence, considers it to be defeatist and constituting an abandonment of traditional forms of struggle by workers.

Chapter 2: Detraditionalization and the Rise of Individualism

1. For example, Paul Heelas (1996) identifies two different schools of thought concerning detraditionalization. He describes these as the 'radical thesis', emphasizing the emergence of a post-traditional society, and the 'coexistence thesis', which stresses the degree of overlap and interaction between the traditional and the modern.

2. Anthony Giddens considers tradition to be a creation of modernity. As he puts it: 'The term "tradition" as it is used today is actually a product of the past two hundred years in Europe' (1999: 39). For a fuller discussion of this position see his chapter on tradition (ch.3) in *Runaway World* (1999).

3. It should be noted that the interpretation of 'cultural imperialism' presented here, though popular, is not universally accepted. For instance, John Tomlinson identifies 'four ways to talk about cultural imperialism' (see Tomlinson, 1991: 19-28).

4. For an alternative interpretation of the consequences of detraditionalization see John Thompson 'Tradition and Self in a Mediated World' (in Heelas, 1996). Rather than individualism, Thompson sees the decline of tradition as leading to an increased reliance upon others.

5. The challenge to tradition also begins to explain why the contemporary period is widely perceived as an 'age of uncertainty'. Tradition is based upon established patterns of behaviour, of ritual and repetition, thereby providing a degree of order and stability. In this sense tradition serves a role of protecting or sheltering us from uncertainty (Giddens, 1994: 104).

6. Martin Jacques (1996) contends we have actually become more morally aware in recent decades: '[t]here has been a proliferation of organisations representing groups facing various forms of discrimination; they in turn have transformed our knowledge of prejudice, rights and the quality of human relationships' (ibid.). It has led, he argues, to people becoming more sensitive to the nature of gender, sexual, ethnic and racial relations.

7. These examples apply to families in all their legitimate diversity, and not simply to the 'traditional family'. . Indeed, the 'traditional' family, as understood and promoted by its defenders, is a relatively recent invention. Anthony Giddens (1999) sees it emerging in the 1950s. Such a family is

typically a heterosexual couple whose relationship or union was based upon romantic love rather than economic necessity, as had been the case in previous centuries. In such a family the mother's role was firmly that of the housewife, while her husband went out to work, and their children during this period often continued to lack both rights and a voice ('they should be seen and not heard').

8. Foucault responded to this type of claim by arguing that we in the West, as inheritors of the Christian moral tradition, find it difficult to base our morality on the precept that we should 'give ourselves more care than anything else in the world' (Martin et al., 1988: 22). 'We are more inclined to see taking care of ourselves as an immorality, as a means of escape from all possible rules' (ibid.). Foucault believes we also inherit a 'secular tradition which respects external law as the basis for morality' (ibid.). This produces a social, essentially ascetic, morality which 'insists that the self is that which one can reject' and is geared instead towards establishing 'rules for acceptable behaviour in relations with others' (ibid.). Indeed, Foucault rejected the very notion of a commonly accepted morality: 'a form of morality acceptable to everybody in the sense that everyone should submit to it, strikes me as catastrophic' (Foucault, 1988a: 254).

9. Interestingly, in a seminar Foucault attended at the University of Vermont, he declared his work on the self was actually inspired by Lasch's book. In particular, he regarded Lasch's description of disillusionment with the modern world and a subsequent turning within to be similar to the situation of the Roman Empire (Martin et al., 1988: 4).

Chapter 3: Globalization and the Individual

1. For the most up-to-date interpretations of the impact of globalization upon welfare states see Robert Sykes, Bruno Palier and Pauline M. Prior (eds), *Globalization and European Welfare States* (2001).

2. Hirst (1999), Pierson (1996) and Callaghan and Tunney (2001) have challenged the notion of the 'welfare state in crisis' and cite national statistics from a range of Western societies suggesting consistent levels of expenditure upon welfare systems. It is of course important to take note of such statistical data, yet the concern here is to identify the broad processes of our time, especially in relation to shifting governmental and popular attitudes and perceptions. This point about attitudes and perceptions is returned to later when it is argued that globalization has come to be internalized as a form of common sense by governments and politicians in many countries. It is a development that has implications for welfare provision in the future.

3. Even Hirst and Thompson concede that the capacity to shape the global economy is limited by the economic doctrines prevalent among the political elites of advanced industrial societies (Hirst and Thompson, 1996: 3).

4. There are of course different approaches within 'mainstream politics'. For instance, Andrew Gamble and Tony Wright (1999) contend in relation to recent developments within European social democracy that it is more

    appropriate to think in terms of new social democracies, rather than a singular new social democracy.

5. Ben Clift (2001) and Frank Vandenbroucke (1999) have examined the extent of social democratic convergence and identify national differences, particularly in the case of the UK. Although both writers concede significant similarities have emerged amongst social democrats over a number of public policy areas. Ben Clift writing at the end of the twentieth century contends: 'The European social democratic parties are more similar now than at any time this century' (Clift, 2001: 71).

6. Geoffrey Garret (1998) challenges the notion that partisan politics has been eroded because of globalization. More specifically, he claims that when powerful left-of-centre parties are allied with strong and centralized trade union movements, social democracy continues to be a distinctive force. However, Garrett's work has been criticized by Colin Hay (2000) who makes a similar point to the position taken in this chapter, declaring that while globalization may not yet have 'laid waste the social democratic welfare state, it may well still be the case that this is precisely the view to which social democrat politicians have increasingly been converted' (ibid., 150-1). Hay concludes 'that social democratic corporatism may not have been undermined by globalization *per se*; but it may very well have been undermined by ideas about globalization – ideas about its corrosive effects on welfare states and encompassing labour market institutions' (ibid., 151).

Chapter 4: Community and Social Capital

1. However, Antony Black (1984) contends the actual situation in Britain was more complex than this, pointing out that securing individual rights and liberties 'was one reason why they acted in unison' (1984: 178).

2. Although writers like Parkin (1997) and Pahl (1996) point to the continuance of co-operative forms of organization. For instance, Parkin notes that there are '500 credit unions and 350 local economic trading systems (LETS) operating in the UK' (Parkin, 1997).

3. For a more positive interpretation of the concept of intimacy see Anthony Giddens (1991, 1992). In particular, Giddens discusses at some length what he terms 'the transformation of intimacy' viewing it as having radical and democratic potential.

4. However, Richard Sennett has been accused of presenting an idealized conception of the nature of public life in previous centuries (see Christopher Lasch, *The Culture of Narcissism*, 1991).

5. This makes the recent attempt to reduce the working week in France all the more interesting. From January 1, 2000 all French companies with more than 20 employees have had to implement a 35-hour working week. However, it is too early to tell if this approach will catch-on and be incorporated by other Western democracies.

6. There is also evidence beginning to emerge that some of the products we are purchasing – such as mobile phones and computers – are serving to blur the boundaries between our working and non-working lives (Ellison, 2001).

7. Daniel Miller (1995) rejects the notion that consumption undermines sociability. Indeed, Miller questions whether there ever was once a historical state of sociability that consumption has eroded (ibid., 23). However, Miller does not address the type of substantive points raised by writers like Gary Cross and Fred Hirsch.

8. Robert Putnam (1996) considers television also has implications for the level of trust there is within a society. He cites evidence indicating that people who watch a lot of television appear to be less trustful of others and are more concerned with crime, tending to over-estimate crime rates. This undoubtedly reflects the extensive coverage of crime on television, ranging from programmes designed to solve crimes to dramas and documentaries about crime. There is also the constant, often sensationalist, reporting of crime in news reports. Putnam concludes that: 'heavy viewing may well increase pessimism about human nature' (ibid., 13).

9. What Eco means by neo- or new medievalism is not that we are literally going back to the Middle Ages, rather there are a number of contemporary developments and preoccupations which have echoes of that period. A similar theme is discussed by Robert D. Kaplan, 'The Coming Anarchy', *The Atlantic Monthly* (February 1994).

Chapter 5: Public-spiritedness and Community

1. Voluntary organizations and the voluntary sector have generated considerable academic debate. As well as funding, other contested issues and themes have centred upon definition, regulation and independence, and relations with other sectors of welfare and social policy provision – specifically the state and the private market (see Alcock, 1996: Harris and Rochester, 2001).

2. Phil Mullan in *The Imaginary Time Bomb: Why an Ageing Population is Not a Social Problem* (1999), presents a different interpretation of recent demographic change. He argues governments have used an ageing population to justify the curbing of their welfare states.

3. See Anthony Arblaster, *The Rise and Decline of Western Liberalism* (1984), for a fuller discussion of the preoccupation of many nineteenth century liberals with instilling in the masses 'civilized' values and attitudes.

4. Although Stephen Holmes in *The Anatomy of Antiliberalism* (1993) argues the liberal stress upon privacy is not an attempt to prioritize it at the expense of the public realm, it is simply a product of the oppressive societies in which many early liberals lived where privacy was regularly abused.

5. For an informative discussion of both the merits and problems associated with privacy in modern societies see Amitai Etzioni, *The Limits of Privacy* (1999).

6. This is evident in the community volunteering schemes that many companies have set-up. As was mentioned earlier in this chapter, there will be a range of reasons for companies behaving in this way, and some will have recognized

there is a correlation between their own profitability and the wellbeing of the communities in which in they operate. There is therefore the possibility of local communities being regenerated in part through self-interest. This issue of motives is discussed in more detail in Chapter 8.

7. For example, see Benjamin Barber, *Strong Democracy: Participatory Politics for a New Age* (1984); John Burnheim, *Is Democracy Possible?* (1985); Carol Gould, *Rethinking Democracy* (1988); Paul Hirst, *Representative Democracy and its Limits* (1990); Anne Phillips, *Engendering Democracy* (1991).

8. In contrast, David Beetham presents a defence of representative democracy. See his essay 'Liberal Democracy and the Limits of Democratization' in D. Held (ed.), *Prospects for Democracy: North, South, East, West* (1993).

9. Another reason for the lack of popular interest in mainstream political parties and processes is undoubtedly the evidence suggesting diminishing faith and trust in politicians in many Western democracies. In part this is a consequence of instances of corruption and other scandals, but at a deeper level the processes associated with detraditionalization (discussed in Chapter 2) – such as the decline of deference and enhanced critical autonomy – must be viewed as contributing to this trend.

Chapter 6: The Retreat into Tribalism

1. Discussion of these issues is made more difficult by the lack of universally accepted definitions of key terms like 'nation', 'ethnicity' and 'nationalism'. This lack of consensus inevitably leads to the blurring of these concepts, and this is undoubtedly what happens here. For a critique of the overlapping or 'interutilization' of these concepts see Walker Connor, 'A Nation is a Nation, is a State, is an Ethnic Group, is a ...', *Ethnic and Racial Studies*, (1978), 1, 4, pp. 379-88. Yet the aim of this chapter is merely to demonstrate the reassurance that can be gained from a sense of shared experience and 'sameness' from particular forms of identity.

2. Ronald Axtmann (1997) contends globalization could usher in heterogeneity, rather than homogeneity, emphasizing the particular ways in which it will be experienced and interpreted by different social groups and societies, each with their own cultures and histories.

3. This claim that class has declined in significance in the contemporary period is contested. See, for example, Ralph Miliband, 'The New Revisionism in Britain', *New Left Review*, (March/April 1985), no.150, pp. 5-27. As well as restating the continuing importance of class in modern societies, Miliband identifies some of the limitations of identity politics.

4. For a defence of the principle of a Queer Nation and the queer movements advocating it, see R. Anthony Slagle, 'In defense of Queer Nation: from identity politics to a politics of difference', *Western Journal of Communications*, (1995).

5. A similar type of dispute took place at the State University of New York at Binghamton – see Monte Williams, 'A campus erupts over multiculturalism', *The New York Times*, 28 June 1996, vol. 145, p. A13 (N).

6. For an informed discussion of the difficulties and complexities involved in striking the right balance between assimilation and multiculturalism, and between liberal individualism and the rights of minority cultures, see Margalit and Halbertal (1994), Kymlicka (1995) and Walzer (1994).

Chapter 7: Communitarianism, Liberalism and Public-spiritedness

1. Other writers who have broadly pursued a similar approach, include Jean Bethke Elshtain, 'The Communitarian Individual' (1995), John Gray, *After Social Democracy* (1996), Jospeh Raz, *The Morality of Freedom* (1986), Philip Selznick, 'Personhood and Moral Obligation' (1995) and Michael Walzer, *Spheres of Justice* (1983).
2. For a fuller discussion of the different types of communitarianisms see Stephen Driver and Luke Martell, 'New Labour's Communitarianisms', *Critical Social Policy*, August/Sept.1997, no. 52.
3. For a useful overview of the different types of neutrality, see Richard Bellamy, *Liberalism and Modern Society* (1992), Chapter 5.
4. For an informative discussion of this complex issue see John O'Neill, *Ecology, Policy and Politics* (1993), particularly Chapter 3.
5. For a more detailed exposition and analysis of Aristotle's conception of the moral virtues see Alasdair MacIntyre, *After Virtue* (1981) and David Ross, *Aristotle* (1995).
6. Citizenship during this period was the prerogative of educated and propertied adult males, and excluded women, children, manual labourers and slaves. This conception of citizenship was clearly a product of its time, and should be rejected. Yet as long as these groups are included within our conceptions of citizenship, Aristotle's work is still of considerable contemporary relevance.
7. See essays by Michael Sandel, 'The Procedural Republic and the Unencumbered Self' and Charles Taylor, 'Atomism' in Shlomo Avineri and Avner de-Shalit, *Communitarianism and Individualism* (1992) for a more detailed critique of the liberal perspective on the individual and society.
8. This necessitates trying to ensure that as far as possible democratically elected governments represent and reflect the will of the people. As we saw in Chapter 5, countries with majority-voting systems such as the UK need to engage in democratic reform to ensure this end.

Chapter 8: Citizenship – A Modest Proposal

1. This idea of incorporating community service guidance into teacher training was inspired by an article written by Rahima C. Wade entitled 'Developing active citizens: community service learning in social studies teacher education', *The Social Studies*, (1995), vol. 86, no. 3, pp. 122-9.

Bibliography

Abercrombie, N. et al. (1980), *The Dominant Ideology Thesis*, Allen and Unwin, London.

Ackerman, B. (1980), *Social Justice and the Liberal State*, Yale UP, New Haven.

Adam, B. (1996), 'Detraditionalization and the Certainty of Uncertain Futures', P. Heelas et al. (eds), *Detraditionalization*, Blackwells, Oxford, pp. 134-48.

Adorno, T. (1991), *The Culture Industry*, Routledge, London.

Adorno, T. and Horkheimer, M. (1972), *Dialectics of Enlightenment*, Verso, London.

Ahmed, A. (1995), 'Ethnic Cleansing: a metaphor for our time?', *Ethnic and Racial Studies*, 18, 1, pp. 2-25.

Albrow, M. (1994), 'The Impact of Globalization on Sociological Concepts: Community, Culture and Milieu', *Innovation*, 7, 4, pp. 371-89.

Alcock, P. (1996), *Social Policy in Britain*, Palgrave, Basingstoke and New York.

Almond, G.A. and Verba, S. (1963), *The Civic Culture: political attitudes and democracy in five nations*, Princeton UP, Princeton.

Almond, G.A. and Verba, S. (eds) (1979), *The Civic Culture revisited*, Sage, London.

Amin, A. (ed.) (1994), *Post-Fordism: A Reader*, Blackwells, Oxford.

Amin, A. (1996), 'The challenge of globalization', *Review of International Political Economy*, 2.

Anderson, B. (1991), *Imagined Communities: Reflections on the Origins and Spread of Nationalism*, Verso, New York.

Anderson, C.W. (1990), *Pragmatic Liberalism*, University of Chicago Press, Chicago and London.

Anderson, D. (ed.) (1993), *The Loss of Virtue. Moral Confusion in Britain and America*, Social Affairs Unit, London.

Anderson, D.S. (1994), 'Corporate retiree volunteerism: an idea whose time has come', *Vital Speeches*, 61, 5, pp. 138-41.

Andison, F.S. (1977), 'TV violence and viewer aggression: A culmination of study results, 1965-1976', *Public Opinion Quarterly*, 41, pp. 314-31.

Appaduri, A. (1990), 'Disjuncture and Difference in the Global Cultural Economy', M. Featherstone (ed.), *Global Culture*, Sage, London, pp. 295-310.

Arblaster, A. (1984), *The Rise and Decline of Western Liberalism*, Basil Blackwell, Oxford.

Aries, P. et al. (eds) (1987), *A History of Private Life*, Harvard UP, Cambridge, MA.

Aristotle (1953), *Ethics: Nicomachean Ethics*, trans. J.A.K. Thomson, Penguin, Harmondsworth.

Aristotle (1981), *The Politics*, T.J. Saunders (ed.), Penguin, Harmondsworth.

Aronowitz, S. (1992), *The Politics of Identity*, Routledge, New York and London.

Arrow, K. (1974), *The Limits of Organization*, Norton, New York.

Ashford, S. and Timms, N. (1993), *What Europe Thinks*, Aldershot, Dartmouth.

Ashley, J. and Hetherington, P. (2002), 'Force the races to mix, says CRE chief', *The Guardian*, 18/3/02, p. 1.

Atkinson, J. (1985), 'Flexibility: Planning for an Uncertain Future', *Manpower Policy and Practice*, 1, pp. 26-9.

——. (1988), 'Recent Changes in the Internal Labour Market Structure in the U.K.', W. Buitelaar (ed.), *Technology and Work: Labour Studies in England, Germany and the Netherlands*, Avebury, Aldershot, pp. 133-49.

Atkinson, J.M. (1978), *Discovering Suicide*, Macmillan, London.

Avineri, S. and De-Shalit, A. (eds), *Communitarianism and Individualism*, Oxford UP, Oxford.

Axelrod, R. (1984), *The Evolution of Cooperation*, Basic Books, New York.

Axtmann, R. (1997), 'Collective Identity and the Democractic Nation-State in the Age of Globalization', A. Cvetkovich and D. Kellner (eds), *Articulating the Global and the Local*, Westview Press, Boulder and Oxford, pp. 33-54.

——. (ed.) (2001), *Balancing Democracy*, Continuum, London and New York.

Balakrishnan, G. (ed.) (1996), *Mapping the Nation*, Verso, London and New York.

Banfield, E. (1958), *The Moral Basis of a Backward Society*, Free Press, New York.

Banks, J.A. (1972), *The Sociology of Social Movements*, Macmillan Press, London.

Barber, B. (1984), *Strong Democracy. Participatory Politics for a New Age*, University of California Press, California and London.

——. (1995), *Jihad vs. McWorld*, Random House, New York.

Barnes, K. (1994), 'Tips for managing telecommuters', *HR Focus*, 71, 11, pp. 9-11.

Barnett, A. (1989), 'Charlie's Army', *New Statesman*, 22/9/89.

Barrett, F. (1992), 'A hitchhikers' guide to growing up', *The Independent*, 29/8/92, p. 43.

Barry, B. (1990), 'How Not to Defend Liberal Institutions', R. Bruce Douglass et al. (eds) (1990), *Liberalism and the Good*, Routledge, London and New York, pp. 44-58.

Barry, N.P. (1989), *An Introduction to Modern Political Theory*, 2nd ed., Macmillan, Basingstoke and London.

Barry Clarke, P. (1996), *Deep Citizenship*, Pluto Press, London and Chicago.

Bates, S. (2000), 'Reformation required', *The Guardian*, 24/6/00.

Batha, E. (2000), 'Austria's problem with foreigners', *BBC News Online*, 4/2/00.

Baudrillard, J. (1981), *For a Critique of the Political Economy of the Sign*, Telos Press, St. Louis.

Bauman, Z. (1990), 'Philosophical affinities of postmodern sociology', *Sociological Review*, 38, 3.

——. (1991), *Modernity and Ambivalence*, Polity Press, Cambridge.

——. (1992), *Intimations of Postmodernity*, Routledge, London.

Bauman, Z. (1993), *Postmodern Ethics*, Blackwells, Oxford.

——. (1996a), 'Morality in the Age of Contingency', P. Heelas et al. (eds), *Detraditionalization*, Blackwells, Oxford, pp. 49-58.

——. (1996b), 'The moth seeks out the lamp', *New Statesman*, 1/11/96, pp. 21-3.

——. (1997), *Postmodernity and its Discontents*, Polity, Cambridge.

——. (2001), *The Individualized Society*, Polity, Cambridge.

Baxter, S. (1994), 'Tories' high on society', *New Statesman and Society*, 4/3/94, 7, 292, p. 22.

Bay, C. (1968), 'Needs, Wants and Political Legitimacy', *Canadian Journal of Political Science*, 1, pp. 241-60.

Beauregard, R.A. and Haila, A. (2000), 'The Unavoidable Continuities of the City', *Globalizing Cities: A New Spatial Order?*, Blackwells, Oxford, pp. 22-36

——. (1992), *Risk Society: Towards a New Modernity*, Sage, London.

——. (1999), *World Risk Society*, Polity Press, Cambridge.

——. (2000), *The Brave New World of Work*, Polity Press, Cambridge.

——. (2000a), *What is Globalization?*, Polity Press, Cambridge.

Beck, U. and Beck-Gernsheim, E. (1994), *The Normal Chaos of Love*, Polity Press, Cambridge.

Beck, U. and Beck-Gernsheim, E. (1996), 'Individualization and "Precarious Freedoms": Perspectives and Controversies of a Subject-orientated Sociology', P.Heelas et al. (eds), *Detraditionalization*, Blackwells, Oxford, pp. 23-48.

Beck, U. and Beck-Gernshem, E. (2002), *Individualization*, Sage, London.

Beck, U., Giddens, A. and Lash, S. (1994), *Reflexive Modernization*, Polity Press, Cambridge.

Beetham, D. (1993), 'Liberal Democracy and the Limits of Democratization', D. Held (ed.), *Prospects for Democracy: North, South, East, West*, Polity Press, Cambridge.

Beirne, M. and Ramsay, H. (1992), *Information technology and workplace democracy*, Routledge, London and New York.

Belk, R.W. (1995), 'Studies in the New Consumer Behaviour', D. Miller (ed.), *Acknowledging Consumption*, Routledge, London and New York, pp. 58-95.

Bell, D. (1960), *The End of Ideology*, Free Press of Glencoe, New York.

——. (1973), *The Coming of Post-Industrial Society*, Basic Books, New York.

——. (1976), *The Cultural Contradictions of Capitalism*, Heinemann, London.

Bellamy, R. (1992), *Liberalism and Modern Society*, The Pennsylvania State UP, Pennsylvania.

Benjamin, W. (1973), 'The Work of Art in the Age of Mechanical Reproduction', *Illuminations*, Fontana, London.

Benn, S. and Gaus, G. (1983), *Public and Private in Social Life*, Croom Helm, Kent.

Ben-Ner, A. (1984), 'On the stability of the cooperative type of organization', *Journal of Comparative Economics*, 8, pp. 247-60.

Ben-Porath, Y. (1980), 'The f-connection: families, friends, and firms and the organization of exchange', *Population Development Review*, 6, pp. 1-30.

Berelson, B. (1952), 'Democratic theory and public opinion', *Public Opinion Quarterly*, 16, pp. 313-30.

Berelson, B. et al. (1954), *Voting*, University of Chicago Press, Chicago.

Berman, M. (1983), *All That Is Solid Melts Into Air*, Verso, London.

Bernstein, R. (1994), 'Foucault: Critique as a Philosophical Ethos', M. Kelly (ed.), *Critique and Power: Recasting the Foucault/Habermas Debate*, MIT Press, Cambridge, Mass. and London, pp. 211-41.

Betz, H-G. (1994), *Radical Right-Wing Populism in Western Europe*, Macmillan, Basingstoke and London.

Beynon, H. (1973), *Working for Ford*, Allen Lane, Harmondsworth.

Bittner, M. (1994), 'The constitutionality of public school community service programs', *The Clearing House*, 68, 2, pp. 115-9.

Bjorgo, T. (1993), 'Role of the Media in Racist Violence', T. Bjorgo & R. Witte (eds), *Racist Violence in Europe*, St. Martin's Press, New York, pp. 96-112.

Black, A. (1984), *Guilds and Civil Society in European Political Thought from the Twelfth Century to the Present*, Methuen and Co., London.

Black, L. (1992), 'Zapping into direct democracy', *The Independent*, 27/6/92.

Blair, T. (1996), *New Britain: my vision of a young country*, Fourth Estate, London.

——. (1997), *Speech to the Party of European Socialists Congress*, Malm, 6/6/97, The Labour Party, London.

——. and Schroeder, G. (1999), 'Europe: The Third Way/ Die Neue Mitte', K. Coates (ed.), *The Third Way to the Servile State*, Spokesman, Nottingham, pp. 27-37.

Bloch, P.H. and Bruce, G.D. (1984), 'Product involvement as leisure behaviour: the case of automobiles and clothing', T. Kinear (ed.), *Advances in Consumer Research*, Association for Consumer Research, Provo., UT, pp. 197-201.

Boldgett, M. (1996), 'Lower costs spur move to more telecommuting', *Computerworld*, 4/11/96, 30, 45, p. 8.

Bornstein, S., Held, D. and Kreiger, J. (eds) (1984), *The State in Capitalist Europe*, Allen and Unwin, London.

Bradley, H. (1996), *Fractured Identities: Changing Patterns of Inequality*, Polity Press, Cambridge.

Bradshaw, J. (1972), 'The concept of social need', *New Society*, 30/3/72.

Braverman, H. (1974), *Labour and Monopoly Capital*, Monthly Review Press, New York.

Brewer, A. (1990), *Marxist Theories of Imperialism: A Critical Survey*, 2nd ed., Routledge, London and New York.

Bridges, T. (1994), *The Culture of Citizenship: Inventing Postmodern Civic Culture*, State University of New York Press, New York.

Bright, M. (1998), 'Britain's selfish young refusing to volunteer', *The Observer*, 22/2/98.

Brown, M.E. (1997), *Nationalism and Ethnic Conflict*, MIT Press, Cambridge, Massachusetts.

Brubaker, R. (1995), 'National minorities, nationalizing states, and external national homelands in the new Europe', *Daedalus*, 124, 2, pp. 107-33.

Bruce Douglass, R. et al. (eds) (1990), *Liberalism and the Good*, Routledge, London and New York.

Budge, I. (1993), 'Direct Democracy: Setting Appropriate Terms of Debate', D. Held (ed.), *Prospects for Democracy*, Polity Press, Cambridge.

Bullock, S. (1996), 'Yes: forced "volunteerism" defeats the purpose', *ABA Journal*, 82, p. 50.

Burbach, R. et al. (1997), *Globalization and its Discontents*, Pluto Press, London.

Burke, E. (1986), *Reflections on the Revolution in France*, Penguin Books, Harmondsworth.

Burnham, L.F. (1994), 'Tyranny from the tyrannized', *Utne Reader*, 61, pp. 133-5.

Burrows, R. and Loader, B. (eds) (1993), *Towards a Post-Fordist Welfare State?*, Routledge, London.

Byrne, D. (1999), *Social exclusion*, Open UP, Buckingham and Philadelphia.

Callaghan, J. and Tunney, S. (2001), 'The End of Social Democracy?', *Politics*, 21, 1, pp. 63-72.

Campbell, B. (1989), 'New Times Towns', S. Hall and M. Jacques (eds), *New Times: The Changing Face of Politics in the 1990s*, Lawrence and Wishart, London, pp. 279-99.

Caplan, R. and Feffer, J. (eds) (1996), *Europe's New Nationalism: States and Minorities in Conflict*, Oxford UP, Oxford.

Carroll, A.B. and Horton, G.T. (1994), 'Do joint corporate social responsibility programs work?', *Business and Society Review*, 90, pp. 24-8.

Carroll, R. (2002), 'Blair and Berlusconi frame deal to free up EU markets', *The Guardian*, 16/ 2/02.

Casey, C. (1995), *Work, Self and Society: After Industrialism*, Routledge, London and New York.

Caudron, S. (1994), 'Volunteer efforts offer low-cost training options', *Personnel Journal*, 73, 6, pp. 39-43.

Chase-Dunn, C. (1989), *Global Formation: Structures of the World Economy*, Basil Blackwell, Oxford.

Chavez, L. (1996), 'Multiculturalism is driving us apart', *USA Today*, 124, no. 2612, pp. 39-42.

Christopherson, S. (1994), 'The Fortress City: Privatized Spaces, Consumer Citizenship', A. Amin (ed.), *Post-Fordism: A Reader*, Blackwells, Oxford, pp. 409-27.

Clark, C.S. (1996), 'The new voluntarism: is America poised for a surge in good works?' *CQ Researcher*, 6, 46, pp. 1083-2003.

Clarke, S. (1988), 'Overaccumulation, class struggle and the regulation approach', *Capital and Class*, 36, pp. 59-92.

——. (1992), 'What in the Ford's name is Fordism', N. Gilbert et al. (eds), *Fordism and Flexibility: Divisions and Change*, Macmillan, London.

Clift, B. (2001), 'New Labour's Third Way and European Social Democracy', S. Ludlam and M.J. Smith (eds), *New Labour in Government*, Macmillan, Basingstoke, pp. 55-72

Coates, K. (ed.), *The Third Way to the Servile State*, Spokesman, Nottingham.

Cockshott, W. Paul and Cottrell, A. (1993), *Towards a New Socialism*, Spokesman, London.

Cohen, G.A. (1984), 'Nozick on appropriation', *New Left Review*, 150, pp. 89-107.

Cohen, P. (1998), 'Daddy Dearest: Do You Really Matter?', *New York Times*, 11/7/98, p. A13.

Connelly, J. (1995), 'Let's hear it for the office', *Fortune*, 131, 4, pp. 221-3.

Connor, W. (1978), 'A Nation is a Nation, is a State, is an Ethnic Group, is a ...', *Ethnic and Racial Studies*, 1, 4, pp. 379-88.

Cooke, P. (1988), 'Modernity, Postmodernity and the City', *Theory, Culture and Society*, 5 (2-3).

Cooper, G. (1997), 'Britain in 2020: review of *Social Trends, 27*', *The Independent*, 30/1/97.

Coriat, B. (1991), 'Technical flexibility and mass production', G. Benko and M. Dunford (eds), *Industrial Change and Regional Development*, Belhaven, London.

Couzens Hoy, D. (ed.) (1986), *Foucault: A Critical Reader*, Basil Blackwell, Oxford.

Cox, R. (1997), 'Economic globalization and the limits to liberal democracy', A.G. McGrew (ed.), *The Transformation of Democracy? Globalization and Territorial Democracy*, Polity, Cambridge.

Crick, B. (2001), *Citizens: Towards a Citizenship Culture*, Oxford, Blackwells.

Cross, G. (1993), *Time and Money: The Making of Consumer Culture*, Routledge, London and New York.

Crouch, C. (1999), 'The Parabola of Working Class Politics', A. Gamble and T. Wright (eds), *The New Social Democracy*, The Political Quarterly, Blackwells, Oxford, pp. 69-83.

Crouch, C. and Marquand, D. (eds) (1995), *Reinventing Collective Action*, Blackwells, Oxford.

Crozier, M. et al. (eds) (1975), *The Crisis of Democracy*, New York UP, New York.

Cvetkovich, A. and Kellner, D. (eds) (1997), *Articulating the Global and the Local*, Westview Press, Boulder and Oxford.

Dahl, R.A. (1982), *Dilemmas of a Pluralist Democracy: Autonomy vs. Control*, Yale UP, New Haven.

Dahrendorf, R. (1996), 'Economic Opportunity, Civil Society and Political Liberty', C. Hewitt de Alcantara (ed.), *Social Futures, Global Visions*, Blackwells, Oxford, pp. 19-38.

Dahya, B. (1974), 'The nature of Pakistani ethnicity in industrial cities in Britain', A. Cohen (ed.), *Urban Ethnicity*, Tavistock, London, pp. 77-118.

Davis Smith, J. (1998), *The 1997 National Survey of Volunteering*, Institute for Volunteering Research, London.

Dawson, J. and Lord, J.D. (1983), *Shopping Centre Development*, Longman, New York.

Deakin, N. (2001), *In Search of Civil Society*, Basingstoke and New York, Palgrave.

Dean, M. (2001), 'The bank it's a credit to join', *Guardian Society*, 8/8/01, p. 5.

DeLue, S.M. (1997), *Political Thinking, Political Theory and Civil Society*, Allyn and Bacon, Boston.

Delve, C. et al. (eds) (1990), *Community service as values education*, Jossey-Bass, San Francisco.

Denny, C. (1998), 'Remote control of the High Street', *The Guardian*, 2/6/98, p. 18.

Deutschmann, C. (1987), 'Economic restructuring and company unionism – the Japanese model', *Economic and Industrial Democracy*, 8, pp. 463-88.

Dews, P. (1989), 'The Return of the Subject in Late Foucault', *Radical Philosophy*, 51, pp. 37-41.

Dhingra, D. (2000), 'Charity begins at work', *Guardian: Office hours*, 4/12/00, p. 5.

Dicken, P. (1986), *Global Shift: Industrial Change in a Turbulent World*, Paul Chapman Publishing, London.

——. (1992), *Global Shift: The Internationalization of Economic Activity*, Chapman and Hall, London.

Dobson, A. (1992), *Green Political Thought*, Routledge, London and New York.

Dohse, K., Jürgens, U. and Malsch, T (1985), 'From Fordism to Toyotism? The social organisation of the labour process in the Japanese automobile industry', *Politics and Society*, 14, 2, pp. 115-46.

Dore, A. (1995), 'Determined to change the way things are', *Times Educational Supplement*, 2/6/95, no. 4118, p. 4A.

Driver, S. and Martell, L. (1997), 'New Labour's Communitarianism', *Critical Social Policy*, 52.

Drucker, P.F. (1991), 'It Profits Us to Strengthen Nonprofits', *The Wall Street Journal*, 19/12/91, A14.

——. (1993), *Post-Capitalist Society*, Butterworth-Heinemann, Oxford.

Dunkin, A. and Baig, E. (1995), 'Taking care of business – without leaving the house', *Business Week*, 17/4/95, no. 3420, pp. 106-8.

Dunning, J.H. (1993), *Multinational Enterprises and the Global Economy*, Addison-Wesley, Wokingham.

Durkheim, E. (1961), *The Elementary Forms of the Religious Life*, first published in 1912, Collier Books, New York.

——. (1961), *Moral Education*, The Free Press, Glencoe.

——. (1964), *The Division of Labour in Society*, Free Press, New York.

——. (1970), *Suicide: A Study in Sociology*, Routledge and Kegan Paul, London.

Dworkin, R. (1978), 'Liberalism', S. Hampshire (ed.), *Public and Private Morality*, Cambridge UP, Cambridge, pp. 113-43.

Eagelton, T. (1990), *The Ideology of the Aesthetic*, Basil Blackwell, Oxford.

——. (1991), *Ideology. An Introduction*, Verso, London and New York.

Eatwell, R. and Wright, A. (1993), *Contemporary Political Ideologies*, Pinter Publishers, London.

Eccleshall, R. et al. (eds) (1984), *Political Ideologies: An introduction*, Unwin Hyman, London.

Eco, U. (1987), *Travels in Hyperreality*, Picador, London.

Economist (1999), 'Is there a crisis?', *The Economist*, 17/7/99.

Edwards, L.N. and Field-Handley, E. (1996), 'Home-based workers: data from the 1990 Census of Population', *Monthly Labor Review*, 119, 11, pp. 26-35.

Ehrenhalt, A. (2000a), 'Appraising Social Capital', *The Responsive Community*, 10, 4, pp. 59-63.

——. (2000b), 'The Empty Square', *The Responsive Community*, 11,1, pp. 59-67.

Elger, T. and Smith, C. (eds), *Global Japanization? The transnational transformation of the labour process*, Routledge, London and New York.

Elliott, G. and Osborne, P. (1991), 'Community as Compulsion? A Reply to Skillen on Citizenship and the State', *Radical Philosophy*, 58, pp. 14-15.

Elliott, L. and Atkinson, D. (1998), *The Age of Insecurity*, Verso, London and New York.

Ellison, M. (2001), 'US workers suffer labour pains', *The Guardian*, 3/9/01.

Elshtain, J.B. (1995), 'The Communitarian Individual', A. Etzioni (ed.), *New Communitarian Thinking: Persons, Virtues, Institutions, and Communities*, University Press of Virginia, Charlottesville and London, pp. 99-109.

Erikson, E. (1965), *Childhood and Society*, Penguin, Harmondsworth.

Esposito, J.L. (1992), *The Islamic Threat: Myth or Reality?*, Oxford UP, Oxford.

Etzioni, A. (1995a), *The Spirit of Community*, Fontana, London.

——. (1995b), 'Old Chestnuts and New Spurs', A. Etzioni (ed.), *New Communitarian Thinking: Persons, Virtues, Institutions, and Communities*, University Press of Virginia, Charlottesville and London, pp. 16-34.

Etzioni, A. (1997a), 'Community watch', *The Guardian*, 28/6/97.

——. (1997b), *The New Golden Rule: Community and Morality in a Democratic Society*, Profile Books, London.

——. (1999), *The Limits of Privacy*, Basic Books, New York.

Featherstone, M. (ed.) (1990), *Global Culture: Nationalism, Globalization and Modernity*, Sage, London.

——. (1991), *Consumer Culture and Postmodernism*, Sage, London.

——. (1995), *Undoing Culture: Globalization, Postmodernism and Identity*, Sage, London.

Fekete, L. and Webber, F. (1994), *Inside racist Europe*, Institute of Race Relations, London.

Fisher, P. (1995), 'Back to the Future', *The Guardian*, 30/9/95.

Forbes, I. and Smith, S. (1983), *Politics and Human Nature*, Pinter Publishers, London.

Ford, G. (1992), *Fascist Europe: The Rise of Racism and Xenophobia*, Pluto Press, London and Boulder, Colorado.

Forester, T. (1988), 'The Myth of The Electronic Cottage', *Futures 20*, 3, pp. 227-40.

Fornas, J. (1995), *Cultural Theory and Late Modernity*, Sage, London.

Fort, M. (1996), 'Why we must make a meal of family life again', *The Observer*, 10/11/96.

Foucault, M. (1980), *Power/Knowledge*, Pantheon, New York.
——. (1984), *The Foucault Reader*, P. Rabinow (ed.), Penguin Books, Harmondsworth.
——. (1987), *The History of Sexuality, Vol.2: The Use of Pleasure*, Penguin, Harmondsworth.
——. (1988a), *Michel Foucault: Politics, Philosophy, Culture - Interviews and Other Writings, 1977-1984*, L.D. Kritzman (ed.), Routledge, New York and London.
——. (1988b), *The History of Sexuality, Vol.3: The Care of the Self*, Penguin, Harmondsworth.
Franklin, J. (ed.) (1998), *The Politics of Risk Society*, Polity Press, Cambridge.
Fraser, E. and Lacey, N. (1993), *The Politics of Community: A Feminist Critique of the Liberal-Communitarian Debate*, Harvester Wheatsheaf, London.
Frazer, E. (1999), *The Problems of Communitarian Politics: Unity and Conflict*, Oxford UP, Oxford.
Friedan, B. (1996), 'To Transcend Identity Politics: A New Paradigm', *Responsive Community*, 6, 2, pp. 4-8.
Friedman, J. (1990), 'Being in the World: Globalization and Localization', M. Featherstone (ed.), *Global Culture*, Sage, London, pp. 311-28.
Frisby, D. (1985), *Fragments of Modernity*, Polity Press, Cambridge.
Freeman, R.B. (1997), 'Working for nothing: the supply of volunteer labor', *Journal of Labor Economics*, 15, 1, pp. S140-67.
Fukuyama, F. (1992), *The End of History and the Last Man*, The Free Press, New York.
——. (1995), *Trust: The Social Virtues and the Creation of Prosperity*, Hamish Hamilton, London.
——. (2000), *The Great Disruption: Human nature and the reconstitution of social order*, Profile Books, London.
Furedi, F. (1997), *Culture of Fear: Risk-Taking and the Morality of Low Expectation*, Cassell, London.
Gambetta, D. (ed.) (1988), *Trust: Making and Breaking Cooperative Relations*, Blackwell, New York.
Gamble, A and Wright, T. (eds) (1999), *The New Social Democracy*, The Political Quarterly, Blackwells, Oxford.
Gans, H. (1982), *The Urban Villagers: Group and Class in the Life of Italian-Americans*, The Free Press, New York.
Garrett, G. (1998), *Partisan Politics in the Global Economy*, Cambridge UP, Cambridge.
Gauthier, D. (1992), 'The Liberal Individual', S. Avineri and A. de-Shalit (eds), *Communitarianism and Individualism*, Oxford UP, Oxford, pp. 151-64.
Gellner, E. (1964), *Thought and Change*, Weidenfeld and Nicholson, London.
——. (1983), *Nations and Nationalism*, Basil Blackwell, Oxford.

Gergen, D. (1997), 'Opportunity knocks: Philadelphia summit issues a new call to national service', *U.S. News and World Report*, 7.4.97., 122, 13, p. 80.

Gershuny, J. and Miles, I. (1983), *The New Service Economy*, Frances Pinter, London.

Gessner, V. and Schade, A. (1990), 'Conflicts of culture in cross-border legal relations', *Theory, Culture and Society*, 7, 2-3.

Gibbins, J.R. (ed.) (1989), *Contemporary Political Culture*, Sage, London.

Giddens, A. (1971), *Capitalism and modern social theory: An analysis of the writings of Marx, Durkheim and Max Weber*, Cambridge UP, Cambridge.

——. (1987), *Social Theory and Modern Sociology*, Polity Press, Cambridge.

——. (1990), *The Consequences of Modernity*, Polity Press, Cambridge.

——. (1991), *Modernity and Self-Identity*, Polity Press, Cambridge.

——. (1992), *The Transformation of Intimacy*, Polity Press, Cambridge.

——. (1994), 'Living in a Post-Traditional Society', U. Beck et al., *Reflexive Modernization*, Polity Press, Cambridge, pp. 56-109.

——. (1998), *The Third Way: The Renewal of Social Democracy*, Polity Press, Cambridge.

——. (1999), *Runaway World: How Globalisation is Reshaping our Lives*, Profile Books, London.

——. (2000), *The Third Way and its Critics*, Polity Press, Cambridge.

Gierke, O.von (1900), *Political Theories of the Middle Age*, trans. F.W. Maitland, vol. 3, Thoemmes Press, Bristol.

Gilbert, P. (1991), *Human Relationships*, Basil Blackwell, Oxford.

Gill, S. (1995), 'Globalization, market civilization and disciplinary neoliberalism', *Millennium*, 24.

Glass, S.T. (1966), *The Responsible Society: The Ideas of Guild Socialism*, London.

Gleeson, D. (1986), 'Life skills training and the politics of personal effectiveness', *Sociological Review*, 34, pp. 381-95.

Glendon, M.A. (1991), *Rights Talk: The Impoverishment of Political Discourse*, Free Press, New York.

Glenny, M. (1992), *The Fall of Yugoslavia*, Penguin, Harmondsworth.

——. (1993), *The Rebirth of History: Eastern Europe in the Age of Democracy*, 2nd ed., Penguin, Harmondsworth.

Godsden, P.H.J.H. (1961), *The Friendly Societies in England, 1815-1875*, Manchester UP, Manchester.

——. (1973), *Self-Help: Voluntary Associations in Nineteenth Century Britain*, WKP, London.

Golding, M. (1972), 'Obligations to future generations', *The Monist*, 56, pp. 85-99.

Goodin, R.E. (1992), *Green Political Theory*, Polity Press, Cambridge.

Gordon, D.M. (1988), 'The Global Economy: New Edifice or Crumbling Foundations?', *New Left Review*, 168, pp. 24-64.

Gorz, A. (1965), 'Work and Consumption', P. Anderson and R. Blackburn (eds), *Towards Socialism*, Collins, London.

——. (1982), *Farewell to the Working Class: An Essay on Post-Industrial Socialism*, Pluto Press, London.

——. (1989), *Critique of Economic Reason*, Verso, London and New York.
——. (1991), 'The New Agenda', R. Blackburn (ed.), *After the Fall*, Verso, London and New York, pp. 287-97.
——. (1994), *Capitalism, Sociology, Ecology*, Verso, London and New York.
Gould, C.C. (1988), *Rethinking democracy: Freedom and social cooperation in politics, economy, and society*, Cambridge UP, Cambridge.
Gouldner, A.W. (1957), *Wildcat Strike*, Routledge and Kegan Paul, London.
Graham, G. (1992), 'Liberalism and Democracy', *Journal of Applied Philosophy*, 9, 2, pp. 149-60.
Gray, J. (1993), *Beyond the New Right: Markets, government and the common environment*, Routledge, London and New York.
——. (1994), 'Against the world', *The Guardian*, 4/1/94.
——. (1995), 'The sad side of cyberspace', *The Guardian*, 10/4/95.
——. (1996), *After Social Democracy*, Demos, London.
——. (1998), *False Dawn: The Delusions of Global Capitalism*, Granta, London.
Grice, A. (2001), 'Riots blamed on "parallel lives" of blacks and whites', *The Independent*, 11/12/01, p. 1.
Grieve Smith, J. (1994), 'Time for a new global vision', *The Observer*, 3/7/94.
Guardian Editorial (2001), 'Your country needs you: Good causes are starved of volunteers', *The Guardian*, 12/1/01.
Guardian Education (2002), 'Why volunteering is a cool thing to do', *The Guardian*, 26/3/02.
Guhenno, J.M. (1995), *The End of the Nation-State*, University of Minnesota Press, Minneapolis.
Guillemard, A-M. (2001), 'Work or Retirement at Career's End? A Third Way Strategy for an Ageing Population', A. Giddens (ed.), *The Global Third Way Debate*, Cambridge, Polity, pp. 233-43.
Gunsteren, H.van (1996), 'Neo-republican citizenship in the practice of education', *Government and Opposition*, 31, 1, pp. 77-100.
Gutman, A. (1992), 'Communitarian Critics of Liberalism', S. Avineri and A. de-Shalit (eds), *Communitarianism and Individualism*, Oxford UP, Oxford, pp. 120-36.
Hall, S. (1996), 'Ethnicity: Identity and Difference', G. Eley and R.G. Suny (eds), *Becoming National: A Reader*, Oxford UP, New York and Oxford, pp. 339-51.
Hall, T. (1998), *Urban Geography*, Routledge, London and New York.
Harman, C. (1996), 'Globalisation: a critique of a new orthodoxy', *International Socialism*, 73, pp. 3-33.
Harper, K. (1998), 'British walking rates show a marked decline', *The Guardian*, 18/6/98.
Harris, G. (1994), *The Dark Side of Europe: The Extreme Right Today*, Edinburgh UP, Edinburgh.
Harris, M. and Rochester, C. (eds) (2001), *Voluntary Organisations and Social Policy in Britain*, Basingstoke and New York, Palgrave.

Hay, C. (2000), 'Globalization, social democracy and the persistence of partisan politics: a commentary on Garrett', *Review of International Political Economy*, 7: 1, pp. 138-52.

Hayek, F.A. (1960), *The Constitution of Liberty*, RKP, London.

Heelas, P., Lash, S. and Morris, P. (eds) (1996), *Detraditionalization: Critical Reflections on Authority and Identity*, Blackwells, Oxford.

Held, D. et al. (1999), *Global Transformations*, Cambridge, Polity Press.

Hewitt, P. (1998), 'Technology and Democracy', J. Franklin (ed.), *The Politics of Risk Society*, Polity Press, Cambridge, pp. 83-9.

Hilpern, K. (2000), 'Strength in numbers', *The Guardian*, 26.6.00.

Hindess, B. (1987), *Freedom, Equality, and the Market: Arguments on Social Policy*, Tavistock, London and New York.

Hirsch, F. (1977), *Social Limits to Growth*, Routledge, London.

Hirschman, A.O. (1982), 'Rival interpretations of market society: civilizing, destructive, or feeble?', *Journal of Economic Literature*, 20, pp. 1463-84.

Hirst, P. (1999), 'Has Globalisation Killed Social Democracy?', A. Gamble and T. Wright (eds), *The New Social Democracy*, The Political Quarterly, Blackwells, Oxford, pp. 84-96.

Hobsbawm, E. and Ranger, T. (1983), *The Invention of Tradition*, Cambridge UP, Cambridge.

Horsman, M. and Marshall, A. (1994), *After the Nation-State: Citizens, Tribalism and the New World Disorder*, Harper-Collins, London.

Howlett, S. and Locke, M. (1999), 'Volunteering for Blair: the Third Way' *Voluntary Action*, 1, 2, pp. 67-76.

Hutchinson, J. and Smith, A.D. (eds) (1994), *Nationalism*, Oxford UP, Oxford and New York.

Hutton, W. (1999), *The Stakeholding Society*, Polity Press, Cambridge.

Ignatieff, M. (1984), *The Needs of Strangers*, Chatto and Windus, London.

——. (1991), 'Citizenship and Moral Narcissism', G. Andrews (ed.), *Citizenship*, London, Lawrence and Wishart, pp. 26-36.

Institute of Personnel Management (1986), *Flexible Patterns of Work*, IPM, London.

Jacobs, J. (1961) *The Death and Life of Great American Cities*, Vintage Books, New York.

Jacques, M. (1996), 'Decline and fallacy', *The Guardian*, 9/11/96.

Jameson, F. (1984), 'Postmodernism, or the cultural logic of late capitalism', *New Left Review*, 146, pp. 53-92.

——. (1984b), 'Postmodernism and the consumer society', H. Foster (ed.), *Postmodern Culture*, Pluto, London.

Jessop, B. (1994), 'Post-Fordism and the State', A. Amin (ed.), *Post-Fordism: A Reader*, Blackwells, Oxford, pp. 251-79.

Joll, J. (1973), *Europe Since 1870: An International History*, Penguin Books, Harmondsworth.

Jones, B. and Kavanagh, D. (1983), *British Politics Today*, 2nd ed., Manchester UP, Manchester.

Jurgens, U (1989), 'The transfer of Japanese management concepts in the international automobile industry', S. Wood (ed.), *The Transformation of Work?*, Routledge, London and New York, pp. 204-18.

Juergensmeyer, M. (1993), *The New Cold War? Religious Nationalism Confronts the Secular State*, University of California Press, Berkeley.

Julius, D.A. (1990), *Global Companies and Public Policies: The Growing Challenge of Foreign Direct Investment*, RIIA/Pinter Publishers, London.

Kaldor, M. (1996), 'Cosmopolitanism Versus Nationalism: The New Divide?', R. Caplan and J. Feffer (eds), *Europe's New Nationalism*, Oxford UP, Oxford, pp. 42-58.

Kant, I. (1970), 'An Answer to the Question: What is Enlightenment?', H. Reiss (ed.), *Kant's Political Writings*, Cambridge UP, Cambridge, pp. 54-60.

Kaplan, R.D. (1994), 'The Coming Anarchy', *The Atlantic Monthly*, Feb. 1994.

Keane, J. (1984), *Public Life and Late Capitalism*, Cambridge UP, Cambridge.

———. (ed.) (1988), *Civil Society and the State*, Verso, London.

———. (1988), *Democracy and Civil Society*, Verso, London.

———. (1991), *The Media and Democracy*, Polity Press, Cambridge.

Kellas, J.G. (1991), *The Politics of Nationalism and Ethnicity*, Macmillan, Basingstoke and London.

Kendall, J. (ed.) (1990), *Combining service and learning: A resource book for community and public service*, 2 vols, National Society for Internships and Experiential Education, Raleigh, NC.

Kennedy, P. (1993), *Preparing for the Twenty-First Century*, Random House, New York.

Kern, H. and Schumann, M. (1987), 'Limits of the Division of Labour', *Economic and Industrial Democracy*, 8, 2, pp. 151-70.

King, A. (1976), *Why is Britain Becoming Harder to Govern?*, BBC Publications, London.

Klein, J. (1994), 'The threat of tribalism', *Newsweek*, 14/3/94, 123, 11, p. 28.

Kornhaber, A. and Woodward, K.L. (1980), *Grandparents/ Grandchildren: The Vital Connection*, New York.

Kraemer, S. and Roberts, J. (eds) (1996), *The Politics of Attachment: Towards a Secure Society*, Free Association Books, London.

Krueger, A. (1993), 'How Computers Have Changed the Wage Structure: Evidence from Microdata', *Quarterly Journal of Economics*, 108.

Kumar, K. (1986), *Prophecy and Progress: The Sociology of Industrial and Post-Industrial Society*, Penguin, Harmondsworth.

———. (1995), *From Post-Industrial to Postmodern Society*, Blackwells, Oxford.

———. (1997), 'Home: The Promise and Predicament of Private Life at the End of the Twentieth Century', J. Weintraub and K. Kumar (eds), *Public and Private in Thought and Practice*, University of Chicago Press, Chicago and London, pp. 204-36.

Kymlicka, W. (1990), *Contemporary Political Philosophy*, Clarendon Press, Oxford.

Kymlicka, W. (1995), *Multicultural Citizenship: A Liberal Theory of Minority Rights*, Clarendon Press, Oxford.

Labour Party (1997), 'Labour Manifesto: Because Britain Deserves Better', *The Times*, 4/4/97, pp. I-IV.

Lane, R.E. (1982), 'Government and self-esteem', *Political Theory*, 10, pp. 5-31.

Lansey, S. (1994a), *After the Gold Rush – The Trouble with Affluence: Consumer Capitalism and the Way Forward*, Henley Centre, Century Books.

——. (1994b), 'The case for arrested development', *Times Higher Education Supplement*, 20/5/94, p. 17.

Lapham, L.H. (1992), 'Who and What is American?', *Harper's*, Jan.1992, 43.

Larmore, C. (1996), *The Morals of Modernity*, Cambridge UP, Cambridge.

Lasch, C. (1977), *Haven in a Heartless World: The Family Besieged*, Basic Books, New York.

——. (1979), *The Culture of Narcissism*, W.W. Norton and Co., New York and London.

——. (1985), *The Minimal Self*, Norton, New York.

——. (1994), *The Revolt of the Elites and the Betrayal of Democracy*, W.W. Norton and Co., New York and London.

Lash, S. (1993), 'Reflexive modernization: the aesthetic dimension', *Theory, Culture and Society*, 10, 1, pp. 1-24.

Lash, S. and Urry, J. (1987), *The End of Organized Capitalism*, Polity Press, Cambridge.

Laslett, P. (1965), *The World We Have Lost*, Methuen, London.

Lawrence, F. (1996), 'My manifesto for the nation', *The Times*, 21/10/96.

Leadbeater, C. (1989), 'Power to the Person', S. Hall and M. Jacques (eds), *New Times*, Lawrence and Wishart, London , pp. 137-49.

——. (1996), 'Let's hear it for the hyphen: We can learn from America in seeking moral consensus', *New Statesman*, 1/11/96, p.10.

——. (1997), *Civic spirit*, Demos, London.

Ledgard, C. (2002), 'No end to overcrowded trains?', *PM*, Radio 4, 22/1/02.

Lewis, R. (1996), 'Making a difference (volunteerism in Canada)', *Maclean's*, 1/7/96, 109, 27, p. 2.

Lichterman, P. (2001), 'Human Nature Fights Back: Review of Francis Fukuyama's *The Great Disruption*', *The Responsive Community*, 11, 3, pp. 71-5.

Lijphart, A. (1989), 'The Structure of Inference', G.A. Almond and S. Verba (eds), *The Civic Culture Revisited*, Sage, London, pp. 37-56.

Linder, H.S. (1970), *The Harried Leisure Class*, Columbia University Press, New York.

Lindenberg, L.N. (ed.) (1976), *Politics and the Future of Industrial Society*, David McKay Company, New York.

Lindley, R. (1986), *Autonomy*, Macmillan, Basingstoke and London.

Lipietz, A. (1992), *Towards a New Economic Order*, Polity Press, Cambridge.

Lipset, S.M. (1960), *Political Man*, Heinemann, London.

Locke, J. (1990), *Two Treatises of Government*, J.M. Dent and Sons, London.
Locke, J. and Pascoe, E. (2000), 'Can a sense of community flourish in cyberspace?', *The Guardian*, 11/3/00.
Luhmann, N. (1979), *Trust and Power*, Wiley, Chichester.
Luhmann, N. (1988), 'Familiarity, confidence, trust: problems and alternatives', D. Gambetta (ed.), *Trust: Making and breaking cooperative relations*, Basil Blackwell, Oxford, pp. 94-107.
——. (1996), 'Complexity, Structural Contingencies and Value Conflicts', P. Heelas et al. (eds), *Detraditionalization*, Blackwells, Oxford, pp. 59-71.
Lukes, S. (1972), *Individualism*, Blackwells, Oxford.
MacDonald, R. (1996), 'Labours of love: voluntary working in a depressed local economy', *Journal of Social Policy*, 25, 1, pp. 19-39.
MacEwan, A. (1994), 'Globalization and Stagnation', R. Miliband and L. Panitch (eds), *Between Globalism and Nationalism*, Socialist Register 1994, The Merlin Press, London, pp. 130-43.
Macfarlane, A. (1978), *The Origins of English Individualism: The family, property and social transition*, Cambridge UP, Cambridge.
MacIntyre, A. (1981), *After Virtue: a study in moral theory*, Duckworth, London.
——. (1991), *How To Seem Virtuous Without Actually Being So*, Lancaster University, Lancaster.
Mackie, J.L. (1977), *Ethics: Inventing Right and Wrong*, Penguin, Harmondsworth.
Maffesoli, M. (1996), *The Time of the Tribes: The Decline of Individualism in Mass Society*, Sage, London.
Mann, M. (1995), 'As the twentieth century ages', *New Left Review*, 214.
——. (1997), 'Has globalization ended the rise and rise of the nation-state?', *Review of International Political Economy*, 4.
Marcuse, H. (1964), *One-Dimensional Man*, Routledge, London.
——. (1971), 'The Movement in a New Era of Repression', *Berkeley Journal of Sociology*, XVI, pp. 1-14.
Marcuse, P. and van Kempen, R. (eds) (2000), *Globalizing Cities: A New Spatial Order?*, Blackwells, Oxford.
Margalit, A. and Halbertal, M. (1994), 'Liberalism and the right to culture', *Social Research*, 61, 3, pp. 491-511.
Marris, P. (1996), *The Politics of Uncertainty: Attachment in private and public life*, Routledge, London and New York.
Marshall, T.H. (1996), 'Citizenship and Social Class', T.H. Marshall and T. Bottomore (eds), *Citizenship and Social Class*, Pluto Classics, London, pp. 1-51.
Martin, A. (1996), 'Citizenship or slavery?', *Utne Reader*, 75, pp. 14-6.
Martin, L.H. et al. (eds) (1988), *Technologies of the Self: A Seminar with Michel Foucault*, Tavistock, London.
Marx, K. (1977), *Karl Marx Selected Writings*, D. McLellan (ed.), Oxford UP, Oxford.

Maslow, A.H. (1970), *Motivation and Personality*, 2nd ed., Harper and Row, New York.

Mathews, J. (1989), *Age of Democracy: The Politics of Post-Fordism*, Oxford UP, Oxford.

McCarthy, A. (1996), 'All together now: going it alone won't do', *Commonweal*, 12/7/96, 123, 13, pp. 7-8.

McCurry, P. (2001), 'Government looks to schools to boost volunteering', *Guardian Society*, 11/7/01.

McLean, I. (1990), *Democracy and New Technology*, Polity Press, Cambridge.

McLellan, D. (1977), *Karl Marx: Selected Writings*, Oxford UP, Oxford.

——. (ed.) (1983), *Marx: the First 100 Years*, Fontana, Oxford.

——. (1986), *Ideology*, Open University Press, Milton Keynes.

McRae, H. (1996), 'People behaving badly (and well)', *The Independent*, 31/10/96.

Meek, J. (1999) 'Number in church on Sunday drops below 1m', *The Guardian*, 13/11/99.

Meiskins Wood, E. (1998), 'Labour, Class, and State in Global Capitalism', E. Meiskins Wood et al. (eds), *Rising from the Ashes? Labor in the Age of "Global" Capitalism*, New York, Monthly Review Press, pp. 3-16.

Melucci, A. (1985), 'The Symbolic Challenge of Contemporary Movements', *Social Research*, 52, 4, pp. 788-816.

——. (1989), *Nomads of the Present: Social Movements and Individual Needs in Contemporary Society*, Hutchinson Radius, London.

Merelman, R.M. (1991), *Partial Visions: Culture and Politics in Britain, Canada and the United States*, University of Wisconsin Press, Madison.

Merton, R.K. (1965), 'Durkheim's *Division of Labour in Society*', R.A. Nisbet (ed.), *Emile Durkheim*, Prentice-Hall, Englewood Cliffs, New Jersey.

Milbank, D. (2001), 'Is Bush a Communitarian?', *The Responsive Community*, 11, 2, pp. 4-7.

Miles, I. (1988a), *Home Informatics: Information Technology and the Transformation of Everyday Life*, Pinter Publishers, London.

——, 'The Electronic Cottage: Myth or Near-Myth?', *Futures* 20, 4, pp. 355-66.

Miles, R. (1994), 'Explaining Racism in Contemporary Europe', A. Rattansi and S.Westwood (eds), *Racism, Modernity & Identity on the Western Front*, Polity Press, Cambridge, pp. 189-221.

Miliband, R. (1985), 'The New Revisionism in Britain', *New Left Review*, 150, pp. 5-27.

Mill, J.S. (1991), *On Liberty and Other Essays*, World's Classics Edition, Oxford UP, Oxford.

Miller, D. (1990), *Market, State and Community: Theoretical Foundations of Market Socialism*, Clarendon Press, Oxford.

——. (1992), 'Community and Citizenship', S. Avineri and A. de-Shalit (eds), *Communitarianism and Individualism*, Oxford UP, Oxford, pp. 85-100.

——. (1995), *Acknowledging Consumption*, Routledge, London and New York.

Misztal, B.A. (1996), *Trust in Modern Societies: The Search for the Bases of Social Order*, Polity Press, Cambridge.

Morris, P. (1996), 'Community Beyond Tradition', P. Heelas et al. (eds), *Detraditionalization*, Blackwells, Oxford, pp. 223-49.

Mort, F, (1989), 'The Politics of Consumption', S. Hall and M. Jacques (eds), *New Times*, Lawrence and Wishart, London, pp. 160-72.

Mulberg, J. (1995), *Social Limits to Economic Theory*, Routledge, London.

Mulgan, G. (1989), 'The Changing Shape of the City', S. Hall and M. Jacques (eds), *New Times*, Lawrence and Wisehart, London, pp. 262-78.

Mulhall, S. and Swift, A. (1992), *Liberals and Communitarians*, Blackwells, Oxford.

Mullan, P. (1999), *The Imaginary Time Bomb: Why an Ageing Population is Not a Social Problem*, London and New York, I.B. Tauris.

Muller, E.N. and Seligson, M.A. (1994), 'Civic culture and democracy: the question of causal relationships', *American Political Science Review*, 88, 3.

Murray, R. (1989), 'Fordism and Post-Fordism', S. Hall and M. Jacques (eds), *New Times*, Lawrence and Wishart, London, pp. 38-54.

Nadwodny, R. (1996), 'Canadians working at home', *Canadian Social Trends*, 40, pp. 16-21.

Nakata, T. (1996), 'Building volunteerism', *Japan Quarterly*, 43, 1, pp. 22-7.

NEDO (1986), *Changing Working Patterns: How Companies Achieve Flexibility to Meet New Needs*, National Economic Development Office, London.

Newhouse, J. (1998), 'Europe's Rising Regionalism', N. Malcolm et al., *A New Europe?*, Foreign Affairs Reader, New York, pp. 19-36.

Nicholson-Lord, D. (1994), 'Consumerism "undermining western society"', *The Independent*, 19/5/94.

Nickel, S. and Bell, B. (1996), 'Changes in the distribution of wages and unemployment in OECD countries', *American Economic Review*, 86, 2, pp. 302-9.

Norton, C. (2000), 'Brown calls for new culture of "civic patriotism"', *The Independent*, 10/2/00.

Nozick, R. (1974), *Anarchy, State and Utopia*, Basic Books, New York.

Nussbaum, M. (1980), 'Aristotelian Social Democracy', R. Bruce Douglass et al. (eds), *Liberalism and the Good*, Routledge, New York and London, pp. 203-52.

Nye, J. (1997), 'In government we don't trust', *Foreign Policy*, 108, pp. 99-111.

OECD (1986), *Labour Market Flexibility*, Organization for Economic Co-operation and Development, Paris.

Offe, C. (1984), *Contradictions of the Welfare State*, Hutchinson, London.

——. *Disorganized Capitalism*, Polity Press, Cambridge.

Office for National Statistics (1997), *Social Trends*, 27.

Ohmae, K. (1990), *The Borderless World*, Collins, London and New York.

O'Leary, B. (2000), 'Peace in Our Time?', *Radio 4: Analysis*, Broadcast: 13/4/00.

O'Neill, J. (1992), 'Altruism, Egoism, and the Market', *The Philosophical Forum*, XXIII, 4, pp. 278-88.

——. (1993), *Ecology, Policy and Politics: Human Well-Being and the Natural World*, Routledge, London and New York.

Oppenheim, C. (2001), 'Enabling Participation? New Labour's Welfare-to-Work Policies', S. White (ed.), *New Labour: The Progressive Future?*, Palgrave, Basingstoke, pp. 77-92.

O'Sullivan, Jack (1996), 'The New Crusaders', *The Independent*, 22/10/96.

O'Sullivan, J. (1996a), 'Mistaken identities', *National Review*, 48, 22, pp. 50-5.

O'Toole, J. (1977), *Work, Learning and the American Future*, Jossey-Bass, San Francisco.

Pahl, R. (1996), 'Friendly Society', *The Politics of Attachment: Towards a Secure Society*, Free Association Books, London, pp. 88-101.

Palmer, C. 'Volunteering steps forward', *The Observer*, 10/9/00.

Panitch, L. (1994), 'Globalization and the State', R. Miliband and L. Panitch (eds), *Between Globalism and Nationalism: Socialist Register 1994*, The Merlin Press, London, pp. 60-93.

Parekh, B. (1993), 'The Cultural Particularity of Liberal Democracy', D. Held (ed.), *Prospects for Democracy*, Polity Press, Cambridge, pp. 156-75.

——. (2000), *Rethinking Multiculturalism: Cultural Diversity and Political Theory*, Palgrave, Basingstoke and New York.

Parkin, S. (1997), 'Your caring, sharing co-op nation', *The Guardian*, 26/4/97.

Parsons, T. (1951), *The Social System*, Free Press, New York.

Passmore, J. (1980), *Man's Responsibility for Nature*, (2nd ed.), Duckworth, London.

Patel, P. and Pavitt, K. (1991), 'Large firms in the production of the world's technology: an important case of "non-globalisation"', *Journal of International Business Studies*, 1, pp. 1-21.

Pateman, C. (1970), *Participation and Democratic Theory*, Cambridge UP, Cambridge.

——. (1985), *The Problem of Political Obligation*, Polity Press, Cambridge.

——. (1989), 'The Civic Culture: A Philosophic Critique', G.A. Almond and S. Verba (eds), *The Civic Culture Revisited*, Sage, London, pp. 57-102.

Perkin, H. (1996), *The Third Revolution: Professional elites in the modern world*, Routledge, London and New York.

Phillips, A. (1991), *Engendering Democracy*, Polity Press, Cambridge.

——. (1993), *Democracy and Difference*, Polity Press, Cambridge.

Phillips, M. (2001), 'It's Completely Voluntary', *BBC Radio 4: Analysis*, 22/11/01.

Pierson, C. (1986), *Marxist Theory and Democratic Politics*, Polity Press, Cambridge.

Pierson, P. (1996), 'The New Politics of the Welfare State', *World Politics*, 48, 2.

Pimlott, B. et al. (eds) (1990), *The Alternative*, W.H. Allen and Co., London.

Piore, M.J. and Sabel, C.F. (1984), *The Second Industrial Divide*, Basic Books, USA.

Popcorn, F. (1992), *The Popcorn Report*, Harper Collins, New York.

Popenoe, D. (1996), *Life Without Father*, Free Press, New York.

Pring, R. (2001), 'Citizenship and Schools', B. Crick (ed.), *Citizens: Towards a Citizenship Culture*, Blackwells, Oxford, pp. 81-9.

Putnam, R.D. (1994), *Making Democracy Work: Civic Traditions in Modern Italy*, Princeton UP, Princeton.

———. (1995), 'Bowling Alone: America's Declining Social Capital', *Journal of Democracy*, 6, pp. 65-78.

———. (1996), 'The strange death of civic America', *The Independent*, 11/3/96, p.13.

Putnam, R. (2000), *Bowling Alone: The Collapse and Revival of American Community*, Simon and Schuster, New York.

Raban, J. (1974), *Soft city*, London.

Randall, V. (1987), *Women and Politics*, 2nd ed., Macmillan, London.

Rawls, J. (1972), *A Theory of Justice*, Oxford UP, Oxford.

Raz, J. (1986), *The Morality of Freedom*, Clarendon Press, Oxford.

Riesman, D. et al. (1950), *The Lonely Crowd: A Study of the Changing American Character*, Yale UP, New Haven.

Richmond, A. (1984), 'Ethnic nationalism and post-industrialism', *Ethnic and Racial Studies*, 7, 1, pp. 4-18.

Ritzer, G. (1993), *The McDonaldization of Society*, Pine Forge Press, Thousand Oaks, CA.

———. (1998), *The McDonaldization Thesis*, Sage Publications, London.

Robbins, K. (2000), 'Encountering Globalization', D. Held and A. McGrew (eds), *The Global Transformations Reader*, Polity Press, Cambridge, pp. 195-201.

Robertson, D. (1985), *The Penguin Dictionary of Politics*, Penguin, Harmondsworth.

Robertson, R. (1992), *Globalization*, Sage, London.

Robison, R. and Goodman, D.S.G. (eds) (1996), *The New Rich in Asia: Mobile Phones, McDonald's and Middle Class Revolution*, Routledge, London & New York.

Roche, G.C. (1977), 'The Relevance of Friedrich A. Hayek', F. Machlup, *Essays on Hayek*, Routledge and Kegan Paul, London and Henley.

Roche, M. (1992), *Rethinking Citizenship: Welfare, Ideology and Change in Modern Society*, Polity Press, Cambridge.

Rorty, R. (1989), *Contigency, Irony and Solidarity*, Cambridge UP, Cambridge.

Rose, R. and Peters, G. (1977), *The political consequences of economic overload*, University of Strathclyde Centre for the Study of Public Policy, Strathclyde.

Rose, N. (1996), 'Authority and the Genealogy of Subjectivity', P. Heelas et al. (eds), *Detraditionalization*, Blackwells, Oxford, pp. 294-327.

Ross, D. (1995), *Aristotle*, 6th edition, Routledge, New York.

Rousseau, J-J (1973), *The Social Contract and Discourses*, J.M. Dent and Son, London.

Ruigrok, W. and van Tulder, R. (1995), *The Logic of International Restructuring*, Routledge, London and New York.

Ryle, S. (1996), 'If the pensioners of today think it's tough...', *The Guardian*, 22/4/96.

Sandel, M. (1982), *Liberalism and the Limits of Justice*, Cambridge UP, Cambridge.

——. (1984), 'Morality and the Liberal Ideal', *The New Republic*, 7/5/84, pp. 15-7.

——. (1992), 'The Procedural Republic and the Unencumbered Self', S. Avineri and A. de-Shalit (eds), *Communitarianism and Individualism*, Oxford UP, Oxford, pp. 12-28.

Sarlvik, B. and Crewe, I. (1983), *Decade of Dealignment: The Conservative Victory of 1979 and Electoral Trends in the 1970s*, Cambridge UP, Cambridge.

Sassoon, D. (1998), 'Fin-de-Siècle Socialism: The United, Modest Left', *New Left Review*, 227, pp. 88-96

——. (1999), 'European Social Democracy and New Labour: Unity in Diversity?', A. Gamble and T. Wright (eds), *The New Social Democracy*, The Political Quarterly, Blackwells, Oxford, pp. 19-36.

Saunders, P. (1993), 'Citizenship in a Liberal Society', B.S. Turner (ed.), *Citizenship and Social Theory*, Sage, London, pp. 57-90.

Savage, M. and Warde, A. (1993), *Urban Sociology, Capitalism and Modernity*, Macmillan, Basingstoke and London.

Sayer, A. (1986), 'New developments in manufacturing: the JIT system', *Capital and Class*, 30, pp. 43-72.

Schlesinger, P. (1991), *Media, State and Nation: Political Violence and Collective Identities*, Sage, London.

Schneider, D. (1994), 'Social Studies teaching: citizenship education and authentic learning', *The Clearing House*, 67, 3, pp. 132-4.

Schor, J. (1991), *The Overworked American: The Unexpected Decline of Leisure in America*, New York.

Schumpter, J.A. (1994), *Capitalism, Socialism and Democracy*, Routledge, London and New York.

Schwarz, H. (1994) *States Versus Markets: History, Geography and the Development of the International Political Economy*, St. Martin's Press, London.

Scott, A. (1990), Ideology and the New Social Movements, Unwin Hyman: London.

Scott, J.C. (1998), *Seeing Like a State: How Certain Schemes to Improve the Human Conditions Have Failed*, Yale UP, New Haven.

Selbourne, D. (1994), *The Principle of Duty*, Sinclair-Stevenson, London.

Selznick, P. (1995), 'Personhood and Moral Obligation', A. Etzioni (ed.), *New Communitarian Thinking: Persons, Virtues, Institutions, and Communities*, University Press of Virginia, Charlottesville and London, pp. 110-25.

Sennett, R. (1986), *The Fall of Public Man*, Faber and Faber, London.

——. (1996), *The Uses of Disorder: Personal Identity and City Life*, Faber and Faber, London.

Shain,Y. (1995), 'Multicultural foreign policy', *Foreign Policy*, 100, pp. 69-88.

Sheard, J. (1995), 'From Lady Bountiful to active citizen: Volunteering and the voluntary sector' J. Davis Smith et al. (eds), *An Introduction to the Voluntary Sector*, London, Routledge.

Sherry, S. (1995), 'Responsible republicanism: educating for citizenship', *University of Chicago Law Review*, 62, 1, pp. 131-208.

Shields, R. (1992a), *Lifestyle Shopping: the Subject of Consumption*, Routledge, London.

——. (1992b), 'The Individual, Consumption Cultures and the Fate of Community', *Lifestyle Shopping: the Subject of Consumption*, Routledge, London, pp. 99-113.

Simmel, G. (1971), 'The metropolis and mental life', D. Levine (ed.), *Georg Simmel, On Individuality and Social Forms*, University of Chicago Press, Chicago and London.

Skillen, T. (1991), 'Active Citizenship as Political Obligation', *Radical Philosophy*, 58, pp. 10-13.

Slagle, R.A. (1995), 'In defense of Queer Nation: from identity politics to a politics of difference', *Western Journal of Communications*, 59, 2, pp. 85-98.

Sleeper, J. (1990), *Closest of Strangers: Liberalism and the Politics of Race in New York*, W.W. Norton and Co., New York.

Smart, J.J.C. and Williams, B. (1973), *Utilitarianism: For and Against*, Cambridge UP, Cambridge.

Smith, A. (1976), *An Inquiry into the Nature and Causes of the Wealth of Nations*, R.H. Campbell et al. (eds), Clarendon Press, Oxford.

Smith, A.D. (1986), *The Ethnic Origins of Nations*, Blackwells, Oxford.

——. (1991), *National Identity*, London, Penguin.

Snell, J. (2000), 'Hidden heroes', *The Guardian*, 2/2/00.

Spence, R. (2002), 'What is a neighbourhood?', *The Independent/ Neighbourhood Renewal Unit*, Special Supplement, 23 Jan. 2002, p. 5.

Standing, G. (1999), *Global Labour Flexibility: Seeking Distributive Justice*, Macmillan, Basingstoke and London.

Starr, A. (2000), *Naming the Enemy: Anti-Corporate Social Movements Confront Globalization*, London, Zed Books.

Stevick, R.A. and Addleman, J.A. (1995), 'Effects of short-term volunteer experience on self-perceptions and prosocial behaviour', *The Journal of Social Psychology*, 135, 5, pp. 663-6.

Street, J. (1994), 'Political culture - from civic culture to mass culture', *British Journal of Political Science*, 24, 1.

Stroud, S. (2002), 'How can we create a volunteering society', *The Independent*, 19/2/02.

Sykes, R., Palier, B. and Prior, P.M. (eds) (2001), *Globalization and European Welfare States* (2001), Palgrave, Basingstoke.

Tam, H. (1998), *Communitarianism: A New Agenda for Politics and Citizenship*, Macmillan, Basingstoke and London.

Tanzi, V. (2001), 'Taxation and the Future of Social Protection', A. Giddens (ed.), *The Global Third Way Debate*, Polity, Cambridge, pp.189-98.

Taylor, C. (1989), *Sources of the Self*, Cambridge UP, Cambridge.

——. (1989a), 'Cross-Purposes: The Liberal-Communitarian Debate', N. Rosenblum (ed.), *Liberalism and the Moral Life*, Harvard UP, Cambridge, MA, pp. 159-82.

Taylor, C. (1992), 'Atomism', S. Avineri and A. de-Shalit (eds), *Communitarianism and Individualism*, Oxford UP, Oxford, pp. 29-50.

Taylor, L. and Walton, P. (1971), 'Industrial Sabotage: Motives and Meanings', S. Cohen (ed.), *Images of Deviance*, Penguin Books, Harmondsworth.

Tester, K. (1997), *Moral Culture*, Sage, London.

Therbon, G. (1984), 'The prospects of labour and the transformation of advanced capitalism', *New Left Review*, 145, pp. 5-38.

Thompson, E.P. (1968), *The Making of the English Working Class*, Penguin, Harmondsworth.

Thompson, G. et al. (eds) (1991), *Markets, Hierarchies and Networks: The Coordination of Social Life*, Sage, London.

Thompson, J.B. (1996), 'Tradition and Self in a Mediated World', P. Heelas et al. (eds), *Detraditionalization*, Blackwell Publishers, Oxford, pp. 89-108.

Thompson, K. (1982), *Emile Durkheim*, Tavistock Publications, London and New York.

Tocqueville, A. de (1969), *Democracy in America*, Doubleday Anchor, New York.

Toffler, A. (1970), *Future Shock*, Random House, New York.

——. (1981), *The Third Wave*, Bantam, New York.

Tolliday, S. & Zeitlin, J. (eds) (1986), *Between Fordism and Flexibility*, Basil Blackwell, Oxford.

Tomaney, J. (1994), 'A New Paradigm of Work Organization and Technology?', A. Amin (ed.), *Post-Fordism: A Reader*, Blackwells, Oxford, pp. 157-94.

Tomlinson, J. (1991), *Cultural Imperialism*, Pinter Publishers, London.

Tonnies, F. (1957), *Community and Society*, C.P. Loomis (ed.), Michigan State UP, East Lansing.

Topf, R. (1989), 'Political Change and Political Culture in Britain, 1959-1987', R. Gibbins (ed.), *Contemporary Political Culture*, Sage, London, pp. 52-80.

Touraine, A. (1985), 'An Introduction to the Study of Social Movements', *Social Research*, 52, 4, pp. 749-87.

Travis, A. (2002), 'Letwin sees "neighbourly society" as the way to beat crime', *The Guardian*, 9/1/02.

Treneman, A. (1996), 'Nothing for something – the Nineties way', *The Independent*, 17/10/96.

UNCTAD (1993), *World Investment Report: Transnational Corporations and Integrated International Production*, UNCTAD, New York.

Unger, R. (1975), *Knowledge and Politics*, New York.

Urry, J. (1989), 'The End of Organised Capitalism', S. Hall and M. Jacques (eds), *New Times*, Lawrence and Wishart, London, pp. 94-102.

U.S. Bureau of the Census (1990), *Statistical Abstract of the United States*, Government Printing Office, Washington, DC.

U.S. Bureau of the Census (1992), *Statistical Abstract of the United States*, Government Printing Office, Washington, DC.

U.S. Bureau of the Census (1993), *Statistical Abstract of the United States*, Government Printing Office, Washington, DC.

Vail, J., Wheelock, J. and Hill, M. (eds) (1999), *Insecure Times: Living with insecurity in contemporary Society*, Routledge, London and New York.

Vaillancourt, F. (1994), 'To volunteer or not: Canada', *Canadian Journal of Economics*, 27, 4, pp. 813-27.

Vandenbroucke, F. (2001), 'European Social Democracy and the Third Way: Convergence, Divisions and Shared Questions', S. White (ed.), *New Labour: The Progressive Future?*, Palgrave, Basingstoke, pp. 161-74.

Veblen, T. (1953), *The Leisure Class*, New American Library, New York.

Verba, S. and Nie, N.H. (1972), *Participation in America: Political Democracy and Social Equality*, Harper and Row, New York.

Vincent, A. (1992), *Modern Political Ideologies*, Blackwell Publishers, Oxford.

Wade, R.C. (1995), 'Developing active citizens: community service learning in social studies teacher education', *The Social Studies*, 86, 3, pp. 122-9.

Waldron, J. (1987), 'Theoretical Foundations of Liberalism', *Philosophical Quarterly*, 37, pp. 127-50.

Walker, D. (2002), 'Get off your bike', *The Guardian*, 30/7/02.

Walker, M. (1995), 'Home alone', *The Guardian*, 22/2/95.

Wallace, I. (1995), *The Global Economic System*, Routledge, London and New York.

Wallerstein, I. (1974), *The Modern World-System*, Academic, New York.

Walzer, M. (1983), *Spheres of Justice: A Defence of Pluralism and Equality*, Blackwells, Oxford.

——. (1989), *The Company of Critics: Social Criticism and Political Commitment in the Twentieth Century*, Peter Halban, London.

——. (1989a), 'The good life', *New Statesman and Society*, 6/10/89, pp. 28-33.

——. (1992), 'Membership', S. Avieri and A. de-Shalit (eds), *Communitarianism and Individualism*, Oxford UP, Oxford, pp. 65-84.

——. (1994), 'Multiculturalism and individualism', *Dissent*, 41, 2, pp. 185-92.

Warnock, M. (1997), 'Utopia and Other Destinations', *Radio 4*, BBC, 12/4/97.

Waters, M. (1995), *Globalization*, Routledge, London.

Weber, M. (1972), 'Politics as a Vocation', in H.H. Gerth and C.W. Mills (eds), *From Max Weber*, Oxford UP, New York, pp. 77-128.

——. (1978), *Economy and Society*, 2 vols., University of California Press, Berkeley.

Weinstein, L. et al. (1995), 'Purpose in life, boredom and volunteerism in a group of retirees', *Psychological Reports*, 76, 2, p. 482.

Welch, S. (1993), *The Concept of Political Culture*, Macmillan, Basingstoke.

White, M. (2001), 'Basildon Man wants to go it alone', *The Guardian*, 20/3/01.

Wieviorka, M. (1994), 'Racism in Europe: Unity and Diversity', A. Rattansi and S. Westwood (eds), *Racism, Modernity and Identity on the Western Front*, Polity Press, Cambridge, pp. 173-88.

Williams, B. (1985), *Ethics and the Limits of Philosophy*, Fontana, London.

Williams, K. et al. (1987), 'The end of mass production?', *Economy and Society*, 16, 3, pp. 405-39.

Williams, M. (1996), 'A campus erupts over multiculturalism', *The New York Times*, 28/10/96, 145, p. A13 (N).

Williams, R. (ed.) (1980), *The impact of field education on student development: Research findings*, Korda Project, Sharon, MA.

Williamson, O.E. (1975), *Markets and Hierarchies: Analysis and antitrust implications*, Free Press, New York.

——. (1985), *The Economic Institutions of Capitalism*, Free Press, New York.

Wilson, W.J. (1987), *The Truly Disadvantaged: The Inner City, the Underclass and Public Policy*, University of Chicago Press, Chicago, IL.

Wilson-Smith, A. (1996), 'Cutting back: in the cash-strapped 1990s government is depending on volunteers to fill the breach', *Macleans*, 1/7/96, 109, 27, pp. 40-2.

Wintour, P. (1996), 'Modern Morality: The Price of Moral Panic', *The Observer*, 3/11/96.

——. (2001), 'Volunteers plan stirs up unions', *The Guardian*, 12/1/01.

Wofford, H., Waldman, S. and Bandow, D. (1996), 'AmeriCorps the beautiful?', *Policy Review*, 79, pp. 28-37.

Wood, S. (1989), *The Transformation of Work? Skill, flexibility and the labour process*, Routledge, London and New York.

Wright, R. (1995), 'Who's really to blame?', *Time*, 6/11/95, 146, 19, pp. 32-8.

Wriston, W. (1992), *The Twilight of Sovereignty*, Charles Scribner and Sons, New York.

Wuthnow, R. (1994), *Sharing the Journey*, Free Press, New York.

Zapler, M. (1994), 'President Clinton swears in 15,000 for national service program', *The Chronicle of Higher Education*, 21/9/94, 41, 4, p. A38.

Zlotkowski, E. (1996), 'Linking service-learning and the academy', *Change*, 28, 1, pp. 20-8.

Zukin, S. (1987), 'Gentrification', *Annual Review of Sociology*.

——. (1988), *Loft Living*, 2nd ed., Hutchinson/Radius, London.

Index